THE BEDFORD SERIES IN HISTORY AND CULTURE

Abraham Lincoln, Slavery, and the Civil War

Selected Writings and Speeches

Related Titles in
THE BEDFORD SERIES IN HISTORY AND CULTURE
Advisory Editors: Lynn Hunt, *University of California, Los Angeles*
David W. Blight, *Yale University*
Bonnie G. Smith, *Rutgers University*
Natalie Zemon Davis, *Princeton University*
Ernest R. May, *Harvard University*

William Lloyd Garrison and the Fight against Slavery:
Selections from THE LIBERATOR
Edited with an Introduction by William E. Cain, *Wellesley College*

Defending Slavery: Proslavery Thought in the Old South:
A Brief History with Documents
Paul Finkelman, *Albany Law School*

NARRATIVE OF THE LIFE OF FREDERICK DOUGLASS, AN AMERICAN SLAVE,
Written by Himself, with Related Documents, Second Edition
Edited with an Introduction by David W. Blight, *Yale University*

DRED SCOTT V. SANDFORD: *A Brief History with Documents*
Paul Finkelman, *Albany Law School*

John Brown's Raid on Harpers Ferry: A Brief History with Documents
Jonathan Earle, *University of Kansas*

The Emancipation Proclamation: A Brief History with Documents
Michael Vorenberg, *Brown University*

INCIDENTS IN THE LIFE OF A SLAVE GIRL, WRITTEN BY HERSELF,
by Harriet Jacobs, with Related Documents
Edited with an Introduction by Jennifer Fleischner, *Adelphi University*

HOSPITAL SKETCHES, *by Louisa May Alcott*
Edited with an Introduction by Alice Fahs, *University of California, Irvine*

The Public Art of Civil War Commemoration: A Brief History
with Documents
Thomas J. Brown, *University of South Carolina*

THE BEDFORD SERIES IN HISTORY AND CULTURE

SECOND EDITION

Abraham Lincoln, Slavery, and the Civil War

Selected Writings and Speeches

Edited by

Michael P. Johnson

Johns Hopkins University

BEDFORD / ST. MARTIN'S   Boston ◆ New York

For Bedford/St. Martin's

Publisher for History: Mary V. Dougherty
Director of Development for History: Jane Knetzger
Executive Editor: William J. Lombardo
Senior Editor: Heidi L. Hood
Developmental Editors: Louise Townsend, Beth Welch
Editorial Assistant: Jennifer Jovin
Production Associate: Samuel Jones
Executive Marketing Manager: Jenna Bookin Barry
Project Management: Books By Design, Inc.
Index: Books By Design, Inc.
Text Design: Claire Seng-Niemoeller
Maps: Mapping Specialists, Ltd.
Cover Design: Richard DiTomassi
Cover Photo: Abraham Lincoln, head-and-shoulders portrait, facing front. Photograph taken
  November 8, 1863, by Alexander Gardner (1821–1882), photographer. Courtesy of the
  Library of Congress, Prints and Photographs Division, LC-DIG-ppmsca-19301.
Composition: Achorn International
Printing and Binding: Haddon Craftsmen, Inc., an RR Donnelley & Sons Company

President: Joan E. Feinberg
Editorial Director: Denise B. Wydra
Editor in Chief: Karen S. Henry
Director of Marketing: Karen R. Soeltz
Director of Production: Susan W. Brown
Associate Director, Editorial Production: Elise S. Kaiser
Manager, Publishing Services: Andrea Cava

Library of Congress Control Number: 2010910699

Manufactured in the United States of America.

5   4   3   2   1   0
f   e   d   c   b   a

For information, write: Bedford/St. Martin's, 75 Arlington Street, Boston, MA 02116
(617-399-4000)

ISBN-13: 978-0-312-55813-0

Acknowledgments
All of the documents in this reader are reproduced courtesy of the Abraham Lincoln
Association.

Distributed outside North America by PALGRAVE MACMILLAN.

Foreword

The Bedford Series in History and Culture is designed so that readers can study the past as historians do.

The historian's first task is finding the evidence. Documents, letters, memoirs, interviews, pictures, movies, novels, or poems can provide facts and clues. Then the historian questions and compares the sources. There is more to do than in a courtroom, for hearsay evidence is welcome, and the historian is usually looking for answers beyond act and motive. Different views of an event may be as important as a single verdict. How a story is told may yield as much information as what it says.

Along the way the historian seeks help from other historians and perhaps from specialists in other disciplines. Finally, it is time to write, to decide on an interpretation and how to arrange the evidence for readers.

Each book in this series contains an important historical document or group of documents, each document a witness from the past and open to interpretation in different ways. The documents are combined with some element of historical narrative—an introduction or a biographical essay, for example—that provides students with an analysis of the primary source material and important background information about the world in which it was produced.

Each book in the series focuses on a specific topic within a specific historical period. Each provides a basis for lively thought and discussion about several aspects of the topic and the historian's role. Each is short enough (and inexpensive enough) to be a reasonable one-week assignment in a college course. Whether as classroom or personal reading, each book in the series provides firsthand experience of the challenge—and fun—of discovering, recreating, and interpreting the past.

Lynn Hunt
David W. Blight
Bonnie G. Smith
Natalie Zemon Davis
Ernest R. May

Preface

This book contains Abraham Lincoln's most important writings and speeches about slavery and the Civil War. The sixty-five letters, speeches, and other writings included here, selected from approximately 120,000 documents in the ten volumes of Lincoln's collected works, portray the range and depth of his thought about the issues that defined his times, his presidency, and his place in history.

Rather than a little of all of Lincoln, this book features most of the essential Lincoln. The history of slavery and the Civil War cannot be fully understood apart from Lincoln, nor can the major contours of his life and thought be separated from these momentous matters, which preoccupied him during his presidency and which continue to compel the attention of many Americans. The focus here on slavery and the Civil War requires overlooking interesting and important topics such as Lincoln's youth in Kentucky, Indiana, and Illinois; his family life; his congressional career; his years as an Illinois lawyer and politician before 1854; and his legendary wit. In addition, by concentrating on the essential documents about slavery and the Civil War, this new edition is much shorter—and ideally more useful in classrooms and more accessible for students—than the previous edition. What this new edition sacrifices in the range and depth of topics is recompensed by thorough, though still selective, coverage of issues at the core of Lincoln's historical significance.

As in the previous edition, the documents are arranged in chapters organized thematically and more or less chronologically. The first two chapters survey Lincoln's emergence as a leader of the new Republican party, first in Illinois, then in the North, and finally as president-elect. The remaining six chapters chronicle Lincoln's attempt to preserve the Union during the bloody war that dominated his four years as president. They illustrate the evolution of Lincoln's political and military policies to place the war aim of freedom alongside that of union. Taken together, the documents provide an extended historical commentary, in Lincoln's own words, on his statement early in 1865 that the Emancipation Proclamation was "the central act of my administration and the great event of the nineteenth century."[1]

To help students understand Lincoln's words, brief headnotes give information about the historical context and significance of each document. By supplying connections between documents, the headnotes allow readers to follow the development of Lincoln's ideas. They also permit otherwise disconnected documents to be read as episodes in a continuous historical narrative, capturing some of the drama, uncertainty, and contingency of Lincoln's experience. Footnotes identify the people, places, and events that Lincoln mentions but that are unfamiliar to most readers today. Quotations from Lincoln's correspondents and from his spoken comments to his contemporaries frequently supplement the footnotes and the headnotes. Other editorial features designed to assist readers include maps and photographs, a chronology, questions to provoke reflection on Lincoln's thoughts, a selected bibliography of sources for further study, and a comprehensive index. In all, the editorial apparatus offers an array of concise, detailed information to help readers explore the many levels of meaning in Lincoln's words.

ACKNOWLEDGMENTS

In the preparation of this second edition, I have been the beneficiary of knowledge, insight, and support from many people. Historians from throughout the nation who used the first edition of this book in their classrooms have shared with me their suggestions about what works best with their students. For their cogent advice about the difficult decision of which Lincoln documents are truly essential and which are extremely important but not quite essential, I am indebted to Stephen Berry, University of Georgia; Stephen Deyle, University of Houston; Nicole Etcheson, Ball State University; Willard Karl Klunder, Wichita State University; David John Marley, Vanguard University; Matthew Mason, Brigham Young University; Jonathan Mercantini, Kean University; Elizabeth White Nelson, University of Nevada, Las Vegas; Joseph

---

[1] Francis B. Carpenter, "Anecdotes and Reminiscences," in Henry J. Raymond, *The Life and Public Service of Abraham Lincoln* (New York, 1865), 764.

Reidy, Howard University; Nathaniel Sheidley, Wellesley College; Amy Dru Stanley, University of Chicago; and Joan Waugh, University of California, Los Angeles.

For years, students at Johns Hopkins have indulged my curiosity about Lincoln and his world. Friends James Roark and David Rankin endured numerous conversations about Lincoln and helped identify mistakes and blind spots. Edward Ayers, Jean Baker, Michael Burlingame, Drew Faust, and two anonymous readers saved me from embarrassing errors of commission and omission. At Bedford/St. Martin's, president Joan E. Feinberg, publisher for history Mary Dougherty, director of development Jane Knetzger, and senior editor Heidi Hood unstintingly supported this project from the outset. Louise Townsend contributed her balanced historical perceptions and her keen editorial eye to the preparation of a sound plan for this revised edition. Supported by editorial assistant Jennifer Jovin, executive editor extraordinaire Beth Welch brought her unsurpassed judgment and sensitive readings to our joint effort to make this new edition shorter and more accessible to students. I completed the first edition of this book while a fellow at the Center for Advanced Study in the Behavioral Sciences, supported in part by the Andrew W. Mellon Foundation. In addition to all of this indispensable help, I have benefited beyond measure from the writings of Lincoln scholars past and present, to whom all who share an interest in Lincoln, slavery, and the Civil War are permanently indebted. In 1876, Frederick Douglass declared, "Any man can say things that are true of Abraham Lincoln, but no man can say anything that is new of Abraham Lincoln."[2] Shelves of fascinating books and articles about Lincoln published since 1876 prove that Douglass spoke prematurely.

Michael P. Johnson

---

[2] Frederick Douglass, "Oration in Memory of Abraham Lincoln," April 14, 1876, in Philip S. Foner, ed., *The Life and Writings of Frederick Douglass* (4 vols.; New York, 1955), IV, 315.

A Note about the Text

The texts reprinted here follow the superb edition of Lincoln's works prepared by Roy P. Basler and published over a half-century ago in 1953.[3] Basler's edition was the first to have access to the massive collection of Lincoln papers, which were not made available for study until July 26, 1947, twenty-one years after the death of Lincoln's last surviving son, Robert Todd Lincoln. Scholars accept Basler's edition as definitive except for a few relatively minor typographic or transcription errors. Some documents are published here in full, but to conserve space I have often abridged documents, trying always to preserve both the substance and the flavor of the complete text. Lincoln's spelling was better than that of most Americans in the mid-nineteenth century, but incorrectly spelled words repeatedly crept into his writing. For example, he frequently wrote the contraction *it's* when the context makes clear that he meant the possessive *its*. Throughout this volume, I have preserved Lincoln's spelling as presented in Basler's *Collected Works* and have not used "[sic]" to alert readers that I am aware of a misspelled word. When Basler suggests alternative readings of a word or phrase, I have silently chosen one that seems to me preferable. For purposes of clarity, I have occasionally inserted a word or two in brackets into Lincoln's text. While remaining faithful to Lincoln's words, punctuation, and capitalization, I have made the following alterations to the format of the documents: each date has been standardized to a month, day, and year style (for example, July 4, 1863) and raised above the text of the document; the place from which Lincoln wrote a document (for example, Washington, D.C.) has been printed flush to the right margin; if Lincoln used a closing

---

[3] Roy P. Basler, Marion Dolores Pratt, and Lloyd A. Dunlap, eds., *The Collected Works of Abraham Lincoln* (8 vols.; New Brunswick, N.J., 1953; supplements 1974, 1990). *The Collected Works* are cited herein as *CW*, followed by the pertinent volume and page numbers.

in a document (for example, *Yours truly*), it has been placed flush to the right margin; if Lincoln signed a document, his signature has been printed in small capital letters below his closing (if there is one) and flush to the right margin. Readers can easily consult the full text of any document abridged in this collection or omitted from it since the Basler edition is widely available in libraries large and small. In addition, all of Lincoln's collected works and a great many related materials are readily available online. Ideally, this edition of Lincoln's writings and speeches will stimulate readers to turn to these and other resources to learn more about Lincoln and his times.

Contents

Maps and Illustrations

(*See following pages.*)

Map 1. *Major Union Campaigns of the Civil War, 1861–1865*
Lincoln's homes in Kentucky, Indiana, and Illinois straddled the legal boundary of slave and free states that the Civil War and the Thirteenth Amendment ultimately erased. Although the war was truly continental in scope, major battles often occurred at important sites of water, rail, or road transportation, testimony to the significance of the movement of men and goods to both the Union and the Confederacy.

Introduction:
Abraham Lincoln, Wordsmith

In the early-morning hours of November 7, 1860, after spending the evening listening to election returns clatter into the telegraph office in Springfield, Illinois, Abraham Lincoln went home, knowing he had received enough popular votes to win a comfortable electoral majority and become the next president of the United States. Since the days of George Washington, twelve other men had been elected to the nation's highest office and had prepared themselves to take the reins of power from an incumbent. Each time the transition proved peaceful and without incident. Power transferred smoothly even when the incumbent and the newly elected president were partisan enemies. Lincoln had every reason to suppose that his election—the first for a member of the relatively new Republican party—would follow the pattern well established by his predecessors: He would take over the presidency from the Democratic incumbent, James Buchanan, and those who lost the election would regroup and try to win the next time, four years later.

On March 4, 1861, Buchanan stepped aside, as all other outgoing presidents had, and Lincoln was inaugurated in an orderly and routine ceremony. But by this time, unlike the immediate aftermath of any previous presidential election, seven slave states had declared their secession from the Union. No other presidential election, before or since, had such violent and ultimately transforming consequences for the nation. During his campaign for the presidency and even during the four-month interval between his election and his inauguration, Lincoln never seriously contemplated civil war or the emancipation of four million slaves. But between his inauguration and his assassination four years later, Lincoln was preoccupied with the Civil War and slavery. His presidency permanently changed the course of American history.

Of course, Lincoln alone did not win the war and free the slaves. Such massive events involved the efforts of millions of Americans—soldiers

1

and civilians, men and women, blacks and whites, northerners and southerners. Lincoln understood the considerable scope of his presidential powers, but he also realized that those powers had severe limits. He knew that he could not effectively exercise his presidential authority without mobilizing the support of millions of ordinary Americans. He needed their consent in the form of their votes, their men of military age, their trust, and their willingness to sacrifice. A political creature to the tips of his toes, Lincoln worked hard to create that consent. Elected with slightly less than 40 percent of the popular vote, he needed no reminder of the nation's deep and bitter divisions both between and within the North and the South. As a lawyer and politician in Illinois, Lincoln had years of experience confronting people with opposing views, dissecting their arguments, and advocating his own. But until he became president, he had never been required to generate consent for the kinds of personal commitment demanded by civil war. No other American president ever faced such a formidable challenge. To build and maintain popular consent—that is, to govern, to win the war, and to save the Union—Lincoln relied on both deeds and words, particularly words that persuaded many Americans to consent to his presidential deeds.

Since boyhood, Lincoln had honed his skill with words. He is often thought of as a backwoods rail-splitter, a farm boy who became president by pluck and luck. Born in 1809, he worked on his father's farms—first in Kentucky, then in Indiana, and finally in Illinois—and he split logs into the fence rails immortalized in his 1860 presidential campaign. But farmwork convinced Lincoln that he wanted to do something else, almost anything else, when he came of age. He told a farmer who hired him in 1829 that "his father taught him to work but never learned him to love it."[1] In 1831, when he was twenty-two, he left his father's farm, moved to the small village of New Salem, Illinois, and began to try his hand at one thing after another—store clerk, merchant, surveyor, postmaster—but never farmer. Barely making ends meet, Lincoln also explored two other occupations that became his lifelong pursuits: lawyer and politician. Both required skill with words, headwork rather than handwork.

---

[1] John Romine interview, September 14, 1865, in Douglas L. Wilson and Rodney O. Davis, eds., *Herndon's Informants: Letters, Interviews, and Statements about Abraham Lincoln* (Urbana, 1998), 118. Cited hereafter as *Herndon's Informants*.

His ultimate achievements depended far more on his ability to turn a phrase, craft a sentence, and construct an argument than on his skill with an ax or a plow. In fact, Lincoln made his living with words. Like many Americans of his time, Lincoln was born into a poor family almost bereft of formal learning. Lincoln's mother, Nancy, could neither read nor write. His father, Thomas, could sign his name but write little else. Looking back on his youth, Lincoln recalled, "There was absolutely nothing to excite ambition for education."[2] Rather than learn the skills of literacy, most of Lincoln's relatives and neighbors trained their eyes on the unforgiving tasks of farming. "I had no books in my house," said one of Lincoln's Illinois friends, "loaned him none—we didn't think about books—papers—We worked—had to live."[3]

Lincoln worked, too, but he stole time before, during, and after chores to read and write. His stepmother, Sarah, recalled that he "studied in the daytime—didnt after night much—went to bed Early—got up Early & then read—Eat his breakfast—go to work in the field with the men."[4] Making time to read while six or seven others in a crowded one-room cabin were still asleep or just stirring to begin the day indicates Lincoln's appetite for learning. Even at work, Lincoln found time to read. One neighbor remembered that when Lincoln "went out to work any where [he] would Carry his books with and would always read whilst resting."[5] After work, when Lincoln "returned to the house," a relative said, "he would go to the Cupboard—Snatch a piece of Corn bread—take down a book—Sit down on a chair—Cock his legs up as high as his head and read. . . . He was a Constant and voracious reader."[6]

Although Sarah Lincoln was illiterate, she brought along several books when she moved into the Lincoln cabin in 1819, among them a Bible, *Aesop's Fables*, John Bunyan's *Pilgrim's Progress*, and William Scott's *Lessons in Elocution*, which included passages from Shakespeare. Lincoln read them all, plus books he obtained from friends and neighbors, such

---

[2] Lincoln to Jesse W. Fell, December 20, 1859, *CW*, III, 511.
[3] Hannah Armstrong interview, [1866], *Herndon's Informants*, 173.
[4] Sarah Lincoln interview, September 8, 1865, *Herndon's Informants*, 107. Lincoln's mother, Nancy Hanks Lincoln, died in 1818, when he was nine years old. His father married Sarah Bush Johnston the next year.
[5] Nathaniel Grigsby interview, September 12, 1865, *Herndon's Informants*, 112–13.
[6] John Hanks interview, [1865–1866], *Herndon's Informants*, 455.

as Parson Weems's *Life of George Washington*, Daniel Defoe's *Robinson Crusoe*, and *The Columbian Orator*, a collection of famous speeches. He worked his way through "an old dog-eared arithmetic" book, and, as Sarah recalled, he "was a Constant reader" of newspapers.

Lincoln's reading led his cousin and childhood companion Dennis Hanks, among many others, to say that "Lincoln was lazy—a very lazy man—He was always reading—scribbling—writing—Ciphering—writing Poetry."[7] Hanks recalled that because Lincoln was "a Constant and I m[a]y Say Stubborn reader, his father . . . Sometimes [had] to slash him for neglecting his work by reading."[8] When Lincoln could be spared from farmwork, he attended school a month or so at a time; in all, he had less than a year of formal schooling. For the most part, he educated himself, starting with disciplined reading.

With access to few books as a youngster, Lincoln developed reading habits that he used throughout his life. An Indiana neighbor remembered, "What Lincoln read he read and re-read—read and Studied thoroughly."[9] William H. Herndon, Lincoln's law partner in Springfield for two decades, claimed that "Mr. Lincoln read less and thought more than any man in his sphere in America."[10] Even while distracted by the endless responsibilities of his presidency, Lincoln borrowed more than 125 items from the Library of Congress on topics ranging from Shakespeare to military tactics.

Lincoln read as if printed words were scarce victuals to be savored and devoured. He had little interest in owning books and never collected a sizable personal library, even after his law practice prospered in the 1850s. Instead, he made a text his by reading and writing. Sarah Lincoln explained that when he "came across a passage that Struck him he would write it down on boards if he had no paper & keep it there till he did get paper—then he would rewrite it—look at it [and] repeat it."[11]

In addition to writing out the core of his reading, Lincoln usually read aloud. This habit often annoyed Herndon, who found it distracting in their small law office. Lincoln explained why he did it: "When I read

[7] Dennis Hanks interview, September 8, 1865, *Herndon's Informants*, 104.

[8] Dennis Hanks interview, June 13, 1865, *Herndon's Informants*, 41

[9] David Turnham interview, September 15, 1865, *Herndon's Informants*, 121.

[10] William H. Herndon, "The Analysis of Mr. Lincoln's Character," in Osborn H. Oldroyd, ed., *The Lincoln Memorial: Album-Immortelles* (New York, 1882), 533.

[11] Sarah Lincoln interview, September 8, 1865, *Herndon's Informants*, 107.

aloud, two senses catch the idea: first, I see what I read; second, I hear it, and therefore can remember it better."[12]

Reading aloud and writing out passages imprinted ideas on Lincoln's mind. Associates marveled at the power of his memory. When a friend mentioned that it seemed easy for Lincoln to remember things, he responded, "No . . . you are mistaken—I am slow to learn and slow to forget that which I have learned—My mind is like a piece of steel, very hard to scratch any thing on it and almost impossible after you get it there to rub it out."[13]

The words engraved on Lincoln's mind came as much from listening as from reading. To a great extent, Lincoln's reading habits grew out of keen listening. In a sense, he listened to books as he did to conversations. As president he told an acquaintance that "after hearing the neighbors talk of an evening with my father . . . I can remember going to my little bedroom, and spending the night . . . trying to make out what was the exact meaning of some of their, to me, dark sayings. I could not sleep . . . until I had put it in language plain enough, as I thought, for any boy I knew to comprehend. This was a kind of passion with me, and it has stuck by me."[14]

Of course, Lincoln did not confine his listening to the log cabin. "He would hear sermons preached," Sarah Lincoln remembered, "come home—take the children out—get on a stump or log and almost repeat it word for word."[15] By dramatizing his command of language, Lincoln pretended to exhort his small flock with holy words. The fun and attention were irresistible, as was the relief from farmwork. By stump preaching, Lincoln launched his apprenticeship as a wordsmith.

Lincoln's apprenticeship took him wherever he could hear people talking, arguing, and laughing. He listened to his father and other men swap tales at the stable, the mill, the spring, the crossroads, and the whiskey barrel. He crowded into rustic courtrooms and listened to people plead their cases, parsing their personal stories by rules of law and local

[12] William Herndon and Jesse K. Weik, *Herndon's Lincoln: The True Story of a Great Life* (3 vols.; Chicago, 1889), II, 332.

[13] Joshua F. Speed to William H. Herndon, December 8, 1866, *Herndon's Informants*, 499.

[14] Francis B. Carpenter, *Six Months at the White House with Abraham Lincoln: The Story of a Picture* (New York, 1866), 312–13.

[15] Ibid.

standards of justice. He listened to politicians explain why they deserved to be elected. Dennis Hanks said that he and Lincoln "learned by sight—scent & hearing—We heard all that was said & talked over & over the questions [we] heard—wore them slick—greasy and threadbare."[16] Not satisfied to listen and discuss, Lincoln projected himself into the leading role of persuader, just as he had after church. A relative recalled that Lincoln "would gather the children together Mount a stump or Log & harang his juvenile audience" with a political speech.[17] Lincoln's long apprenticeship at stump speaking meant that in 1832, when he first ran for the Illinois legislature, he already had plenty of practice expressing his thoughts before an inquisitive audience. Lincoln also began to "Pettifog [argue] before [the] Justice of the Peace" shortly after moving to New Salem in 1831.[18] Although he had no legal credentials, an old book of Illinois laws and the countless disputes he had witnessed made him enough of a lawyer to argue cases for his neighbors, for free.

A courtroom advocate long before he became a lawyer in 1836, a stump speaker long before he first ran for office in 1832, Lincoln also had a long apprenticeship in the art of storytelling. He absorbed jokes, yarns, and scandals from every source. More than any other single trait, Lincoln's associates recalled his ability to tell a funny story, whether on the stump, in the courtroom, or later in the White House. He once described laughter as "the joyous, beautiful, universal evergreen of life."[19] He delighted in condensing a telling observation into a witty quip. For example, in 1863, he explained that he intended to pardon soldiers sentenced to be executed for cowardice because "it would frighten the poor devils too terribly to shoot them."[20]

Beyond sharing a laugh with his audience, Lincoln used stories to illustrate his ideas. An Indiana neighbor pointed out that Lincoln "argued much from Analogy and Explained things hard for us to understand by

[16] Dennis Hanks interview, September 8, 1865, *Herndon's Informants*, 105.
[17] A. H. Chapman statement, before September 8, 1865, *Herndon's Informants*, 102.
[18] William G. Greene interview, May 30, 1865, *Herndon's Informants*, 20.
[19] John G. Nicolay, "Lincoln's Literary Experiments," *Century Magazine* 47 (April 1894): 832.
[20] Tyler Dennett, ed., *Lincoln and the Civil War in the Diaries and Letters of John Hay* (New York, 1939), 68–69.

stories . . . that we might instantly see the force & bearing of what he said."[21] Lincoln's stories bridged the abstract ideas of books and laws to everyday lives. Stories made common sense out of uncommon ideas. Stories deployed a vocabulary of experience rather than professional expertise. With stories, Lincoln built the foundation for persuasion and consent. During the Civil War, he told a Republican leader, "I have found in the course of a long experience that common people . . . are more easily influenced and informed through the medium of a broad illustration than in any other way, and as to what the hyper-critical few may think, I don't care."[22]

Lincoln's stories contributed to the frequent impression among genteel, educated people that he was a hick, an impression reinforced by his mannerisms and appearance. A lawyer recalled that when he first saw Lincoln in court in 1854, "he had the appearance of a rough intelligent farmer."[23] Appearances, of course, can be deceiving. Leonard Swett, an eminent Illinois attorney and Lincoln's longtime friend and frequent courtroom adversary, declared that Lincoln was "considered by the people of this country as a frank, guileless, unsophisticated man. There never was a greater mistake."[24] Having witnessed Lincoln try many cases, Swett observed, "Any man who took Lincoln for a simple minded man would very soon wake [up] with his back in a ditch."[25]

Behind Lincoln's courtroom artfulness lay careful preparation that continued through his presidential years. Swett noted that when Lincoln appeared in court, "the first impression he generally conveyed was, that he had stated the case of his adversary better and more forcibly, than his opponent could state it himself. . . . The force of his logic was in conveying to the minds of others the same clear and thorough analysis he had in his own."[26] In many ways, Lincoln's style of argument was an outgrowth of his reading habit of distilling every subject to its essence. He confided to a congressman in 1863 that "a peculiarity of his own life

---

[21] Nathaniel Grigsby interview, September 12, 1865, *Herndon's Informants*, 114–15.

[22] Herbert Joseph Edwards and John Erskine Hankins, *Lincoln the Writer* (Orono, Maine, 1962), 26.

[23] Henry C. Whitney statement, [1887?], *Herndon's Informants*, 648.

[24] Leonard Swett to William H. Herndon, January 17, 1866, *Herndon's Informants*, 168.

[25] Swett statement included in Henry C. Whitney to Herndon, August 29, 1887, *Herndon's Informants*, 636.

[26] Leonard Swett to William H. Herndon, January 17, 1866, *Herndon's Informants*, 167.

from his earliest manhood had been that he habitually studied the opposite side of every disputed question, of every law case, of every political issue, more exhaustively, if possible, than his own side . . . [with] the result . . . that in all his long practice at the bar he had never once been surprised in court by the strength of his adversary's case, often finding it much weaker than he had feared."[27]

The style of analysis Lincoln deployed in his legal arguments pervaded his writings and speeches. In an age of inflated political rhetoric, Lincoln valued reason. "Reason," he declared in a speech in 1838, "cold, calculating, unimpassioned reason, must furnish all the materials for our future support and defence."[28] Although Lincoln was capable of unsurpassed eloquence, for the most part his language was lean, plain, and direct. Lincoln's rhetorical style reflected the clarity and precision of his thoughts. In general, he chose words with unusual care to say just what he meant—no more, no less. During his presidency, Lincoln commented, "It is very common in this country to find great facility of expression and less common to find great lucidity of thought. The combination of the two in one person is very uncommon but whenever you do find it, you have a great man."[29] Perhaps half-consciously, Lincoln described himself.

Lincoln's lifelong habit of writing contributed to the clarity of his thoughts. In addition to writing out passages from his reading, Lincoln often crystallized his thoughts by writing them down. Major speeches he painstakingly wrote and rewrote. He never wrote a book, although his famous 1858 debates with Stephen A. Douglas were published in book form. He wrote a number of anonymous, mostly satirical pieces for the Springfield newspaper. But mostly he wrote speeches, letters, and—once he became president—official documents.

Lincoln declared that writing—"the art of communicating thoughts to the mind, through the eye—is the great invention of the world . . . great, very great in enabling us to converse with the dead, the absent,

---

[27] Allen Thorndike Rice, ed., *Reminiscences of Abraham Lincoln by Distinguished Men of His Time* (New York, 1886), 333–34.

[28] "Address to the Young Men's Lyceum of Springfield, Illinois," January 27, 1838, *CW*, I, 115.

[29] Edward Dicey, "Washington during the War," *Macmillan's Magazine* 6 (May 1862): 24.

and the unborn, at all distances of time and space."[30] Printing enormously expanded the range of writing by communicating to thousands what had previously been available to only a few.

Most Americans, of course, never saw Lincoln or heard him speak. But printing brought his ideas to millions. Published in newspapers throughout the North, Lincoln's writings and speeches were widely read, discussed, and criticized. "The image of the man went out with his words," the famous abolitionist Frederick Douglass observed, "and those who read them knew him."[31] If Lincoln had not become president, he would have remained a gifted but obscure Illinois lawyer, forgotten by all but a small circle of friends and relatives. Yet Lincoln's words, along with many other developments, elevated him to the presidency. In the Civil War's fourth year, Lincoln mused, "It is strange that I, a boy brought up in the woods, and seeing, as it were, but little of the world, should be drifted to the very apex of this great event."[32] That boy brought up in the woods had become a master wordsmith through a lifelong apprenticeship of reading, speaking, and writing. Because he was president, his words about slavery and the Civil War had profound influence then and still. Above all, his words helped fashion the popular consent upon which his presidency depended. Lincoln should be remembered as a preeminent political leader whose language did more than that of any president since Thomas Jefferson to define the meaning of America.

[30] "Second Lecture on Discoveries and Inventions," February 11, 1859, *CW*, III, 359–60.

[31] Frederick Douglass, "Oration in Memory of Abraham Lincoln," April 14, 1876, in Philip S. Foner, ed., *The Life and Writings of Frederick Douglass* (4 vols.; New York, 1955), IV, 315. I am indebted to David Rankin for this quotation.

[32] Don E. Fehrenbacher and Virginia Fehrenbacher, eds., *Recollected Words of Abraham Lincoln* (Stanford, Calif., 1996), 31.

1

Becoming a Republican

Abraham Lincoln spent most of his political life as a loyal member of the Whig party. From the time he first stepped forward as a candidate for political office in 1832, Lincoln declared his support for policies that would aid economic development, policies endorsed by Whigs throughout the nation. He believed that internal improvements—roads, canals, and railroads—should be built to connect inland farms, towns, navigable waterways, and more distant markets. He favored tariffs to provide revenues to fund internal improvements and to protect American manufacturers from foreign competition. He advocated banks to help capitalize these improvements and to make credit more readily available to borrowers. Henry Clay, the national leader of the Whig party, termed these central tenets of Whig faith "the American System." Clay and other Whigs believed that the American System would create an economic infrastructure that encouraged trade among people in the North, South, and West, thereby producing prosperity, making the sections interdependent, and strengthening the nation.

As a Whig, Lincoln was elected to four terms in the Illinois legislature between 1834 and 1840 and to one term in Congress in 1846. He campaigned energetically for other Whig candidates, but after the Mexican War (1846–1848), when the status of slavery in the newly acquired territories became controversial, Whig party ties began to fray. Southern Whigs tended to claim that the new territories should be open to slavery; most northern Whigs argued that slavery should be barred. Slavery and questions of sectional loyalty began to crowd the economic issues of the American System out of the political spotlight, weakening the Whig party's national appeal. Whigs were still strong enough to play a major role in crafting the Compromise of 1850, intended to settle the question of slavery in the territories. The compromise balanced the admission of California as a free state and the elimination of the slave trade in the

Figure 1. *Congressman-Elect*
The first known photograph of Lincoln, this portrait was made in Springfield in 1846, shortly after his election to Congress. It portrays the successful young lawyer and Whig politician in splendid clothing that betrays no hint of his log cabin origins.

Reproduced from the Collections of the Library of Congress.

District of Columbia with the organization of the Utah and New Mexico territories without specifying the status of slavery and a new fugitive slave law that favored slaveholders by increasing punishments for aiding slaves to escape and requiring northern citizens to help catch runaway slaves. Finally, it seemed, the compromise had removed the troublesome question of slavery from political contention.

In 1854, the Kansas-Nebraska Act exploded the Whig party and blasted deep fissures among Democrats, permanently altering the nation's political landscape. In flight from the Whig party, whose southern wing endorsed Kansas-Nebraska, many northern Whigs began to align themselves with the newly formed Republican party. Lincoln became a founding member of the Republican party in Illinois in 1856 and campaigned for the Republicans' presidential nominee, John C. Frémont. The 1856 election revealed the emerging sectional chasm in party loyalties. James Buchanan, the Democratic candidate, was elected president with majorities in every slave state but one. Frémont carried all but five free states, demonstrating the Republicans' appeal in the North.

The Kansas-Nebraska Act provoked Lincoln into renewed political activity. At first reluctant to abandon his roots in the Whig party, he soon became a leading Republican spokesman in Illinois. In the heat of partisan battle, Lincoln repeatedly explained his views of the place of slavery and black people in American society, the meaning of freedom in the life of the Republic, and the profound value of the Constitution and the Union in preserving the nation's experiment in self-government. Lincoln believed that these issues distinguished his political allies (first Whigs, then Republicans) from their foes in the Democratic party. The speeches and writings in this chapter document the ideas that defined Lincoln's Republican convictions and, ultimately, his policies as president.

THE KANSAS-NEBRASKA ACT

Passage of the Kansas-Nebraska Act in May 1854 ignited a political firestorm. James M. McPherson, one of the foremost historians of the Civil War, declared that the "law may have been the most important single event pushing the nation toward civil war."[1] But why did a single piece

---

[1] James M. McPherson, *Battle Cry of Freedom: The Civil War Era* (New York, 1988), 121.

of legislation about a thinly populated region most Americans had no desire to settle or even to visit cause such an uproar?

The major reason the Kansas-Nebraska Act created controversy was that it repealed the provision of the Missouri Compromise that prohibited slavery from the Kansas-Nebraska region, overturning the longstanding political settlement of the status of slavery in this territory (see Map 2). In effect, the Kansas-Nebraska Act opened to slavery land that had previously been slave-free, which outraged many northerners, especially northern Whigs such as Lincoln. Stephen A. Douglas, Democratic U.S. senator from Illinois and architect of the Kansas-Nebraska Act, wanted to organize the Kansas-Nebraska territory in order to encourage settlement and to permit a transcontinental railroad to be built through the region, with the railroad's eastern terminus at Chicago in his home state. Without repealing the Missouri Compromise, Douglas could not get slave state congressmen to support the Kansas-Nebraska legislation. Douglas argued that repeal of the Missouri Compromise did not matter much. For one thing, few masters would bring their slaves into the territory because the climate and topography did not favor slave-grown crops such as cotton and tobacco. More important, Douglas pointed out, the Kansas-Nebraska Act permitted settlers to decide for themselves all questions regarding slavery in the region. If they wanted to prohibit slavery, they could vote to do so. What could be more democratic? This doctrine of popular sovereignty had been approved by Congress in the Compromise of 1850 for settling the question of slavery in the Utah and New Mexico territories. Why should it cause such turmoil now, just four years later?

Lincoln addressed that question in the fall of 1854 when, in a prelude to the more famous Lincoln-Douglas debates of 1858, he confronted Douglas at Peoria, Illinois. Lincoln's speech signaled both his opposition to Kansas-Nebraska and his renewed political ambition. Lincoln's Peoria speech, later published in the *Illinois State Journal*, examined the history of disputes about the status of slavery in the territories and explained why the Kansas-Nebraska Act was wrong and dangerous. In the following selection, Lincoln outlined themes that remained central to his thinking about slavery, freedom, African Americans, the Constitution, and the Union. His speech illustrates why Kansas-Nebraska catalyzed the metamorphosis of old Whigs into new Republicans.

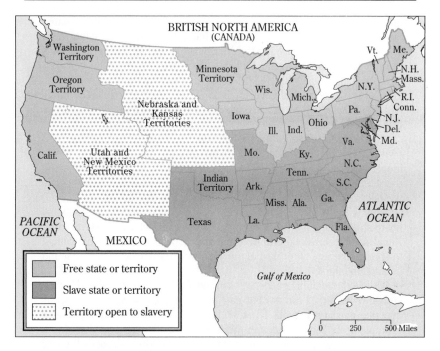

Map 2. *Kansas-Nebraska Act, 1854*
Compared to the states east of the Mississippi River, the immense size of the Kansas and Nebraska territories roughly equaled all the free states or all the slave states, an illustration of the high stakes in the Kansas-Nebraska controversy.

1

Speech on the Kansas-Nebraska Act at Peoria, Illinois
October 16, 1854

. . . Preceding the Presidential election of 1852, each of the great political parties, democrats and whigs, met in convention, and adopted resolutions endorsing the compromise of '50; as a "finality," a final settlement, so far as these parties could make it so, of all slavery agitation. . . .

During this long period of time Nebraska had remained, substantially an uninhabited country, but now emigration to, and settlement within it began to take place. It is about one third as large as the present United States, and its importance so long overlooked, begins to come into view. The restriction of slavery by the Missouri Compromise directly applies to it; in fact, was first made, and has since been maintained, expressly for it. . . . On January 4th, 1854, Judge Douglas[2] introduces a new bill to give Nebraska territorial government. . . . Before long the bill is so modified as to make two territories instead of one; calling the Southern one Kansas.

Also, about a month after the introduction of the bill, on the judge's own motion, it is so amended as to declare the Missouri Compromise inoperative and void; and, substantially, that the People who go and settle there may establish slavery, or exclude it, as they may see fit. In this shape the bill passed both branches of congress, and became a law.

This is the *repeal* of the Missouri Compromise. . . . I think, and shall try to show, that it is wrong; wrong in its direct effect, letting slavery into Kansas and Nebraska—and wrong in its prospective principle, allowing it to spread to every other part of the wide world, where men can be found inclined to take it.

This *declared* indifference, but as I must think, covert *real* zeal for the spread of slavery, I can not but hate. I hate it because of the monstrous injustice of slavery itself. I hate it because it deprives our republican example of its just influence in the world—enables the enemies of free institutions, with plausibility, to taunt us as hypocrites—causes the real friends of freedom to doubt our sincerity, and especially because it forces so many really good men amongst ourselves into an open war with the very fundamental principles of civil liberty—criticising the Declaration of Independence, and insisting that there is no right principle of action but *self-interest*.

Before proceeding, let me say I think I have no prejudice against the Southern people. They are just what we would be in their situation. If slavery did not now exist amongst them, they would not introduce it. If it did now exist amongst us, we should not instantly give it up. This I believe of the masses north and south. Doubtless there are individuals, on both sides, who would not hold slaves under any circumstances; and others who would gladly introduce slavery anew, if it were out of existence. We know that some southern men do free their slaves, go north, and become tip-top abolitionists; while some northern ones go south, and become most cruel slave-masters.

When southern people tell us they are no more responsible for the origin of slavery, than we; I acknowledge the fact. When it is said that the institution exists; and that it is very difficult to get rid of it, in any

---

[2] Although Douglas was a U.S. senator, Lincoln referred to him as "Judge" because he served on the Illinois Supreme Court for two years before he was elected to Congress in 1843.

satisfactory way, I can understand and appreciate the saying. I surely will not blame them for not doing what I should not know how to do myself. If all earthly power were given me, I should not know what to do, as to the existing institution. My first impulse would be to free all the slaves, and send them to Liberia,—to their own native land. But a moment's reflection would convince me, that whatever of high hope, (as I think there is) there may be in this, in the long run, its sudden execution is impossible. If they were all landed there in a day, they would all perish in the next ten days; and there are not surplus shipping and surplus money enough in the world to carry them there in many times ten days. What then? Free them all, and keep them among us as underlings? Is it quite certain that this betters their condition? I think I would not hold one in slavery, at any rate; yet the point is not clear enough for me to denounce people upon. What next? Free them, and make them politically and socially, our equals? My own feelings will not admit of this; and if mine would, we well know that those of the great mass of white people will not. Whether this feeling accords with justice and sound judgment, is not the sole question, if indeed, it is any part of it. A universal feeling, whether well or ill-founded, can not be safely disregarded. We can not, then, make them equals. It does seem to me that systems of gradual emancipation might be adopted; but for their tardiness in this, I will not undertake to judge our brethren of the south.

When they remind us of their constitutional rights, I acknowledge them, not grudgingly, but fully, and fairly; and I would give them any legislation for the reclaiming of their fugitives, which should not, in its stringency, be more likely to carry a free man into slavery, than our ordinary criminal laws are to hang an innocent one.

But all this; to my judgment, furnishes no more excuse for permitting slavery to go into our own free territory, than it would for reviving the African slave trade by law. The law which forbids the bringing of slaves *from* Africa; and that which has so long forbid the taking them *to* Nebraska, can hardly be distinguished on any moral principle; and the repeal of the former could find quite as plausible excuses as that of the latter. . . .

Some men, mostly whigs, who condemn the repeal of the Missouri Compromise, nevertheless hesitate to go for its restoration, lest they be thrown in company with the abolitionist. Will they allow me as an old whig to tell them good humoredly, that I think this is very silly? Stand with anybody that stands RIGHT. Stand with him while he is right and PART with him when he goes wrong. Stand WITH the abolitionist in restoring the Missouri Compromise; and stand AGAINST him when he attempts to repeal the fugitive slave law. In the latter case you stand with the southern disunionist. What of that? You are still right. In both cases you are right. In both cases you oppose the dangerous extremes. In both you stand on middle ground and hold the ship level and steady. In both you are national and nothing less than national. This is good old whig ground. To desert such ground, because of any company, is to be less than a whig—less than a man—less than an American.

I particularly object to the new position which the avowed principle of this Nebraska law gives to slavery in the body politic. I object to it because it assumes that there CAN BE MORAL RIGHT in the enslaving of one man by another. I object to it as a dangerous dalliance for a free people—a sad evidence that, feeling prosperity we forget right—that liberty, as a principle, we have ceased to revere. I object to it because the fathers of the republic eschewed, and rejected it. The argument of "Necessity" was the only argument they ever admitted in favor of slavery; and so far, and so far only as it carried them, did they ever go. They found the institution existing among us, which they could not help; and they cast blame upon the British King for having permitted its introduction. BEFORE the constitution, they prohibited its introduction into the north-western Territory—the only country we owned, then free from it. AT the framing and adoption of the constitution, they forbore to so much as mention the word "slave" or "slavery" in the whole instrument. In the provision for the recovery of fugitives, the slave is spoken of as a "PERSON HELD TO SERVICE OR LABOR." In that prohibiting the abolition of the African slave trade for twenty years, that trade is spoken of as "The migration or importation of such persons as any of the States NOW EXISTING, shall think proper to admit," &c. These are the only provisions alluding to slavery. Thus, the thing is hid away, in the constitution, just as an afflicted man hides away a wen [cyst] or a cancer, which he dares not cut out at once, lest he bleed to death; with the promise, nevertheless, that the cutting may begin at the end of a given time. Less than this our fathers COULD not do; and MORE they WOULD not do. Necessity drove them so far, and farther, they would not go. But this is not all. The earliest Congress, under the constitution, took the same view of slavery. They hedged and hemmed it in to the narrowest limits of necessity.

In 1794, they prohibited an out-going slave-trade—that is, the taking of slaves FROM the United States to sell.

In 1798, they prohibited the bringing of slaves from Africa, INTO the Mississippi Territory—this territory then comprising what are now the States of Mississippi and Alabama. This was TEN YEARS before they had the authority to do the same thing as to the States existing at the adoption of the constitution.

In 1800 they prohibited AMERICAN CITIZENS from trading in slaves between foreign countries—as, for instance, from Africa to Brazil.

In 1803 they passed a law in aid of one or two State laws, in restraint of the internal slave trade.

In 1807, in apparent hot haste, they passed the law, nearly a year in advance, to take effect the first day of 1808—the very first day the constitution would permit—prohibiting the African slave trade by heavy pecuniary and corporal penalties.

In 1820, finding these provisions ineffectual, they declared the trade piracy, and annexed to it, the extreme penalty of death. While all this was passing in the general government, five or six of the original slave States had adopted systems of gradual emancipation; and by which the institution was rapidly becoming extinct within these limits.

Thus we see, the plain unmistakable spirit of that age, towards slavery, was hostility to the PRINCIPLE, and toleration, ONLY BY NECESSITY.

But NOW it is to be transformed into a "sacred right." Nebraska brings it forth, places it on the high road to extension and perpetuity; and, with a pat on its back, says to it, "Go, and God speed you." Henceforth it is to be the chief jewel of the nation—the very figure-head of the ship of State. Little by little, but steadily as man's march to the grave, we have been giving up the OLD for the NEW faith. Near eighty years ago we began by declaring that all men are created equal; but now from that beginning we have run down to the other declaration, that for SOME men to enslave OTHERS is a "sacred right of self-government." These principles can not stand together. They are as opposite as God and mammon [material riches]; and whoever holds to the one, must despise the other. When [a pro-Nebraska congressman] . . . called the Declaration of Independence "a self-evident lie" he only did what consistency and candor require all other Nebraska men to do. . . . If this had been said . . . in old Independence Hall, seventy-eight years ago, the very door-keeper would have throttled the man, and thrust him into the street.

Let no one be deceived. The spirit of seventy-six and the spirit of Nebraska, are utter antagonisms; and the former is being rapidly displaced by the latter.

Fellow countrymen—Americans south, as well as north, shall we make no effort to arrest this? . . . Is there no danger to liberty itself, in discarding the earliest practice, and first precept of our ancient faith? In our greedy chase to make profit of the negro, let us beware, lest we "cancel and tear to pieces" even the white man's charter of freedom.

Our republican robe is soiled, and trailed in the dust. Let us repurify it. Let us turn and wash it white, in the spirit, if not the blood, of the Revolution. Let us turn slavery from its claims of "moral right," back upon its existing legal rights, and its arguments of "necessity." Let us return it to the position our fathers gave it; and there let it rest in peace. Let us re-adopt the Declaration of Independence, and with it, the practices, and policy, which harmonize with it. Let north and south—let all Americans—let all lovers of liberty everywhere—join in the great and good work. If we do this, we shall not only have saved the Union; but we shall have so saved it, as to make, and to keep it, forever worthy of the saving. We shall have so saved it, that the succeeding millions of free happy people, the world over, shall rise up, and call us blessed, to the latest generations. . . .

JUSTIFICATIONS OF SLAVERY

In his speeches, Lincoln explained his opposition to slavery in terms of the nation's commitment to the ideals of freedom and equality. In a brief, undated note evidently written to crystallize his thoughts, Lincoln condensed his critique of arguments often used to justify the existence of slavery. The note subverts the conventional racial defense of slavery as the proper place for black people by showing that the same arguments could be employed to defend enslavement of anybody, including whites.

2

Fragment on Slavery

Possibly 1854

If A. can prove, however conclusively, that he may, of right, enslave B.—why may not B. snatch the same argument, and prove equally, that he may enslave A?—

You say A. is white, and B. is black. It is *color*, then; the lighter, having the right to enslave the darker? Take care. By this rule, you are to be slave to the first man you meet, with a fairer skin than your own.

You do not mean *color* exactly?—You mean the whites are *intellectually* the superiors of the blacks, and, therefore have the right to enslave them? Take care again. By this rule, you are to be slave to the first man you meet, with an intellect superior to your own.

But, say you, it is a question of *interest*; and, if you can make it your *interest*, you have the right to enslave another. Very well. And if he can make it his interest, he has the right to enslave you.

"WHERE I NOW STAND"

The furor over slavery renewed by the Kansas-Nebraska Act strained Lincoln's relationship with Joshua Speed, one of his oldest and best friends. The two men shared a room and even slept in the same bed for several years after Lincoln arrived in Springfield in 1837.[3] Speed grew up in a wealthy Kentucky family that owned some seventy slaves on a

---

[3] Crowded housing often required men to share a bed. Travelers commonly slept in the same bed with complete strangers. Although a few writers have suggested that Lincoln was homosexual, persuasive evidence of the claim does not exist.

plantation near Louisville. In 1841, Speed moved back to Kentucky, and Lincoln visited him there late that summer. In 1855, when their differences about slavery threatened to disrupt their long friendship, Lincoln tried to reassure Speed that, under the Constitution, slaveholders could not be deprived of their slave property. Yet Lincoln's moral opposition to slavery and his insistence that the expansion of slavery was intolerable separated him from both his old friend and his old attachment to the Whig party. Although Lincoln's views threatened—as he said—to "unwhig" him, he affirmed his personal sympathies for Speed and other slaveholders, despite deep political differences. Lincoln's unusual respect for people who held views in conflict with his own, evident in the following letter, continued to characterize his thoughts and actions after he became president.

3

Letter to Joshua F. Speed
August 24, 1855

Springfield, [Illinois]

Dear Speed:

. . . You suggest that in political action now, you and I would differ. I suppose we would; not quite as much, however, as you may think. You know I dislike slavery; and you fully admit the abstract wrong of it. So far there is no cause of difference. But you say that sooner than yield your legal right to the slave—especially at the bidding of those who are not themselves interested, you would see the Union dissolved. I am not aware that *any one* is bidding you to yield that right; very certainly *I* am not. I leave that matter entirely to yourself. I also acknowledge *your* rights and *my* obligations, under the constitution, in regard to your slaves. I confess I hate to see the poor creatures hunted down, and caught, and carried back to their stripes [whippings], and unrewarded toils; but I bite my lip and keep quiet. In 1841 you and I had together a tedious low-water trip, on a Steam Boat from Louisville to St. Louis. You may remember, as I well do, that from Louisville to the mouth of the Ohio there were, on board, ten or a dozen slaves, shackled together with irons. That sight was a continual torment to me; and I see something like it every time I touch the Ohio, or any other slave-border.[4] It is hardly fair for you to assume, that I have

[4] Back in 1841, Lincoln described the slaves on the steamboat in a letter to Joshua Speed's half sister Mary without mentioning that the sight "was a continual torment"

no interest in a thing which has, and continually exercises, the power of making me miserable. You ought rather to appreciate how much the great body of the Northern people do crucify their feelings, in order to maintain their loyalty to the constitution and the Union.

I do oppose the extension of slavery, because my judgment and feelings so prompt me; and I am under no obligation to the contrary. If for this you and I must differ, differ we must. You say if you were President, you would send an army and hang the leaders of the Missouri outrages upon the Kansas elections;[5] still, if Kansas fairly votes herself a slave state, she must be admitted, or the Union must be dissolved. But how if she votes herself a slave state *unfairly*—that is, by the very means for which you say you would hang men? Must she still be admitted, or the Union be dissolved? That will be the phase of the question when it first becomes a practical one. In your assumption that there may be a *fair* decision of the slavery question in Kansas, I plainly see you and I would differ about the Nebraska-law. I look upon that enactment not as a *law*, but as *violence* from the beginning. It was conceived in violence, passed in violence, is maintained in violence, and is being executed in violence. I say it was *conceived* in violence, because the destruction of the Missouri Compromise, under the circumstances, was nothing less than violence. It was *passed* in violence, because it could not have passed at all but for the votes of many members, in violent disregard of the known will of their constituents. It is *maintained* in violence because the elections since, clearly demand it's repeal, and this demand is openly disregarded. *You* say men ought to be hung for the way they are executing that law; and *I* say the way it is being executed is quite as good as any of its antecedents. It is being executed

---

to him. Lincoln wrote, "By the way; a fine example was presented on board the boat for contemplating the effect of *condition* upon human happiness. A gentleman had purchased twelve negroes in different parts of Kentucky and was taking them to a farm in the South. They were chained six and six together . . . so that the negroes were strung together precisely like so many fish upon a trot-line. In this condition they were being separated forever from the scenes of their childhood, their friends, their fathers and mothers, and brothers and sisters, and many of them, from their wives and children, going into perpetual slavery where the lash of the master is proverbially more ruthless and unrelenting than any other where; and yet amid all these distressing circumstances, as we would think them, they were the most cheerful and apparantly happy creatures on board. One, whose offence for which he had been sold was an over-fondness for his wife, played the fiddle almost continually; and the others danced, sung, cracked jokes, and played various games with cards from day to day. How true it is that 'God tempers the wind to the shorn lamb,' or in other words, that He renders the worst of human conditions tolerable, while He permits the best, to be nothing better than tolerable." *CW*, I, 259–61.

[5] Thousands of proslavery Missourians crossed the border into Kansas and voted illegally in the fall of 1854 for a proslavery delegate to Congress and in March 1855 for proslavery members of the territorial legislature, easily defeating free-soil candidates.

in the precise way which was intended from the first; else why does no Nebraska man express astonishment or condemnation? . . .

That Kansas will form a Slave constitution, and, with it, will ask to be admitted into the Union, I take to be an already settled question; and so settled by the very means you so pointedly condemn. By every principle of law, ever held by any court, North or South, every negro taken to Kansas is free; yet in utter disregard of this—in the spirit of violence merely—that beautiful Legislature gravely passes a law to hang men who shall venture to inform a negro of his legal rights. This is the substance, and real object of the law. . . .

In my humble sphere, I shall advocate the restoration of the Missouri Compromise, so long as Kansas remains a territory;[6] and when, by all these foul means, it seeks to come into the Union as a Slave-state, I shall oppose it. I am very loth, in any case, to withhold my assent to the enjoyment of property *acquired*, or *located*, in good faith; but I do not admit that *good faith*, in taking a negro to Kansas, to be held in slavery, is a *possibility* with any man. Any man who has sense enough to be the controller of his own property, has too much sense to misunderstand the outrageous character of this whole Nebraska business. But I digress. In my opposition to the admission of Kansas I shall have some company; but we may be beaten. If we are, I shall not, on that account, attempt to dissolve the Union. On the contrary, if we succeed, there will be enough of us to take care of the Union. I think it probable, however, we shall be beaten. Standing as a unit among yourselves, you can, directly, and indirectly, bribe enough of our men to carry the day—as you could on an open proposition to establish monarchy. Get hold of some man in the North, whose position and ability is such, that he can make the support of your measure—whatever it may be—a *democratic party necessity*, and the thing is done. . . .

You say if Kansas fairly votes herself a free state, as a christian you will rather rejoice at it. All decent slave-holders *talk* that way; and I do not doubt their candor. But they never *vote* that way. Although in a private letter, or conversation, you will express your preference that Kansas shall be free, you would vote for no man for Congress who would say the same thing publicly. No such man could be elected from any district in any slave-state. . . . The slave-breeders and slave-traders, are a small, odious and detested class, among you; and yet in politics, they dictate the course of all of you, and are as completely your masters, as you are the masters of your own negroes.

You enquire where I now stand. That is a disputed point. I think I am a whig; but others say there are no whigs, and that I am an abolitionist.

---

[6] The Missouri Compromise provided that slavery was prohibited from the territory that by 1854 had become Kansas.

When I was at Washington I voted for the Wilmot Proviso[7] as good as forty times, and I never heard of any one attempting to unwhig me for that. I now do no more than oppose the *extension* of slavery.

I am not a Know-Nothing.[8] That is certain. How could I be? How can any one who abhors the oppression of negroes, be in favor of degrading classes of white people? Our progress in degeneracy appears to me to be pretty rapid. As a nation, we began by declaring that "*all men are created equal.*" We now practically read it "all men are created equal, *except negroes.*" When the Know-Nothings get control, it will read "all men are created equal, except negroes, *and foreigners, and catholics.*" When it comes to this I should prefer emigrating to some country where they make no pretence of loving liberty—to Russia, for instance, where despotism can be taken pure, and without the base alloy of hypocracy. . . .

> And yet let me say I am Your friend forever
> A. LINCOLN

[7] In August 1846, David Wilmot—a first-term Democratic congressman from Pennsylvania—proposed an amendment providing that slavery and involuntary servitude would never be permitted to exist in any territory acquired as a result of the Mexican War. The Wilmot Proviso became the focal point of heated debate between proslavery and free-soil forces. The proviso never became law. Free-soil majorities in the House of Representatives supported it, but it stalled in the Senate, where slave state senators who opposed the proviso counterbalanced those from free states who favored it.

[8] The Know-Nothing (or American) party, organized as a secret society in 1854, was anti-immigrant, anti-Catholic, and—for the most part—anti-Democratic, since many Irish Catholic immigrants who flooded into the nation after 1845 voted for Democrats. Unlike Lincoln, many former Whigs gravitated toward the Know-Nothings after the Kansas-Nebraska Act.

THE *DRED SCOTT* DECISION

In March 1857, the U.S. Supreme Court announced its decision in the *Dred Scott* case. Scott, a Missouri slave whose master had taken him north where slavery was prohibited, had filed suit to obtain his freedom. Many Americans hoped that the Court's decision would finally settle the slavery controversy. They were disappointed. Chief Justice Roger B. Taney, a Maryland Democrat and former slaveholder who had been appointed to the Court in 1836 by President Andrew Jackson, wrote the majority opinion. Taney held that Congress had no constitutional power to regulate slavery in the territories and that black people—even if they were free—had no rights under the Constitution. Taney's purpose, as Don E. Fehrenbacher, the preeminent historian of the *Dred Scott* case has written, was "to launch a sweeping counterattack on the antislavery movement and to reinforce the bastions of slavery at every rampart and parapet."[9] Taney's opinion effectively declared the Republican party's opposition to the expansion of slavery unconstitutional, putting Lincoln and other Republicans in the uncomfortable position of defending a policy that had been ruled illegal by the highest court in the land.

Late in June, Lincoln spoke out against Taney's decision in Springfield, two weeks after hearing Stephen A. Douglas defend the Court's verdict. In his speech, subsequently published in the *Illinois State Journal* and other newspapers, Lincoln argued that while he and other Republicans vehemently disagreed with Taney, they did not resist the Court's ruling. Above all, Lincoln attacked Taney's claim that the Declaration of Independence and the Constitution did not apply to blacks. Lincoln affirmed the humanity and political rights of black people and contrasted his Republican convictions with the Democrats' determination to oppress blacks in every way. Since Douglas and other Democrats appealed to the widespread belief in white supremacy among northern voters by accusing Republicans of advocating social equality for blacks, Lincoln took care to explain his view of the limits of racial equality.

[9] Don E. Fehrenbacher, *The* Dred Scott *Case: Its Significance in American Law and Politics* (New York, 1978), 341.

4

Speech on the Dred Scott *Decision*

June 26, 1857

Springfield, Illinois

. . . And now as to the Dred Scott decision. That decision declares two propositions—first, that a negro cannot sue in the U.S. Courts; and secondly, that Congress cannot prohibit slavery in the Territories. It was made by a divided court[10]—dividing differently on the different points. Judge Douglas . . . denounces all who question the correctness of that decision, as offering violent resistance to it. But who resists it? Who

[10] On the principal issues, the Court was divided seven to two.

has, in spite of the decision, declared Dred Scott free, and resisted the authority of his master over him?

Judicial decisions have two uses—first, to absolutely determine the case decided, and secondly, to indicate to the public how other similar cases will be decided when they arise. For the latter use, they are called "precedents" and "authorities."

We believe, as much as Judge Douglas, (perhaps more) in obedience to, and respect for the judicial department of government. We think its decisions on Constitutional questions, when fully settled, should control, not only the particular cases decided, but the general policy of the country, subject to be disturbed only by amendments of the Constitution as provided in that instrument itself. More than this would be revolution. But we think the Dred Scott decision is erroneous. We know the court that made it, has often over-ruled its own decisions, and we shall do what we can to have it to over-rule this. We offer no *resistance* to it. . . .

If this important decision had been made by the unanimous concurrence of the judges, and without any apparent partisan bias, and in accordance with legal public expectation, and with the steady practice of the departments throughout our history, and had been in no part, based on assumed historical facts which are not really true; or, if wanting in some of these, it had been before the court more than once, and had there been affirmed and re-affirmed through a course of years, it then might be, perhaps would be, factious, nay, even revolutionary, to not acquiesce in it as a precedent.

But when, as it is true we find it wanting in all these claims to the public confidence, it is not resistance, it is not factious, it is not even disrespectful, to treat it as not having yet quite established a settled doctrine for the country. . . . [T]he Chief Justice does not directly assert, but plainly assumes, as a fact, that the public estimate of the black man is more favorable now than it was in the days of the Revolution. This assumption is a mistake. In some trifling particulars, the condition of that race has been ameliorated; but, as a whole, in this country, the change between then and now is decidedly the other way; and their ultimate destiny has never appeared so hopeless as in the last three or four years. In two of the five States—New Jersey and North Carolina—that then gave the free negro the right of voting, the right has since been taken away; and in a third—New York—it has been greatly abridged; while it has not been extended, so far as I know, to a single additional State, though the number of the States has more than doubled. In those days, as I understand, masters could, at their own pleasure, emancipate their slaves; but since then, such legal restraints have been made upon emancipation, as to amount almost to prohibition. In those days, Legislatures held the unquestioned power to abolish slavery in their respective States; but now it is becoming quite fashionable for State Constitutions to withhold that power from the Legislatures. In those days, by common consent, the spread of the black man's bondage to new countries was prohibited; but now, Congress decides that it *will* not continue the prohibition, and the Supreme Court decides that it *could* not if it would. In those days, our Declaration of Independence was held sacred by all, and thought to include all; but now, to aid in making the bondage of the negro universal and eternal, it is assailed, and sneered at, and construed, and hawked at, and torn, till, if its framers could rise from their graves, they could not at all recognize it. All the powers of earth seem rapidly combining against him.[11] Mammon [greed] is after him; ambition follows, and philosophy follows, and the Theology of the day is fast joining the cry. They have him in his prison house; they have searched his person, and left no prying instrument with him. One after another they have closed the heavy iron doors upon him, and now they have him, as it were, bolted in with a lock of a hundred keys, which can never be unlocked without the concurrence of every key; the keys in the hands of a hundred different men, and they scattered to a hundred different and distant places; and they stand musing as to what invention, in all the dominions of mind and matter, can be produced to make the impossibility of his escape more complete than it is.

It is grossly incorrect to say or assume, that the public estimate of the negro is more favorable now than it was at the origin of the government. . . .

There is a natural disgust in the minds of nearly all white people, to the idea of an indiscriminate amalgamation of the white and black races; and Judge Douglas evidently is basing his chief hope, upon the chances of being able to appropriate the benefit of this disgust to himself. If he can, by much drumming and repeating, fasten the odium of that idea upon his adversaries, he thinks he can struggle through the storm. He therefore clings to this hope, as a drowning man to the last plank. . . . He finds the Republicans insisting that the Declaration of Independence includes ALL men, black as well as white; and forthwith he boldly denies that it includes negroes at all, and proceeds to argue gravely that all who contend it does, do so only because they want to vote, and eat, and sleep, and marry with negroes! He will have it that they cannot be consistent else. Now I protest against that counterfeit logic which concludes that, because I do not want a black woman for a *slave* I must necessarily want her for a *wife*. I need not have her for either, I can just leave her alone. In some respects she certainly is not my equal; but in her natural right to eat the bread she earns with her own hands without asking leave of any one else, she is my equal, and the equal of all others.

Chief Justice Taney, in his opinion in the Dred Scott case, admits that the language of the Declaration is broad enough to include the whole

[11] By "him," Lincoln means "the Negro."

human family, but he and Judge Douglas argue that the authors of that instrument did not intend to include negroes, by the fact that they did not at once, actually place them on an equality with the whites. Now this grave argument comes to just nothing at all, by the other fact, that they did not at once, or *ever afterwards*, actually place all white people on an equality with one or another. And this is the staple argument of both the Chief Justice and the Senator, for doing this obvious violence to the plain unmistakable language of the Declaration. I think the authors of that notable instrument intended to include *all* men, but they did not intend to declare all men equal *in all respects*. They did not mean to say all were equal in color, size, intellect, moral developments, or social capacity. They defined with tolerable distinctness, in what respects they did consider all men created equal — equal in "certain inalienable rights, among which are life, liberty, and the pursuit of happiness." This they said, and this meant. They did not mean to assert the obvious untruth, that all were then actually enjoying that equality, nor yet, that they were about to confer it immediately upon them. In fact they had no power to confer such a boon. They meant simply to declare the *right*, so that the *enforcement* of it might follow as fast as circumstances should permit. They meant to set up a standard maxim for free society, which should be familiar to all, and revered by all; constantly looked to, constantly labored for, and even though never perfectly attained, constantly approximated, and thereby constantly spreading and deepening its influence, and augmenting the happiness and value of life to all people of all colors everywhere. The assertion that "all men are created equal" was of no practical use in effecting our separation from Great Britain; and it was placed in the Declaration, not for that, but for future use. Its authors meant it to be, thank God, it is now proving itself, a stumbling block to those who in after times might seek to turn a free people back into the hateful paths of despotism. They knew the proneness of prosperity to breed tyrants, and they meant when such should re-appear in this fair land and commence their vocation they should find left for them at least one hard nut to crack. . . .

I have said that the separation of the races is the only perfect preventive of amalgamation [of the races]. I have no right to say all the members of the Republican party are in favor of this, nor to say that as a party they are in favor of it. There is nothing in their platform directly on the subject. But I can say a very large proportion of its members are for it, and that the chief plank in their platform — opposition to the spread of slavery — is most favorable to that separation.

Such separation, if ever effected at all, must be effected by colonization; and no political party, as such, is now doing anything directly for colonization. Party operations at present only favor or retard colonization incidentally. The enterprise is a difficult one; but "when there is a will there is a way"; and what colonization needs most is a hearty will. Will springs from the two elements of moral sense and self-interest. Let us be brought to believe it is morally right, and, at the same time, favorable to, or, at least, not against, our interest, to transfer the African to his native clime, and we shall find a way to do it, however great the task may be. . . .

How differently the respective courses of the Democratic and Republican parties incidentally bear on the question of forming a will—a public sentiment—for colonization, is easy to see. The Republicans inculcate, with whatever of ability they can, that the negro is a man; that his bondage is cruelly wrong, and that the field of his oppression ought not to be enlarged. The Democrats deny his manhood; deny, or dwarf to insignificance, the wrong of his bondage; so far as possible, crush all sympathy for him, and cultivate and excite hatred and disgust against him; compliment themselves as Union-savers for doing so; and call the indefinite outspreading of his bondage "a sacred right of self-government." . . .

2

Leading the Republican Party

By 1858, Lincoln stood in the front ranks of Republicans in Illinois; two years later, he headed the Republican ticket in the campaign for president of the United States. Lincoln's skill in defining doctrines that appealed to the most important constituencies in the emerging Republican coalition contributed to his remarkable ascension as a party leader. In speech after speech during his 1858 campaign against Stephen A. Douglas for the U.S. Senate and afterward, Lincoln explained his views of how Republicans differed from Democrats, freedom from slavery, and whites from blacks. His insistence on fundamental human equality and the immorality of slavery sharply distinguished Republicans from many Democrats who denied both propositions. His respect for constitutional restraints on federal action against slavery reassured conservative former Whigs in the North that at least this Republican did not intend to translate his moral opposition to slavery into a call for immediate abolition and thereby precipitate a constitutional crisis and possibly disunion. His refusal to scapegoat German and Irish immigrants contrasted with the nativism of the Know-Nothing (or American) party, while his reluctance to criticize Know-Nothings in public left the door to the Republican party conveniently open to former Whigs who had found a temporary home in the American party. His repeated attacks on Douglas's perversion of the hallowed ideals of the Declaration of Independence also invited anti-Nebraska Democrats to affirm their traditional beliefs—which he claimed Douglas had abandoned—by migrating to the Republican party.

In June 1858, Lincoln was the unanimous selection of the Illinois Republican convention to run against Douglas for the U.S. Senate. After his "House Divided" speech (Document 5) and his celebrated debates with Douglas, Lincoln began to attract attention in Republican circles throughout the North. Although Lincoln lost the senatorial race, he remained a leading Republican spokesman, and when the party met for its 1860 convention in Chicago, he enjoyed the united support of the Illinois delegation for the presidential nomination. Republicans knew they could win the presidency if they nominated a candidate who maintained their majorities in the states carried by Frémont in 1856 and who added victories in Pennsylvania and either Indiana or Illinois. On the third ballot, they nominated Lincoln.

Unlike presidential aspirants today, Lincoln did not give speeches to promote his candidacy. In fact, he seldom left home. During and after the presidential campaign, he maintained an active correspondence and met with countless visitors and office-seekers, but he avoided speaking out on the developing crisis. He believed that his previous speeches had thoroughly explained the policies he would pursue as president. The following selections from Lincoln's political speeches between his 1858 nomination for the U.S. Senate and his victory in the 1860 presidential election document both Lincoln's ideas and what any interested person of the era could have known about them.

A HOUSE DIVIDED

Lincoln delivered his famous "House Divided" speech shortly after the Illinois Republican convention selected him to run for the U.S. Senate against Democratic incumbent Stephen A. Douglas. Lincoln did not originate the "house divided" metaphor. It appears several times in the Bible, and it had been used in recent years by both proslavery and antislavery advocates. Lincoln employed the metaphor to emphasize his view that slavery was on the verge of becoming national, rather than remaining confined to the southern states. Lincoln argued that leading Democrats, headed by Douglas, conspired to pass the Kansas-Nebraska Act, to repeal the Missouri Compromise, and most recently to undermine the Constitution with the *Dred Scott* decision, all with the intent to make slavery legal throughout the nation. Although no such conspiracy really existed, it was possible—as Lincoln pointed out—that the Supreme Court would soon declare that the principles of the *Dred Scott* decision applied not just to federal territories but also to states, thereby preventing states such as Illinois from excluding slavery.

Lincoln paid special attention to Douglas's indifference to the spread of slavery because of recent events in Kansas. Late in 1857, voters in Kansas had approved the Lecompton constitution, which would make Kansas a slave state. The constitution passed easily because antislavery Kansans boycotted the election, protesting the proslavery dominance of the convention that had drafted the constitution. Early in 1858, Democratic president James Buchanan recommended that Congress admit Kansas to the Union, organized as a slave state under the Lecompton constitution. Douglas and other northern Democrats joined Republicans in denouncing the constitution as the result of an unfair and unrepresentative election. Douglas's opposition to Lecompton made some Republicans flirt with the possibility of supporting him rather than Lincoln in the Illinois Senate race. In what amounted to the opening salvo in the senatorial campaign, Lincoln tried to end that flirtation by showing that a Republican was a far safer choice than a Democrat in the looming crisis of the house divided. Lincoln's speech was published in the *Illinois State Journal*, reprinted in other papers, and read by many people outside Illinois.

5

"House Divided" Speech[1]

June 16, 1858

Springfield, Illinois

If we could first know *where* we are, and *whither* we are tending, we could then better judge *what* to do, and *how* to do it.

We are now far into the *fifth* year, since a policy was initiated, with the *avowed* object, and *confident* promise, of putting an end to slavery agitation.

Under the operation of that policy, that agitation has not only, *not ceased*, but has *constantly augmented*.

In *my* opinion, it *will* not cease, until a *crisis* shall have been reached, and passed.

"A house divided against itself cannot stand."

I believe this government cannot endure, permanently half *slave* and half *free*.

I do not expect the Union to be *dissolved*—I do not expect the house to *fall*—but I *do* expect it will cease to be divided.

---

[1] The text of this speech follows that in Abraham Lincoln, *Selected Speeches and Writings*, ed. Don E. Fehrenbacher (New York, 1992), 131–32.

It will become *all* one thing, or *all* the other.

Either the *opponents* of slavery, will arrest the further spread of it, and place it where the public mind shall rest in the belief that it is in course of ultimate extinction; or its *advocates* will push it forward, till it shall become alike lawful in *all* the States, *old* as well as *new*—*North* as well as *South*.

Have we no *tendency* to the latter condition?

Let any one who doubts, carefully contemplate that now almost complete legal combination—piece of *machinery* so to speak—compounded of the Nebraska doctrine, and the Dred Scott decision. Let him consider not only *what work* the machinery is adapted to do, and *how well* adapted; but also, let him study the *history* of its construction, and trace, if he can, or rather *fail*, if he can, to trace the evidences of design, and concert of action, among its chief bosses, from the beginning.

The new year of 1854 found slavery excluded from more than half the States by State Constitutions, and from most of the national territory by Congressional prohibition.

Four days later, commenced the struggle, which ended in repealing that Congressional prohibition.

This opened all the national territory to slavery; and was the first point gained.

But, so far, *Congress* only, had acted; and an *indorsement* by the people, *real* or apparent, was indispensable, to *save* the point already gained, and give chance for more.

This necessity had not been overlooked; but had been provided for, as well as might be, in the notable argument of "*squatter sovereignty,*" otherwise called "*sacred right of self government,*" which latter phrase, though expressive of the only rightful basis of any government, was so perverted in this attempted use of it as to amount to just this: That if any *one* man, choose to enslave *another*, no *third* man shall be allowed to object.

That argument was incorporated into the Nebraska bill itself, in the language which follows: *"It being the true intent and meaning of this act not to legislate slavery into any Territory or state, nor to exclude it therefrom; but to leave the people thereof perfectly free to form and regulate their domestic institutions in their own way, subject only to the Constitution of the United States."*

Then opened the roar of loose declamation in favor of "Squatter Sovereignty," and "Sacred right of self government."

"But," said opposition members, "let us be more *specific*—let us *amend* the bill so as to expressly declare that the people of the territory *may* exclude slavery." "Not we," said the friends of the measure; and down they voted the amendment.

While the Nebraska bill was passing through congress, a *law case*, involving the question of a negroe's freedom, by reason of his owner having voluntarily taken him first into a free state and then a territory covered by the congressional prohibition, and held him as a slave, for a long time in each, was passing through the U.S. Circuit Court for the District of Missouri; and both Nebraska bill and law suit were brought to a decision in the same month of May, 1854. The negroe's name was "Dred Scott," which name now designates the decision finally made in the case.

Before the *then* next Presidential election, the law case came to, and was argued in the Supreme Court of the United States; but the *decision* of it was deferred until *after* the election. . . .

The Presidential inauguration came, and still no decision of the court; but the *incoming* President, in his inaugural address, fervently exhorted the people to abide by the forthcoming decision, *whatever it might be.*

Then, in a few days, came the decision.

The reputed author[2] of the Nebraska bill finds an early occasion to make a speech at this capitol indorsing the Dred Scott Decision, and vehemently denouncing all opposition to it.

The new President, too, seizes the early occasion . . . to *indorse* and strongly *construe* that decision, and to express his *astonishment* that any different view had ever been entertained.

At length a squabble springs up between the President and the author of the Nebraska bill, on the *mere* question of *fact*, whether the Lecompton constitution was or was not, in any just sense, made by the people of Kansas; and in that squabble the latter declares that all he wants is a fair vote for the people, and that he *cares* not whether slavery be voted *down* or voted *up*. I do not understand his declaration that he cares not whether slavery be voted down or voted up, to be intended by him other than as an *apt definition* of the *policy* he would impress upon the public mind—the *principle* for which he declares he has suffered much, and is ready to suffer to the end.

And well may he cling to that principle. If he has any parental feeling, well may he cling to it. That principle, is the only *shred* left of his original Nebraska doctrine. Under the Dred Scott decision, "squatter sovereignty" squatted out of existence, tumbled down like temporary scaffolding. . . . His late *joint* struggle with the Republicans, against the Lecompton Constitution, involves nothing of the original Nebraska doctrine. That struggle was made on a point, the right of a people to make their own constitution, upon which he and the Republicans have never differed.

The several points of the Dred Scott decision, in connection with Senator Douglas' "care not" policy, constitute the piece of machinery, in its *present* state of advancement. . . .

The *working* points of that machinery are:

First, that no negro slave, imported as such from Africa, and no descendant of such slave can ever be a *citizen* of any State, in the sense of that term as used in the Constitution of the United States.

[2] Stephen A. Douglas.

This point is made in order to deprive the negro, in every possible event, of the benefit of this provision of the United States Constitution, which declares that—

"The citizens of each State shall be entitled to all privileges and immunities of citizens in the several States."

Secondly, that "subject to the Constitution of the United States," neither *Congress* nor a *Territorial Legislature* can exclude slavery from any United States territory.

This point is made in order that individual men may *fill up* the territories with slaves, without danger of losing them as property, and thus to enhance the chances of *permanency* to the institution through all the future.

Thirdly, that whether the holding a negro in actual slavery in a free State, makes him free, as against the holder, the United States courts will not decide, but will leave to be decided by the courts of any slave State the negro may be forced into by the master.

This point is made, not to be pressed *immediately*; but, if acquiesced in for a while, and apparently *indorsed* by the people at an election, *then* to sustain the logical conclusion that what Dred Scott's master might lawfully do with Dred Scott, in the free State of Illinois, every other master may lawfully do with any other *one*, or one *thousand* slaves, in Illinois, or in any other free State.

Auxiliary to all this, and working hand in hand with it, the Nebraska doctrine, or what is left of it, is to *educate* and *mould* public opinion, at least *Northern* public opinion, to not *care* whether slavery is voted *down* or voted *up*.

This shows exactly where we now *are*; and *partially* also, whither we are tending.

It will throw additional light on the latter, to go back, and run the mind over the string of historical facts already stated. Several things will *now* appear less *dark* and *mysterious* than they did *when* they were transpiring. The people were to be left "perfectly free" "subject only to the Constitution." What the *Constitution* had to do with it, outsiders could not *then* see. Plainly enough *now*, it was an exactly fitted *niche*, for the Dred Scott decision to afterwards come in, and declare the *perfect freedom* of the people, to be just no freedom at all. . . .

We can not absolutely *know* that all these exact adaptations are the result of preconcert. But when we see a lot of framed timbers, different portions of which we know have been gotten out at different times and places and by different workmen—Stephen, Franklin, Roger and James,[3] for instance—and when we see these timbers joined together, and see they exactly make the frame of a house or a mill, all the tenons and mortices exactly fitting, and all the lengths and proportions of the different

[3] Senator Stephen A. Douglas, former president Franklin Pierce, Chief Justice of the Supreme Court Roger B. Taney, and President James Buchanan, all Democrats.

pieces exactly adapted to their respective places, and not a piece too many or too few—not omitting even scaffolding—or, if a single piece be lacking, we can see the place in the frame exactly fitted and prepared to yet bring such piece in—in *such* a case, we find it impossible to not *believe* that Stephen and Franklin and Roger and James all understood one another from the beginning, and all worked upon a common *plan* or *draft* drawn up before the first lick was struck.

It should not be overlooked that, by the Nebraska bill, the people of a *State* as well as *Territory*, were to be left *"perfectly free" "subject only to the Constitution."*

Why mention a *State*? They were legislating for *territories*, and not *for* or *about* States. Certainly the people of a State *are* and *ought to be* subject to the Constitution of the United States; but why is mention of this *lugged* into this merely *territorial* law? Why are the people of a *territory* and the people of a *state* therein *lumped* together, and their relation to the Constitution therein treated as being *precisely* the same?

While the opinion of *the Court*, by Chief Justice Taney, in the Dred Scott case, and the separate opinions of all the concurring Judges, expressly declare that the Constitution of the United States neither permits Congress nor a Territorial legislature to exclude slavery from any United States territory, they all *omit* to declare whether or not the same Constitution permits a *state*, or the people of a State, to exclude it.

Possibly, this was a mere *omission*; but who can be *quite* sure. . . .

The nearest approach to the point of declaring the power of a State over slavery, is made by Judge Nelson.[4] He approaches it more than once, using the precise idea, and *almost* the language too, of the Nebraska act. On one occasion his exact language is, "except in cases where the power is restrained by the Constitution of the United States, the law of the State is supreme over the subject of slavery within its jurisdiction."

In what *cases* the power of the *states* is so restrained by the U.S. Constitution, is left an *open* question, precisely as the same question, as to the restraint on the power of the *territories* was left open in the Nebraska act. Put *that* and *that* together, and we have another nice little niche, which we may, ere long, see filled with another Supreme Court decision, declaring that the Constitution of the United States does not permit a *state* to exclude slavery from its limits.

And this may especially be expected if the doctrine of "care not whether slavery be voted *down* or voted *up*," shall gain upon the public mind sufficiently to give promise that such a decision can be maintained when made.

Such a decision is all that slavery now lacks of being alike lawful in all the States.

---

[4] Samuel Nelson was a Supreme Court justice who wrote a separate opinion in the *Dred Scott* case that Lincoln refers to here.

Welcome or unwelcome, such decision is probably coming, and will soon be upon us, unless the power of the present political dynasty shall be met and overthrown.

We shall *lie down* pleasantly dreaming that the people of *Missouri* are on the verge of making their State *free*; and we shall *awake* to the *reality*, instead, that the *Supreme* Court has made *Illinois* a *slave* State.

To meet and overthrow the power of that dynasty, is the work now before all those who would prevent that consummation.

That is *what* we have to do.

But *how* can we best do it?

There are those who denounce us *openly* to their *own* friends, and yet whisper *us softly*, that *Senator Douglas* is the *aptest* instrument there is, with which to effect that object. . . .

They remind us that *he* is a very *great man*, and that the largest of *us* are very small ones. Let this be granted. But . . . [h]ow can he oppose the advances of slavery? He don't *care* anything about it. His avowed *mission is impressing* the "public heart" to *care* nothing about it.

A leading Douglas Democratic newspaper thinks Douglas' superior talent will be needed to resist the revival of the African slave trade.

Does Douglas believe an effort to revive that trade is approaching? He has not said so. Does he *really* think so? But if it is, how can he resist it? For years he has labored to prove it a *sacred right* of white men to take negro slaves into the new territories. Can he possibly show that it is *less* a sacred right to *buy* them where they can be bought cheapest? And, unquestionably they can be bought *cheaper in Africa* than in *Virginia*.

He has done all in his power to reduce the whole question of slavery to one of a mere *right of property*; and as such, how can *he* oppose the foreign slave trade—how can he refuse that trade in that "property" shall be "perfectly free." . . .

But clearly, he is not *now* with us—he does not *pretend* to be—he does not *promise* to *ever* be.

Our cause, then, must be intrusted to, and conducted by its own undoubted friends—those whose hands are free, whose hearts are in the work—who *do care* for the result.

Two years ago the Republicans of the nation mustered over thirteen hundred thousand strong.[5]

We did this under the single impulse of resistance to a common danger, with every external circumstance against us.

Of *strange, discordant*, and even, *hostile* elements, we gathered from the four winds, and *formed* and fought the battle through, under the constant hot fire of a disciplined, proud, and pampered enemy.

---

[5] John C. Frémont, the Republican candidate for president, received more than 1.3 million votes in the 1856 presidential election. The winner, Democrat James Buchanan, received 1.8 million votes.

Did we brave all *then*, to *falter* now? . . .
The result is not doubtful. We shall not fail—if we stand firm, we shall not fail.
Wise councils may *accelerate* or *mistakes delay* it, but, sooner or later the victory is *sure* to come.

THE LINCOLN-DOUGLAS DEBATES

The Lincoln-Douglas debates highlighted the 1858 senatorial campaign in Illinois. Both men gave dozens of other speeches during the campaign, each of them traveling thousands of miles. Lincoln, knowing that he faced an uphill battle in a predominantly Democratic state, hoped to improve his prospects by challenging Douglas to face-to-face debates. Douglas, by far the better-known and more prominent candidate, reluctantly agreed to seven debates, one in each of Illinois's congressional districts, with the exception of the districts centering on Chicago and Springfield, where the candidates had already appeared. Each debate followed a similar format: The candidates alternated speaking first; the leadoff speaker had one hour, the second speaker had an hour and a half, followed by a half-hour rebuttal by the first speaker. These three-hour marathons of political analysis attracted huge crowds. Newspapers sent reporters to describe the scene and transcribe every word. Neither candidate presented strikingly new ideas. Instead, they emphasized the differences between themselves and between their parties.

Douglas argued that Lincoln and the Republicans were in fact abolitionists whose zeal to end slavery would ride roughshod over the property rights of slave owners, explicitly protected by the Constitution, and would be likely to precipitate disunion, even civil war. Worse, Douglas declared, Lincoln's insistence on the equality of whites and blacks violated the rights and privileges of white citizens of Illinois because it grew out of a misunderstanding of the Declaration of Independence, which was never intended to apply to anyone but whites. Douglas proclaimed that "this Government was made by our fathers on the white basis. It was made by white men for the benefit of white men and their posterity forever."[6] Far more important than any misplaced sympathy for slaves, Douglas repeatedly pointed out, was the sacred principle of democracy.

---

[6] Robert W. Johannsen, ed., *The Lincoln-Douglas Debates of 1858* (New York, 1965), 216.

Voters should be able to decide for themselves about slavery, as they did about other fundamental matters. He announced, "I care more for the great principle of self-government, the right of the people to rule, than I do for all the negroes in Christendom."[7]

Lincoln responded to Douglas's assertions by defining clearly what he and other Republicans stood for. Although Republicans believed that slavery was wrong, Lincoln insisted that they did not intend to harm it where it already existed, only to prevent it from expanding—hardly an abolitionist agenda. Lincoln reiterated that he did not advocate or desire full political or social equality for blacks, although blacks and whites did share the same inalienable rights to life, liberty, and the pursuit of happiness affirmed in the Declaration of Independence. Lincoln took care to detail his views of the limits of racial equality, understanding full well that the vast majority of Illinois voters considered black people inferior and wanted nothing to do with them. In 1848, for example, 70 percent of Illinois voters favored prohibiting blacks from entering the state, a plan put into effect by the legislature in 1853. Above all, Lincoln emphasized that Republicans, unlike Democrats, believed that slavery was morally wrong.

Lincoln's arguments did not elevate him to the U.S. Senate. Since the Illinois legislature, not the voters at large, elected U.S. senators, neither Lincoln nor Douglas appeared on the popular ballot. In the November election, Democrats maintained their edge in the legislature and re-elected Douglas to the Senate by a margin of 54 to 46. "I am glad I made the late race," Lincoln wrote an old Whig friend. "It gave me a hearing on the great and durable question of the age, which I could have had in no other way; and though I now sink out of view, and shall be forgotten, I believe I have made some marks which will tell for the cause of civil liberty long after I am gone."[8]

Lincoln did not "sink out of view," of course. Prominent Republicans outside Illinois noticed his speeches and recognized him as an attractive moderate, positioned between the more militant antislavery Republicans and the more conservative old Whigs—notice that Lincoln promoted by having the debates published in book form. Lincoln's performance in the senatorial campaign also consolidated his leadership in the Illinois Republican party, a matter of significance when Republicans gathered in Chicago two years later to nominate a candidate for president. The ideas

[7] Ibid., 326.
[8] Lincoln to Anson G. Henry, *CW*, III, 339.

Lincoln expressed on "the great and durable question of the age" in the following selections from his debates with Douglas became even more important when the defeated senatorial candidate became president of the United States and confronted the crisis of the Union.

6

First Lincoln-Douglas Debate

August 21, 1858

Ottawa, Illinois

... This is the true complexion of all I have ever said in regard to the institution of slavery and the black race. This is the whole of it, and anything that argues me into his idea of perfect social and political equality with the negro, is but a specious and fantastic arrangement of words, by which a man can prove a horse chestnut to be a chestnut horse. [Laughter.] I will say here, while upon this subject, that I have no purpose directly or indirectly to interfere with the institution of slavery in the States where it exists. I believe I have no lawful right to do so, and I have no inclination to do so. I have no purpose to introduce political and social equality between the white and the black races. There is a physical difference between the two, which in my judgment will probably forever forbid their living together upon the footing of perfect equality, and inasmuch as it becomes a necessity that there must be a difference, I, as well as Judge Douglas, am in favor of the race to which I belong, having the superior position. I have never said anything to the contrary, but I hold that notwithstanding all this, there is no reason in the world why the negro is not entitled to all the natural rights enumerated in the Declaration of Independence, the right to life, liberty and the pursuit of happiness. [Loud cheers.] I hold that he is as much entitled to these as the white man. I agree with Judge Douglas he is not my equal in many respects—certainly not in color, perhaps not in moral or intellectual endowment. But in the right to eat the bread, without leave of anybody else, which his own hand earns, *he is my equal and the equal of Judge Douglas and the equal of every living man.* [Great applause.] ...

I ask the attention of the people here assembled and elsewhere, to the course that Judge Douglas is pursuing every day as bearing upon this question of making slavery national. ... In the first place what is necessary to make the institution national? Not war. There is no danger that the people of Kentucky will shoulder their muskets and with a young nigger stuck on every bayonet march into Illinois and force them upon us. There is no danger of our going over there and making war upon them. Then what is necessary for the nationalization of slavery? It is simply the next Dred Scott decision. It is merely for the Supreme Court to decide that no *State* under the Constitution can exclude it, just as they have already decided that under the Constitution neither Congress nor the Territorial Legislature can do it. . . .

Henry Clay, my beau ideal of a statesman, the man for whom I fought all my humble life—Henry Clay once said of a class of men who would repress all tendencies to liberty and ultimate emancipation, that they must, if they would do this, go back to the era of our Independence, and muzzle the cannon which thunders its annual joyous return; they must blow out the moral lights around us; they must penetrate the human soul, and eradicate there the love of liberty; and then and not till then, could they perpetuate slavery in this country! [Loud cheers.] To my thinking, Judge Douglas is, by his example and vast influence, doing that very thing in this community, [cheers,] when he says that the negro has nothing in the Declaration of Independence. Henry Clay plainly understood the contrary. Judge Douglas is going back to the era of our Revolution, and to the extent of his ability, muzzling the cannon which thunders its annual joyous return. When he invites any people willing to have slavery, to establish it, he is blowing out the moral lights around us. [Cheers.] When he says he "cares not whether slavery is voted down or voted up,"—that it is a sacred right of self government—he is in my judgment penetrating the human soul and eradicating the light of reason and the love of liberty in this American people. [Enthusiastic and continued applause.] And now I will only say that when, by all these means and appliances, Judge Douglas shall succeed in bringing public sentiment to an exact accordance with his own views—when these vast assemblages shall echo back all these sentiments—when they shall come to repeat his views and to avow his principles, and to say all that he says on these mighty questions—then it needs only the formality of the second Dred Scott decision, which he endorses in advance, to make Slavery alike lawful in all the States—old as well as new, North as well as South.

7

Fourth Lincoln-Douglas Debate

September 18, 1858

Charleston, Illinois
While I was at the hotel to-day an elderly gentleman called upon me to know whether I was really in favor of producing a perfect equality between the negroes and white people. [Great laughter.] . . . I will say then that I am not, nor ever have been in favor of bringing about in any way the social

and political equality of the white and black races, [applause]—that I am not nor ever have been in favor of making voters or jurors of negroes, nor of qualifying them to hold office, nor to intermarry with white people; and I will say in addition to this that there is a physical difference between the white and black races which I believe will for ever forbid the two races living together on terms of social and political equality. And inasmuch as they cannot so live, while they do remain together there must be the position of superior and inferior, and I as much as any other man am in favor of having the superior position assigned to the white race. I say upon this occasion I do not perceive that because the white man is to have the superior position the negro should be denied everything. I do not understand that because I do not want a negro woman for a slave I must necessarily want her for a wife. [Cheers and laughter.] My understanding is that I can just let her alone. I am now in my fiftieth year, and I certainly never have had a black woman for either a slave or a wife. So it seems to me quite possible for us to get along without making either slaves or wives of negroes. I will add to this that I have never seen to my knowledge a man, woman or child who was in favor of producing a perfect equality, social and political, between negroes and white men. . . . I have never had the least apprehension that I or my friends would marry negroes if there was no law to keep them from it, [laughter] but as Judge Douglas and his friends seem to be in great apprehension that they might, if there were no law to keep them from it, [roars of laughter] I give him the most solemn pledge that I will to the very last stand by the law of this State, which forbids the marrying of white people with negroes. [Continued laughter and applause.] I will add one further word, which is this, that I do not understand there is any place where an alteration of the social and political relations of the negro and the white man can be made except in the State Legislature—not in the Congress of the United States—and as I do not really apprehend the approach of any such thing myself, and as Judge Douglas seems to be in constant horror that some such danger is rapidly approaching, I propose as the best means to prevent it that the Judge be kept at home and placed in the State Legislature to fight the measure. [Uproarious laughter and applause.] . . .

Judge Douglas has said to you that he has not been able to get from me an answer to the question whether I am in favor of negro citizenship. So far as I know, the Judge never asked me the question before. [Applause.] He shall have no occasion to ever ask it again, for I tell him very frankly that I am not in favor of negro citizenship. [Renewed applause.] . . . Now my opinion is that the different States have the power to make a negro a citizen under the Constitution of the United States if they choose. The Dred Scott decision decides that they have not that power. If the State of Illinois had that power I should be opposed to the exercise of it. [Cries of "good," "good," and applause.] That is all I have to say about it. . . .

8

Fifth Lincoln-Douglas Debate
October 7, 1858

Galesburg, Illinois

The Judge has alluded to the Declaration of Independence, and insisted that negroes are not included in that Declaration; and that it is a slander upon the framers of that instrument, to suppose that negroes were meant therein; and he asks you: Is it possible to believe that Mr. Jefferson, who penned the immortal paper, could have supposed himself applying the language of that instrument to the negro race, and yet held a portion of that race in slavery? Would he not at once have freed them? . . . I believe the entire records of the world, from the date of the Declaration of Independence up to within three years ago, may be searched in vain for one single affirmation, from one single man, that the negro was not included in the Declaration of Independence. I think I may defy Judge Douglas to show that he ever said so, that Washington ever said so, that any President ever said so, that any member of Congress ever said so, or that any living man upon the whole earth ever said so, until the necessities of the present policy of the Democratic party, in regard to slavery, had to invent that affirmation. [Tremendous applause.] And I will remind Judge Douglas and this audience, that while Mr. Jefferson was the owner of slaves, as undoubtedly he was, in speaking upon this very subject, he used the strong language that "he trembled for his country when he remembered that God was just"; and I will offer the highest premium in my power to Judge Douglas if he will show that he, in all his life, ever uttered a sentiment at all akin to that of Jefferson. [Great applause and cries of "Hit him again," "good," "good."] . . .

When the Judge says, in speaking on this subject, that I make speeches of one sort for the people of the Northern end of the State, and of a different sort for the Southern people, he assumes that I do not understand that my speeches will be put in print and read North and South. . . . And I have not supposed, and do not now suppose, that there is any conflict whatever between them. ["They are all good speeches!" "Hurrah for Lincoln!"] But the Judge will have it that if we do not confess that there is a sort of inequality between the white and black races, which justifies us in making them slaves, we must, then, insist that there is a degree of equality that requires us to make them our wives. [Loud applause, and cries, "Give it to him"; "Hit him again."] . . . I have all the while maintained, that in so far as it should be insisted that there was an equality between the white and black races that should produce a perfect social and political equality, it was an impossibility. This you have seen in my printed speeches, and with it I have said, that in their right to "life, liberty and the pursuit of happiness," as proclaimed in that old Declaration, the inferior races are our equals. [Long-continued cheering.] And these declarations I have constantly made in reference to the abstract moral question, to contemplate and consider when we are legislating about any new country [territory] which is not already cursed with the actual presence of the evil—slavery. I have never manifested any impatience with the necessities that spring from the actual presence of black people amongst us, and the actual existence of slavery amongst us where it does already exist; but I have insisted that, in legislating for new countries, where it does not exist, there is no just rule other than that of moral and abstract right! With reference to those new countries, those maxims as to the right of a people to "life, liberty and the pursuit of happiness," were the just rules to be constantly referred to. . . .

The essence of the Dred Scott case is compressed into the sentence which I will now read: "Now, as we have already said in an earlier part of this opinion, upon a different point, the right of property in a slave is distinctly and expressly affirmed in the Constitution." . . . I believe that the right of property in a slave *is not* distinctly and expressly affirmed in the Constitution, and Judge Douglas thinks it *is*. I believe that the Supreme Court and the advocates of that decision may search in vain for the place in the Constitution where the right of property in a slave is distinctly and expressly affirmed. . . . This is but an opinion, and the opinion of one very humble man; but it is my opinion that the Dred Scott decision, as it is, never would have been made in its present form if the party that made it had not been sustained previously by the elections. My own opinion is, that the new Dred Scott decision, deciding against the right of the people of the States to exclude slavery, will never be made, if that party is not sustained by the elections. [Cries of "Yes, yes."] I believe, further, that it is just as sure to be made as to-morrow is to come, if that party shall be sustained. ["We won't sustain it, never, never."] . . .

9

Sixth Lincoln-Douglas Debate
October 13, 1858

Quincy, Illinois

We have in this nation this element of domestic slavery. It is a matter of absolute certainty that it is a disturbing element. It is the opinion of all the great men who have expressed an opinion upon it, that it is a dangerous element. We keep up a controversy in regard to it. That controversy necessarily springs from difference of opinion, and if we can learn exactly—can reduce to the lowest elements—what that difference of opinion is, we perhaps shall be better prepared for discussing the different systems of policy that we would propose in regard to that disturbing element. I suggest that the difference of opinion, reduced to its lowest terms, is no other than the difference between the men who think slavery a wrong and those who do not think it wrong. The Republican party think it wrong—we think it is a moral, a social and a political wrong. We think it is a wrong not confining itself merely to the persons or the States where it exists, but that it is a wrong in its tendency, to say the least, that extends itself to the existence of the whole nation. Because we think it wrong, we propose a course of policy that shall deal with it as a wrong. We deal with it as with any other wrong, in so far as we can prevent its growing any larger, and so deal with it that in the run of time there may be some promise of an end to it. We have a due regard to the actual presence of it amongst us and the difficulties of getting rid of it in any satisfactory way, and all the constitutional obligations thrown about it. I suppose that in reference both to its actual existence in the nation, and to our constitutional obligations, we have no right at all to disturb it in the States where it exists, and we profess that we have no more inclination to disturb it than we have the right to do it. . . . Where we suppose we have the constitutional right [such as in the congressionally controlled District of Columbia], we restrain ourselves in reference to the actual existence of the institution and the difficulties thrown about it. We also oppose it as an evil so far as it seeks to spread itself. We insist on the policy that shall restrict it to its present limits. We don't suppose that in doing this we violate anything due to the actual presence of the institution, or anything due to the constitutional guarantees thrown around it.

We oppose the Dred Scott decision in a certain way, upon which I ought perhaps to address you a few words. We do not propose that when Dred Scott has been decided to be a slave by the court, we, as a mob, will decide him to be free. We do not propose that, when any other one, or one thousand, shall be decided by that court to be slaves, we will in any violent way disturb the rights of property thus settled; but we nevertheless do oppose that decision as a political rule which shall be binding on the voter, to vote for nobody who thinks it wrong, which shall be binding on the members of Congress or the President to favor no measure that does not actually concur with the principles of that decision. We do not propose to be bound by it as a political rule in that way, because we think it lays the foundation not merely of enlarging and spreading out what we consider an evil, but it lays the foundation for spreading that evil into the States themselves. We propose so resisting it as to have it reversed if we can, and a new judicial rule established upon this subject.

I will add this, that if there be any man who does not believe that slavery is wrong in the three aspects which I have mentioned, or in any one of them, that man is misplaced, and ought to leave us. While, on the other hand, if there be any man in the Republican party who is impatient over the necessity springing from its actual presence, and is impatient of the constitutional guarantees thrown around it, and would act in disregard of these, he too is misplaced standing with us. He will find his place somewhere else; for we have a due regard, so far as we are capable of understanding them, for all these things. This, gentlemen, as well as I can give it, is a plain statement of our principles in all their enormity.

I will say now that there is a sentiment in the country contrary to me—a sentiment which holds that slavery is not wrong, and therefore it goes for policy that does not propose dealing with it as a wrong. That policy is the Democratic policy, and that sentiment is the Democratic sentiment. . . . [T]urn it in any way you can, in all the arguments sustaining the Democratic policy, and in that policy itself, there is a careful, studied exclusion of the idea that there is anything wrong in slavery. Let us understand this. I am not, just here, trying to prove that we are right and they are wrong. I have been stating where we and they stand, and trying to show what is the real difference between us; and I now say that whenever we can get the question distinctly stated—can get all these men who believe that slavery is in some of these respects wrong, to stand and act with us in treating it as a wrong—then, and not till then, I think we will in some way come to an end of this slavery agitation. [Prolonged cheers.] . . .

10

Seventh Lincoln-Douglas Debate

October 15, 1858

Alton, Illinois

I have stated upon former occasions, and I may as well state again, what I understand to be the real issue in this controversy between Judge Douglas and myself. On the point of my wanting to make war between the free and the slave States, there has been no issue between us. So, too, when he assumes that I am in favor of introducing a perfect social and political equality between the white and black races. These are false issues, upon which Judge Douglas has tried to force the controversy. There is no foundation in truth for the charge that I maintain either of these propositions. The real issue in this controversy—the one pressing upon every mind—is the sentiment on the part of one class that looks upon the institution of slavery *as a wrong*, and of another class that *does not* look upon it as a wrong. The sentiment that contemplates the institution of slavery in this country as a wrong is the sentiment of the Republican party. It is the sentiment around which all their actions—all their arguments circle—from which all their propositions radiate. They look upon it as being a moral, social and political wrong; and while they contemplate it as such, they nevertheless have due regard for its actual existence among us, and the difficulties of getting rid of it in any satisfactory way and to all the constitutional obligations thrown about it. Yet having a due regard for these, they desire a policy in regard to it that looks to its not creating any more danger. They insist that it should as far as may be, *be treated* as a wrong, and one of the methods of treating it as a wrong is to *make provision that it shall grow no larger.* [Loud applause.] They also desire a policy that looks to a peaceful end of slavery at sometime, as being wrong. These are the views they entertain in regard to it as I understand them; and all their sentiments—all their arguments and propositions are brought within this range. . . .

On this subject of treating it as a wrong, and limiting its spread, let me say a word. Has any thing ever threatened the existence of this Union save and except this very institution of Slavery? What is it that we hold most dear amongst us? Our own liberty and prosperity. What has ever threatened our liberty and prosperity save and except this institution of Slavery? If this is true, how do you propose to improve the condition of things by enlarging Slavery—by spreading it out and making it bigger? You may have a wen [cyst] or a cancer upon your person and not be able to cut it out lest you bleed to death; but surely it is no way to cure it, to engraft it and spread it over your whole body. That is no proper way of treating what you regard a wrong. You see this peaceful way of dealing with it as a wrong—restricting the spread of it, and not allowing it to go into new countries where it has not already existed. That is the peaceful way, the old-fashioned way, the way in which the fathers themselves set us the example.

On the other hand, I have said there is a sentiment which treats it as *not* being wrong. That is the Democratic sentiment of this day. I do not mean to say that every man who stands within that range positively asserts that it is right. That class will include all who positively assert that it is right, and all who like Judge Douglas treat it as indifferent and do not say it is either right or wrong. . . . You may turn over everything in the Democratic policy from beginning to end, whether in the shape it takes on the statute book [the Kansas-Nebraska Act], in the shape it takes in the Dred Scott decision, in the shape it takes in conversation or the shape it takes in short maxim-like arguments—it everywhere carefully excludes the idea that there is anything wrong in it.

That is the real issue. That is the issue that will continue in this country when these poor tongues of Judge Douglas and myself shall be silent. It is the eternal struggle between these two principles—right and wrong—throughout the world. They are the two principles that have stood face to face from the beginning of time; and will ever continue to struggle.

The one is the common right of humanity and the other the divine right of kings. It is the same principle in whatever shape it develops itself. It is the same spirit that says, "You work and toil and earn bread, and I'll eat it." [Loud applause.] No matter in what shape it comes, whether from the mouth of a king who seeks to bestride the people of his own nation and live by the fruit of their labor, or from one race of men as an apology for enslaving another race, it is the same tyrannical principle. . . . Whenever the issue can be distinctly made, and all extraneous matter thrown out so that men can fairly see the real difference between the parties, this controversy will soon be settled, and it will be done peaceably too. There will be no war, no violence. It will be placed again where the wisest and best men of the world, placed it. . . .

THE 1860 CAMPAIGN FOR PRESIDENT

After losing to Douglas in the fall election, Lincoln traveled throughout the Midwest addressing Republican groups and stressing themes he had developed in his speeches since 1854. When his name began to be mentioned as a possible presidential candidate, he was "flattered, and gratified," he wrote an Illinois newspaper editor in the spring of 1859, but he added, "I must, in candor, say I do not think myself fit for the Presidency."[9] In truth, Lincoln did not have an auspicious record for a presidential aspirant: His national political experience was limited to one term in Congress ten years earlier; he had never served as governor of Illinois or even mayor of Springfield.

Lincoln's strongest political qualifications for the presidency were his ideas outlining a moderate Republicanism that had wide appeal among northern voters. Other Republican candidates were ostensibly better qualified than Lincoln, especially William H. Seward, U.S. senator and former governor of New York, and Salmon P. Chase, governor of Ohio. But compared to Lincoln, both Seward and Chase were more fervently antislavery and more closely associated with abolitionism. In a presidential election, their ideas threatened to alienate centrist voters who, like Lincoln, tended to view both abolitionists and proslavery militants as extremists who jeopardized the Union.

When Lincoln received an invitation to speak to a gathering of Republicans in New York in February 1860, he jumped at the chance to present his ideas to an audience of sophisticated easterners right in Seward's backyard. Knowing the importance of the occasion, Lincoln crafted his

[9] Lincoln to Thomas J. Pickett, *CW*, III, 377.

speech with care. His address contrasted Republican doctrines with the distorted and misleading convictions of white southerners and Democrats, as the following selection illustrates. The enthusiastic response to the speech, which was published in the *New York Tribune* and reprinted as a pamphlet, elevated Lincoln to many Republicans' second choice for the presidential nomination, behind the front-runners Seward and Chase. The excitement caused Lincoln to confess to a Republican friend who asked if he intended to compete for the nomination, "I will be entirely frank. The taste is in my mouth a little."[10]

[10] Lincoln to Lyman Trumbull, *CW*, IV, 45.

11

Address at Cooper Institute
February 27, 1860

New York City

... It is surely safe to assume that the thirty-nine framers of the original Constitution, and the seventy-six members of the Congress which framed the amendments thereto, taken together, do certainly include those who may be fairly called "our fathers who framed the Government under which we live." And so assuming, I defy any man to show that any one of them ever, in his whole life, declared that, in his understanding, any proper division of local from federal authority, or any part of the Constitution, forbade the Federal Government to control as to slavery in the federal territories. . . . To those who now so declare, I give, not only "our fathers who framed the Government under which we live," but with them all other living men within the century in which it was framed, among whom to search, and they shall not be able to find the evidence of a single man agreeing with them.

Now, and here, let me guard a little against being misunderstood. I do not mean to say we are bound to follow implicitly in whatever our fathers did. To do so, would be to discard all the lights of current experience—to reject all progress—all improvement. What I do say is, that if we would supplant the opinions and policy of our fathers in any case, we should do so upon evidence so conclusive, and argument so clear, that even their great authority, fairly considered and weighed, cannot stand; and most surely not in a case whereof we ourselves declare they understood the question better than we. . . .

Let all who believe that "our fathers, who framed the Government under which we live, understood this question just as well, and even better, than we do now," speak as they spoke, and act as they acted upon it. This is all Republicans ask—all Republicans desire—in relation to slavery. As those fathers marked it, so let it be again marked, as an evil not to be extended, but to be tolerated and protected only because of and so far as its actual presence among us makes that toleration and protection a necessity. Let all the guaranties those fathers gave it, be, not grudgingly, but fully and fairly maintained. For this Republicans contend, and with this, so far as I know or believe, they will be content.

And now, if they would listen—as I suppose they will not—I would address a few words to the Southern people.

I would say to them:—You consider yourselves a reasonable and a just people; and I consider that in the general qualities of reason and justice you are not inferior to any other people. Still, when you speak of us Republicans, you do so only to denounce us as reptiles, or, at the best, as no better than outlaws. You will grant a hearing to pirates or murderers, but nothing like it to "Black Republicans." In all your contentions with one another, each of you deems an unconditional condemnation of "Black Republicanism" as the first thing to be attended to. Indeed, such condemnation of us seems to be an indispensable prerequisite—license, so to speak—among you to be admitted or permitted to speak at all. Now, can you, or not, be prevailed upon to pause and to consider whether this is quite just to us, or even to yourselves? . . .

You say we are sectional. We deny it. That makes an issue; and the burden of proof is upon you. You produce your proof; and what is it? Why, that our party has no existence in your section—gets no votes in your section. The fact is substantially true; but does it prove the issue? If it does, then in case we should, without change of principle, begin to get votes in your section, we should thereby cease to be sectional. You cannot escape this conclusion; and yet, are you willing to abide by it? If you are, you will probably soon find that we have ceased to be sectional, for we shall get votes in your section this very year. You will then begin to discover, as the truth plainly is, that your proof does not touch the issue. The fact that we get no votes in your section, is a fact of your making, and not of ours. And if there be fault in that fact, that fault is primarily yours, and remains so until you show that we repel you by some wrong principle or practice. If we do repel you by any wrong principle or practice, the fault is ours; but this brings you to where you ought to have started—to a discussion of the right or wrong of our principle. If our principle, put in practice, would wrong your section for the benefit of ours, or for any other object, then our principle, and we with it, are sectional, and are justly opposed and denounced as such. Meet us, then, on the question of whether our principle, put in practice, would wrong your section; and so meet us as if it were possible that something may be said on our side. Do you accept the challenge? No! Then you really believe that the principle which "our fathers who framed the Government under which we live" thought so clearly right as to adopt it, and indorse it again and again, upon their official oaths, is in fact so clearly wrong as to demand your condemnation without a moment's consideration. . . .

But you say you are conservative—eminently conservative—while we are revolutionary, destructive, or something of the sort. What is conservatism? Is it not adherence to the old and tried, against the new and untried? We stick to, contend for, the identical old policy on the point in controversy which was adopted by "our fathers who framed the Government under which we live"; while you with one accord reject, and scout, and spit upon that old policy, and insist upon substituting something new. True, you disagree among yourselves as to what that substitute shall be. You are divided on new propositions and plans, but you are unanimous in rejecting and denouncing the old policy of the fathers. Some of you are for reviving the foreign slave trade; some for a Congressional Slave-Code for the Territories; some for Congress forbidding the Territories to prohibit Slavery within their limits; some for maintaining Slavery in the Territories through the judiciary; some for the "gur-reat pur-rinciple" that "if one man would enslave another, no third man should object," fantastically called "Popular Sovereignty"; but never a man among you in favor of federal prohibition of slavery in federal territories, according to the practice of "our fathers who framed the Government under which we live." Not one of all your various plans can show a precedent or an advocate in the century within which our Government originated. Consider, then, whether your claim of conservatism for yourselves, and your charge of destructiveness against us, are based on the most clear and stable foundations.

Again, you say we have made the slavery question more prominent than it formerly was. We deny it. We admit that it is more prominent, but we deny that we made it so. It was not we, but you, who discarded the old policy of the fathers. We resisted, and still resist, your innovation; and thence comes the greater prominence of the question. Would you have that question reduced to its former proportions? Go back to that old policy. What has been will be again, under the same conditions. If you would have the peace of the old times, readopt the precepts and policy of the old times.

You charge that we stir up insurrections among your slaves. We deny it; and what is your proof? Harper's Ferry! John Brown!![11] John Brown was no Republican; and you have failed to implicate a single Republican in his Harper's Ferry enterprise. If any member of our party is guilty in that matter, you know it or you do not know it. If you do know it, you are inexcusable for not designating the man and proving the fact. If you do

---

[11] John Brown, intending to incite a slave insurrection, led a group of five black and seventeen white abolitionists in an attack on the federal armory at Harpers Ferry, Virginia, on October 16, 1859. Authorities quickly suppressed the attack, and the State of Virginia tried Brown for treason and executed him.

not know it, you are inexcusable for asserting it, and especially for persisting in the assertion after you have tried and failed to make the proof. You
need not be told that persisting in a charge which one does not know to
be true, is simply malicious slander.

Some of you admit that no Republican designedly aided or encouraged
the Harper's Ferry affair; but still insist that our doctrines and declarations necessarily lead to such results. We do not believe it. We know we
hold to no doctrine, and make no declaration, which were not held to
and made by "our fathers who framed the Government under which we
live." . . . Every Republican man knew that, as to himself at least, your
charge was a slander. . . . Republican doctrines and declarations are
accompanied with a continual protest against any interference whatever
with your slaves, or with you about your slaves. Surely, this does not
encourage them to revolt. True, we do, in common with "our fathers, who
framed the Government under which we live," declare our belief that slavery is wrong; but the slaves do not hear us declare even this. For anything
we say or do, the slaves would scarcely know there is a Republican party. I
believe they would not, in fact, generally know it but for your misrepresen-
tations of us, in their hearing. In your political contests among yourselves,
each faction charges the other with sympathy with Black Republicanism;
and then, to give point to the charge, defines Black Republicanism to simply be insurrection, blood and thunder among the slaves.

Slave insurrections are no more common now than they were before
the Republican party was organized. What induced the Southampton
insurrection,[12] twenty-eight years ago, in which, at least, three times as
many lives were lost as at Harper's Ferry? You can scarcely stretch your
very elastic fancy to the conclusion that Southampton was "got up by
Black Republicanism." In the present state of things in the United States,
I do not think a general, or even a very extensive slave insurrection, is
possible. The indispensable concert of action cannot be attained. The
slaves have no means of rapid communication; nor can incendiary freemen, black or white, supply it. The explosive materials are everywhere
in parcels; but there neither are, nor can be supplied, the indispensable
connecting trains.

Much is said by Southern people about the affection of slaves for their
masters and mistresses; and a part of it, at least, is true. A plot for an upris-
ing could scarcely be devised and communicated to twenty individuals
before some one of them, to save the life of a favorite master or mistress,
would divulge it. . . . Occasional poisonings from the kitchen, and open or
stealthy assassinations in the field, and local revolts extending to a score

---

[12] In 1831, in Southampton County, Virginia, a group of about sixty slaves led by Nat
Turner initiated a slave insurrection that killed more than seventy white men, women,
and children. White officials wasted no time capturing, trying, and executing the rebels,
while vengeful whites tortured and killed hundreds of other slaves.

or so, will continue to occur as the natural results of slavery; but no general insurrection of slaves, as I think, can happen in this country for a long time. Whoever much fears, or much hopes for such an event, will be alike disappointed.

In the language of Mr. Jefferson, uttered many years ago, "It is still in our power to direct the process of emancipation, and deportation, peaceably, and in such slow degrees, as that the evil will wear off insensibly; and their places be . . . filled up by free white laborers. If, on the contrary, it is left to force itself on, human nature must shudder at the prospect held up."

Mr. Jefferson did not mean to say, nor do I, that the power of emancipation is in the Federal Government. He spoke of Virginia; and, as to the power of emancipation, I speak of the slaveholding States only. The Federal Government, however, as we insist, has the power of restraining the extension of the institution—the power to insure that a slave insurrection shall never occur on any American soil which is now free from slavery.

John Brown's effort was peculiar. It was not a slave insurrection. It was an attempt by white men to get up a revolt among slaves, in which the slaves refused to participate. In fact, it was so absurd that the slaves, with all their ignorance, saw plainly enough it could not succeed. That affair, in its philosophy, corresponds with the many attempts, related in history, at the assassination of kings and emperors. An enthusiast broods over the oppression of a people till he fancies himself commissioned by Heaven to liberate them. He ventures the attempt, which ends in little else than his own execution. . . .

And how much would it avail you, if you could, by the use of John Brown, Helper's Book,[13] and the like, break up the Republican organization? Human action can be modified to some extent, but human nature cannot be changed. There is a judgment and a feeling against slavery in this nation, which cast at least a million and a half of votes. You cannot destroy that judgment and feeling—that sentiment—by breaking up the political organization which rallies around it. You can scarcely scatter and disperse an army which has been formed into order in the face of your heaviest fire; but if you could, how much would you gain by forcing the sentiment which created it out of the peaceful channel of the ballot-box, into some other channel? What would that other channel probably be? Would the number of John Browns be lessened or enlarged by the operation?

But you will break up the Union rather than submit to a denial of your Constitutional rights.

---

[13] In 1857, Hinton Rowan Helper, a white North Carolinian, published *The Impending Crisis of the South*, a vehement attack on slavery and slaveholders for impoverishing slaveless southern whites and the South in general. Republicans distributed thousands of copies of Helper's book during the 1860 presidential campaign.

That has a somewhat reckless sound; but it would be palliated, if not fully justified, were we proposing, by the mere force of numbers, to deprive you of some right, plainly written down in the Constitution. But we are proposing no such thing.

When you make these declarations, you have a specific and well-understood allusion to an assumed Constitutional right of yours, to take slaves into the federal territories, and to hold them there as property. But no such right is specifically written in the Constitution. That instrument is literally silent about any such right. We, on the contrary, deny that such a right has any existence in the Constitution, even by implication.

Your purpose, then, plainly stated, is, that you will destroy the Government, unless you be allowed to construe and enforce the Constitution as you please, on all points in dispute between you and us. You will rule or ruin in all events.

This, plainly stated, is your language. Perhaps you will say the Supreme Court [in its *Dred Scott* decision] has decided the disputed Constitutional question in your favor. Not quite so. But waiving the lawyer's distinction between dictum and decision, the Court have decided the question for you in a sort of way. The Court have substantially said, it is your Constitutional right to take slaves into the federal territories, and to hold them there as property. When I say the decision was made in a sort of way, I mean it was made in a divided Court, by a bare majority of the Judges, and they not quite agreeing with one another in the reasons for making it; that it is so made as that its avowed supporters disagree with one another about its meaning, and that it was mainly based upon a mistaken statement of fact—the statement in the opinion that "the right of property in a slave is distinctly and expressly affirmed in the Constitution."

An inspection of the Constitution will show that the right of property in a slave is not "*distinctly* and *expressly* affirmed" in it. . . .

And then it is to be remembered that "our fathers, who framed the Government under which we live"—the men who made the Constitution—decided this same Constitutional question in our favor, long ago—decided it without division among themselves, when making the decision; without division among themselves about the meaning of it after it was made, and, so far as any evidence is left, without basing it upon any mistaken statement of facts.

Under all these circumstances, do you really feel yourselves justified to break up this Government, unless such a court decision as yours is, shall be at once submitted to as a conclusive and final rule of political action? But you will not abide the election of a Republican President! In that supposed event, you say, you will destroy the Union; and then, you say, the great crime of having destroyed it will be upon us! That is cool. A highwayman holds a pistol to my ear, and mutters through his teeth, "Stand and deliver, or I shall kill you, and then you will be a murderer!"

To be sure, what the robber demanded of me—my money—was my own; and I had a clear right to keep it; but it was no more my own than my vote is my own; and the threat of death to me, to extort my money, and the threat of destruction to the Union, to extort my vote, can scarcely be distinguished in principle.

A few words now to Republicans. *It is exceedingly desirable that all parts of this great Confederacy shall be at peace, and in harmony, one with another. Let us Republicans do our part to have it so. Even though much provoked, let us do nothing through passion and ill temper. Even though the southern people will not so much as listen to us, let us calmly consider their demands, and yield to them if, in our deliberate view of our duty, we possibly can.* Judging by all they say and do, and by the subject and nature of their controversy with us, let us determine, if we can, what will satisfy them.

Will they be satisfied if the Territories be unconditionally surrendered to them? We know they will not. In all their present complaints against us, the Territories are scarcely mentioned. Invasions and insurrections are the rage now. Will it satisfy them, if, in the future, we have nothing to do with invasions and insurrections? We know it will not. We so know, because we know we never had anything to do with invasions and insurrections; and yet this total abstaining does not exempt us from the charge and the denunciation.

The question recurs, what will satisfy them? Simply this: We must not only let them alone, but we must, somehow, convince them that we do let them alone. This, we know by experience, is no easy task. We have been so trying to convince them from the very beginning of our organization, but with no success. In all our platforms and speeches we have constantly protested our purpose to let them alone; but this has had no tendency to convince them. Alike unavailing to convince them, is the fact that they have never detected a man of us in any attempt to disturb them.

These natural, and apparently adequate means all failing, what will convince them? This, and this only: cease to call slavery *wrong*, and join them in calling it *right*. And this must be done thoroughly—done in *acts* as well as in *words*. Silence will not be tolerated—we must place ourselves avowedly with them. . . . We must arrest and return their fugitive slaves with greedy pleasure. We must pull down our Free State constitutions. The whole atmosphere must be disinfected from all taint of opposition to slavery, before they will cease to believe that all their troubles proceed from us.

I am quite aware they do not state their case precisely in this way. Most of them would probably say to us, "Let us alone, *do* nothing to us, and *say* what you please about slavery." But we do let them alone—have never disturbed them—so that, after all, it is what we say, which dissatisfies them. They will continue to accuse us of doing, until we cease saying.

I am also aware they have not, as yet, in terms, demanded the overthrow of our Free-State Constitutions. Yet those Constitutions declare the wrong of slavery, with more solemn emphasis, than do all other sayings against it; and when all these other sayings shall have been silenced, the overthrow of these Constitutions will be demanded, and nothing be left to resist the demand. It is nothing to the contrary, that they do not demand the whole of this just now. Demanding what they do, and for the reason they do, they can voluntarily stop nowhere short of this consummation. Holding, as they do, that slavery is morally right, and socially elevating, they cannot cease to demand a full national recognition of it, as a legal right, and a social blessing.

Nor can we justifiably withhold this, on any ground save our conviction that slavery is wrong. If slavery is right, all words, acts, laws, and constitutions against it, are themselves wrong, and should be silenced, and swept away. If it is right, we cannot justly object to its nationality—its universality; if it is wrong, they cannot justly insist upon its extension—its enlargement. All they ask, we could readily grant, if we thought slavery right; all we ask, they could as readily grant, if they thought it wrong. Their thinking it right, and our thinking it wrong, is the precise fact upon which depends the whole controversy. Thinking it right, as they do, they are not to blame for desiring its full recognition, as being right; but, thinking it wrong, as we do, can we yield to them? Can we cast our votes with their view, and against our own? In view of our moral, social, and political responsibilities, can we do this?

Wrong as we think slavery is, we can yet afford to let it alone where it is, because that much is due to the necessity arising from its actual presence in the nation; but can we, while our votes will prevent it, allow it to spread into the National Territories, and to overrun us here in these Free States? If our sense of duty forbids this, then let us stand by our duty, fearlessly and effectively. Let us be diverted by none of those sophistical contrivances wherewith we are so industriously plied and belabored—contrivances such as groping for some middle ground between the right and the wrong, vain as the search for a man who should be neither a living man nor a dead man—such as a policy of "don't care" on a question about which all true men do care—such as Union appeals beseeching true Union men to yield to Disunionists, reversing the divine rule, and calling, not the sinners, but the righteous to repentance—such as invocations to Washington, imploring men to unsay what Washington said, and undo what Washington did.

Neither let us be slandered from our duty by false accusations against us, nor frightened from it by menaces of destruction to the Government nor of dungeons to ourselves. LET US HAVE FAITH THAT RIGHT MAKES MIGHT, AND IN THAT FAITH, LET US, TO THE END, DARE TO DO OUR DUTY AS WE UNDERSTAND IT.

After Lincoln received the Republican nomination for the presidency, he stayed in Springfield, corresponding with scores of Americans about matters large and small, but saying as little as possible in public, as was customary in presidential campaigns. Throughout the North, however, Republicans staged rallies, organized parades, and waved banners proclaiming enthusiasm for "Honest Abe the Rail-Splitter."

Lincoln's public reticence and Republican electioneering proved successful. Although Lincoln won just under 40 percent of the popular vote, he carried every northern state except New Jersey (where he split the electoral vote with Douglas), easily compiling an electoral vote majority of 180. The nominee of the National Democratic party, Lincoln's old rival Douglas, polled nearly 30 percent of the popular vote but won only in Missouri, accounting for just 12 electoral votes. John Bell, the nominee of the Constitutional Union party, carried the border states of Virginia, Kentucky, and Tennessee, winning 39 electoral votes and 13 percent of the popular vote. Every other southern state voted for John C. Breckinridge, nominee of the Southern Democratic party, who amassed 72 electoral votes and 18 percent of the popular vote. Never before had a presidential election created such deep sectional fissures.

3

From Secession to War

Lincoln's victory in the November 1860 presidential election provoked secessionists to launch a campaign to lead southern states out of the Union. Four months later, when Lincoln took the oath of office, seven Deep South states—South Carolina, Mississippi, Florida, Alabama, Georgia, Louisiana, and Texas—had seceded and seized many federal facilities, including forts, arsenals, and customhouses. As president-elect, Lincoln had no official power. He could do little more than watch as outgoing president James Buchanan declared that although secession was illegal, he could do nothing about it.

While the nation drifted toward dissolution, Lincoln used his influence as the leader of the Republican party, writing privately to political leaders to demand that his own party hold firm to its opposition to the extension of slavery and to reassure southerners that a Republican administration posed no threat. In February 1861, Lincoln broke his public silence, speaking at nearly every whistle-stop on his long train journey from Springfield to Washington. As the documents in this chapter illustrate, the ideas Lincoln outlined in these public speeches and private letters structured his inaugural address on March 4 and defined the basic assumptions that guided his subsequent responses to the secession crisis.

THE LIMITS OF COMPROMISE

While voters across the South chose delegates to state conventions that would decide whether to secede, President-elect Lincoln remained in Springfield, deluged with the requests of office-seekers and the advice of friends and foes. In Washington, House and Senate committees considered compromise proposals that might forestall disunion. In a series of private letters, from which the following selections are drawn, Lincoln made it clear that he was willing to conciliate the slave states but that no compromise that permitted the expansion of territory open to slavery would be acceptable. After South Carolina officially seceded on December 20, followed by six other Deep South states by February 1, Lincoln began to formulate his views on secession.

12

Letter to Lyman Trumbull

December 10, 1860

Private, & confidential

Springfield, Ills.

Hon. L. Trumbull[1]

My dear Sir: Let there be no compromise on the question of *extending* slavery. If there be, all our labor is lost, and, ere long, must be done again. The dangerous ground—that into which some of our friends have a hankering to run—is Pop[ular] Sov[ereignty]. Have none of it. Stand firm. The tug has to come, & better now, than any time hereafter.

Yours as ever
A. LINCOLN

---

[1] Trumbull, a U.S. senator from Illinois and a Republican, was in Washington, where committees in both the House and the Senate were considering proposals to reach a compromise on sectional differences.

13

Letter to John A. Gilmer

December 15, 1860

Strictly confidential.

Springfield, Ill.

Hon. John A. Gilmer[2]

My dear Sir—Yours of the 10th is received.[3] I am greatly disinclined to write a letter on the subject embraced in yours; and I would not do so, even privately as I do, were it not that I fear you might misconstrue my silence. Is it desired that I shall shift the ground upon which I have been elected? I can not do it. You need only to acquaint yourself with that ground, and press it on the attention of the South. It is all in print and easy of access. May I be pardoned if I ask whether even you have ever attempted to procure the reading of the Republican platform, or my speeches, by the Southern people? If not, what reason have I to expect that any additional production of mine would meet a better fate? It would make me appear as if I repented for the crime of having been elected, and was anxious to apologize and beg forgiveness. To so represent me, would be the principal use made of any letter I might now thrust upon the public. My old record cannot be so used; and that is precisely the reason that some new declaration is so much sought.

Now, my dear sir, be assured, that I am not questioning *your* candor; I am only pointing out, that, while a new letter would hurt the cause which I think a just one, you can quite as well effect every patriotic object with the old record. Carefully read . . . the volume of Joint Debates between Senator Douglas and myself, with the Republican Platform adopted at Chicago, and all your questions will be substantially answered. I have no thought of recommending the abolition of slavery in the District of Columbia, nor the slave trade among the slave states, even on the conditions indicated; and if I were to make such recommendation, it is quite clear Congress would not follow it.

As to employing slaves in Arsenals and Dockyards,[4] it is a thing I never thought of in my life, to my recollection, till I saw your letter; and I may say of it, precisely as I have said of the two points above.

---

[2] Gilmer, a congressman from North Carolina and a former Whig, opposed secession.

[3] Gilmer's letter asked Lincoln to answer a series of questions about his position by issuing a public announcement.

[4] Lincoln had no plans to replace white workingmen in federal arsenals or dockyards with black slaves.

As to the use of patronage [to appoint Republican sympathizers to federal offices] in the slave states, where there are few or no Republicans, I do not expect to inquire for the politics of the appointee, or whether he does or not own slaves. I intend in that matter to accommodate the people in the several localities, if they themselves will allow me to accommodate them. In one word, I never have been, am not now, and probably never shall be, in a mood of harassing the people, either North or South.

On the territorial question, I am inflexible, as you see my position in the book. On that, there is a difference between you and us; and it is the only substantial difference. You think slavery is right and ought to be extended; we think it is wrong and ought to be restricted. For this, neither has any just occasion to be angry with the other.

As to the state laws,[5] mentioned in your sixth question, I really know very little of them. I never have read one. If any of them are in conflict with the fugitive slave clause, or any other part of the constitution, I certainly should be glad of their repeal; but I could hardly be justified, as a citizen of Illinois, or as President of the United States, to recommend the repeal of a statute of Vermont, or South Carolina.

With the assurance of my highest regards I subscribe myself

Your obt. Servt.,

A. LINCOLN

---

[5] Southern leaders demanded that northern states repeal laws — often called "personal liberty laws" — intended to impede enforcement of the federal fugitive slave law.

14

Letter to Alexander H. Stephens

December 22, 1860

For your own eye only.

Springfield, Ills.

Hon. A. H. Stephens[6]

My dear Sir

Your obliging answer[7] to my short note is just received, and for which please accept my thanks. I fully appreciate the present peril the country is in, and the weight of responsibility on me.

---

[6] Stephens, a former Whig from Georgia who had served in Congress with Lincoln, opposed secession. After Georgia seceded, he supported the decision and was chosen vice president of the Confederacy in February 1861.

[7] Stephens's letter urged Lincoln to "do what you can to save our common country" by declaring publicly that he did not intend to harm slavery. *CW*, IV, 161.

Do the people of the South really entertain fears that a Republican administration would, *directly*, or *indirectly*, interfere with their slaves, or with them, about their slaves? If they do, I wish to assure you, as once a friend, and still, I hope, not an enemy, that there is no cause for such fears.

The South would be in no more danger in this respect, than it was in the days of Washington. I suppose, however, this does not meet the case. You think slavery is *right* and ought to be extended; while we think it is *wrong* and ought to be restricted. That I suppose is the rub. It certainly is the only substantial difference between us.

Yours very truly
A. LINCOLN

INAUGURATION AS PRESIDENT

On February 11, Lincoln and his family boarded a special train for the trip to Washington. Instead of making a beeline for the capital, the train proceeded slowly across Indiana into southern Ohio, jogged north to Pittsburgh and Cleveland, then moved east and south through New York, New Jersey, and Pennsylvania before finally arriving in Washington on February 23. At every stop, huge crowds turned out to catch a glimpse of the new president, the first to be born west of the Appalachian Mountains. Lincoln took advantage of these brief public encounters to proclaim his devotion to the Union and his determination to preserve it. He ridiculed secession and sought to rally support for the Union among all citizens, regardless of how they had voted in the presidential election. Newspapers avidly reported Lincoln's speeches, spreading his views to a national audience for the first time since his election. The same newspapers also carried dispatches from Montgomery, Alabama, where the newly organized Confederacy selected Jefferson Davis of Mississippi, a former senator and secretary of war, as its president on February 18, while Lincoln was midway on his journey to Washington.

When Lincoln took the oath of office—administered by Chief Justice Roger B. Taney, whose *Dred Scott* decision Lincoln had denounced repeatedly—the controversy over the extension of slavery had been eclipsed by the formation of the Confederacy. In his inaugural address, Lincoln explained that he would govern according to the Constitution. Attempting to reassure unionists in the slave states, he explained that he did not intend to interfere with slavery where it existed, protected by the federal Constitution and state laws. He contrasted his devotion to the Constitution with secession, which he believed violated the Constitution's assumption of a perpetual Union. Secession was anarchy, he declared. Safety, peace, and democratic order lay within the Union, Lincoln argued, while secession offered danger, bloodshed, and lawlessness. In sum, Lincoln coupled an intransigent defense of the Union with a promise of benign government under the Constitution for all Americans, South and North. Lincoln's insistence that the Union was unbroken and unbreakable remained the bedrock principle of his presidency.

15

First Inaugural Address
March 4, 1861

Fellow citizens of the United States:

In compliance with a custom as old as the government itself, I appear before you to address you briefly, and to take, in your presence, the oath prescribed by the Constitution of the United States, to be taken by the President "before he enters on the execution of his office."

I do not consider it necessary, at present, for me to discuss those matters of administration about which there is no special anxiety, or excitement.

Apprehension seems to exist among the people of the Southern States, that by the accession of a Republican Administration, their property, and their peace, and personal security, are to be endangered. There has never been any reasonable cause for such apprehension. Indeed, the most ample evidence to the contrary has all the while existed, and been open to their inspection. It is found in nearly all the published speeches of him who now addresses you. I do but quote from one of those speeches when I declare that "I have no purpose, directly or indirectly, to interfere with the institution of slavery in the States where it exists. I believe I have no lawful right to do so, and I have no inclination to do so." Those who nominated and elected me did so with full knowledge that I had made this, and many similar declarations, and had never recanted them. And more than this, they placed in the platform, for my acceptance, and as a law to themselves, and to me, the clear and emphatic resolution which I now read:

"*Resolved*, That the maintenance inviolate of the rights of the States, and especially the right of each State to order and control its own domestic institutions according to its own judgment exclusively, is essential to that balance of power on which the perfection and endurance of our political fabric depend; and we denounce the lawless invasion by armed force of the soil of any State or Territory, no matter under what pretext, as among the gravest of crimes."

I now reiterate these sentiments: and in doing so, I only press upon the public attention the most conclusive evidence of which the case is susceptible, that the property, peace and security of no section are to be in anywise endangered by the now incoming Administration. I add too, that all the protection which, consistently with the Constitution and the laws, can be given, will be cheerfully given to all the States when lawfully demanded, for whatever cause—as cheerfully to one section, as to another.

There is much controversy about the delivering up of fugitives from service or labor. The clause I now read is as plainly written in the Constitution as any other of its provisions:

"No person held to Service or labor in one State, under the laws thereof, escaping into another, shall, in consequence of any law or regulation therein, be discharged from such service or labor, but shall be delivered up on claim of the party to whom such service or labor may be due."

It is scarcely questioned that this provision was intended by those who made it, for the reclaiming of what we call fugitive slaves; and the intention of the law-giver is the law. All members of Congress swear their support to the whole Constitution—to this provision as much as to any other. To the proposition, then, that slaves whose cases come within the terms of this clause, "shall be delivered up," their oaths are unanimous. Now, if they would make the effort in good temper, could they not, with nearly equal unanimity, frame and pass a law, by means of which to keep good that unanimous oath?

There is some difference of opinion whether this clause should be enforced by national or by state authority; but surely that difference is not a very material one. If the slave is to be surrendered, it can be of but little consequence to him, or to others, by which authority it is done. And should any one, in any case, be content that his oath shall go unkept, on a merely unsubstantial controversy as to *how* it shall be kept?

Again, in any law upon this subject, ought not all the safeguards of liberty known in civilized and humane jurisprudence to be introduced, so that a free man be not, in any case, surrendered as a slave? And might it not be well, at the same time, to provide by law for the enforcement of that clause in the Constitution which guarranties that "The citizens of each State shall be entitled to all previleges and immunities of citizens in the several States?"

I take the official oath to-day, with no mental reservations, and with no purpose to construe the Constitution or laws, by any hypercritical rules. And while I do not choose now to specify particular acts of Congress as proper to be enforced, I do suggest, that it will be much safer for all, both in official and private stations, to conform to, and abide by, all those acts which stand unrepealed, than to violate any of them, trusting to find impunity [exemption from punishment] in having them held to be unconstitutional.

It is seventy-two years since the first inauguration of a President under our national Constitution. During that period fifteen different and greatly distinguished citizens, have, in succession, administered the executive branch of the government. They have conducted it through many perils; and, generally, with great success. Yet, with all this scope for precedent, I now enter upon the same task for the brief constitutional term of four years, under great and peculiar difficulty. A disruption of the Federal Union heretofore only menaced, is now formidably attempted.

I hold, that in contemplation of universal law, and of the Constitution, the Union of these States is perpetual. Perpetuity is implied, if not expressed, in the fundamental law of all national governments. It is safe to assert that no government proper, ever had a provision in its organic law for its own termination. Continue to execute all the express provisions of our national Constitution, and the Union will endure forever—it being impossible to destroy it, except by some action not provided for in the instrument itself.

Again, if the United States be not a government proper, but an association of States in the nature of contract merely, can it, as a contract, be peaceably unmade, by less than all the parties who made it? One party to a contract may violate it—break it, so to speak; but does it not require all to lawfully rescind it?

Descending from these general principles, we find the proposition that, in legal contemplation, the Union is perpetual, confirmed by the history of the Union itself. The Union is much older than the Constitution. It was formed in fact, by the Articles of Association in 1774. It was matured and continued by the Declaration of Independence in 1776. It was further matured and the faith of all the then thirteen States expressly plighted and engaged that it should be perpetual, by the Articles of Confederation in 1778. And finally, in 1787, one of the declared objects for ordaining and establishing the Constitution, was "*to form a more perfect union.*"

But if destruction of the Union, by one, or by a part only, of the States, be lawfully possible, the Union is *less* perfect than before the Constitution, having lost the vital element of perpetuity.

It follows from these views that no State, upon its own mere motion, can lawfully get out of the Union,—that *resolves* and *ordinances* to that effect are legally void; and that acts of violence, within any State or States, against the authority of the United States, are insurrectionary or revolutionary, according to circumstances.

I therefore consider that, in view of the Constitution and the laws, the Union is unbroken; and, to the extent of my ability, I shall take care, as the Constitution itself expressly enjoins upon me, that the laws of the Union be faithfully executed in all the States. Doing this I deem to be only a simple duty on my part; and I shall perform it, so far as practicable, unless my rightful masters, the American people, shall withhold the requisite means, or, in some authoritative manner, direct the contrary. I trust this will not be regarded as a menace, but only as the declared purpose of the Union that it *will* constitutionally defend, and maintain itself.

In doing this there needs to be no bloodshed or violence; and there shall be none, unless it be forced upon the national authority. The power confided to me, will be used to hold, occupy, and possess the property, and places belonging to the government, and to collect the duties and imposts [taxes]; but beyond what may be necessary for these objects, there will be no invasion — no using of force against, or among the people anywhere. Where hostility to the United States, in any interior locality, shall be so great and so universal, as to prevent competent resident citizens from holding the Federal offices, there will be no attempt to force obnoxious strangers among the people for that object. While the strict legal right may exist in the government to enforce the exercise of these offices, the attempt to do so would be so irritating, and so nearly impracticable with all, that I deem it better to forego, for the time, the uses of such offices.

The mails, unless repelled, will continue to be furnished in all parts of the Union. So far as possible, the people everywhere shall have that sense of perfect security which is most favorable to calm thought and reflection. The course here indicated will be followed, unless current events, and experience, shall show a modification, or change, to be proper; and in every case and exigency, my best discretion will be exercised, according to circumstances actually existing, and with a view and a hope of a peaceful solution of the national troubles, and the restoration of fraternal sympathies and affections.

That there are persons in one section, or another who seek to destroy the Union at all events, and are glad of any pretext to do it, I will neither affirm or deny; but if there be such, I need address no word to them. To those, however, who really love the Union, may I not speak?

Before entering upon so grave a matter as the destruction of our national fabric, with all its benefits, its memories, and its hopes, would it not be wise to ascertain precisely why we do it? Will you hazard so desperate a step, while there is any possibility that any portion of the ills you fly from, have no real existence? Will you, while the certain ills you fly to, are greater than all the real ones you fly from? Will you risk the commission of so fearful a mistake?

All profess to be content in the Union, if all constitutional rights can be maintained. Is it true, then, that any right, plainly written in the Constitution, has been denied? I think not. Happily the human mind is so constituted, that no party can reach to the audacity of doing this. Think, if you can, of a single instance in which a plainly written provision of the Constitution has ever been denied. If, by the mere force of numbers, a majority should deprive a minority of any clearly written constitutional right, it might, in a moral point of view, justify revolution — certainly would, if such right were a vital one. But such is not our case. All the vital rights of minorities, and of individuals, are so plainly assured to them, by affirmations and negations, guarranties and prohibitions, in the Constitution, that controversies never arise concerning them. But no organic law can ever be framed with a provision specifically applicable to every question which may occur in practical administration. No foresight can anticipate, nor any document of reasonable length contain express provisions for all possible questions. Shall fugitives from labor be surrendered by national or by State authority? The Constitution does not expressly say. *May* Congress prohibit slavery in the territories? The Constitution does not expressly say. *Must* Congress protect slavery in the territories? The Constitution does not expressly say.

From questions of this class spring all our constitutional controversies, and we divide upon them into majorities and minorities. If the minority will not acquiesce, the majority must, or the government must cease. There is no other alternative; for continuing the government, is acquiescence on one side or the other. If a minority, in such case, will secede rather than acquiesce, they make a precedent which, in turn, will divide and ruin them; for a minority of their own will secede from them, whenever a majority refuses to be controlled by such minority. For instance, why may not any portion of a new confederacy, a year or two hence, arbitrarily secede again, precisely as portions of the present Union now claim to secede from it. All who cherish disunion sentiments, are now being educated to the exact temper of doing this. Is there such perfect identity of interests among the States to compose a new Union, as to produce harmony only, and prevent renewed secession?

Plainly, the central idea of secession, is the essence of anarchy. A majority, held in restraint by constitutional checks, and limitations, and always changing easily, with deliberate changes of popular opinions and sentiments, is the only true sovereign of a free people. Whoever rejects it, does, of necessity, fly to anarchy or to despotism. Unanimity is impossible; the rule of a minority, as a permanent arrangement, is wholly inadmissible; so that, rejecting the majority principle, anarchy, or despotism in some form, is all that is left.

I do not forget the position assumed by some, that constitutional questions are to be decided by the Supreme Court; nor do I deny that such decisions must be binding in any case, upon the parties to a suit, as to the object of that suit, while they are also entitled to very high respect and consideration, in all paralel cases, by all other departments of the government. And while it is obviously possible that such decision may be erroneous in any given case, still the evil effect following it, being limited to that particular case, with the chance that it may be over-ruled, and never become a precedent for other cases, can better be borne than could the evils of a different practice. At the same time the candid citizen must confess that if the policy of the government, upon vital questions, affecting the whole people, is to be irrevocably fixed by decisions of the

Supreme Court, the instant they are made, in ordinary litigation between parties, in personal actions, the people will have ceased, to be their own rulers, having, to that extent, practically resigned their government, into the hands of that eminent tribunal. Nor is there, in this view, any assault upon the court, or the judges. It is a duty, from which they may not shrink, to decide cases properly brought before them; and it is no fault of theirs, if others seek to turn their decisions to political purposes.

One section of our country believes slavery is *right*, and ought to be extended, while the other believes it is *wrong*, and ought not to be extended. This is the only substantial dispute. The fugitive slave clause of the Constitution, and the law for the suppression of the foreign slave trade, are each as well enforced, perhaps, as any law can ever be in a community where the moral sense of the people imperfectly supports the law itself. The great body of the people abide by the dry legal obligation in both cases, and a few break over in each. This, I think, cannot be perfectly cured; and it would be worse in both cases *after* the separation of the sections, than before. The foreign slave trade, now imperfectly suppressed, would be ultimately revived without restriction, in one section; while fugitive slaves, now only partially surrendered, would not be surrendered at all, by the other.

Physically speaking, we cannot separate. We cannot remove our respective sections from each other, nor build an impassable wall between them. A husband and wife may be divorced, and go out of the presence, and beyond the reach of each other; but the different parts of our country cannot do this. They cannot but remain face to face; and intercourse, either amicable or hostile, must continue between them. Is it possible then to make that intercourse more advantageous, or more satisfactory, *after* separation than *before*? Can aliens make treaties easier than friends can make laws? Can treaties be more faithfully enforced between aliens, than laws can among friends? Suppose you go to war, you cannot fight always; and when, after much loss on both sides, and no gain on either, you cease fighting, the identical old questions, as to terms of intercourse, are again upon you.

This country, with its institutions, belongs to the people who inhabit it. Whenever they shall grow weary of the existing government, they can exercise their *constitutional* right of amending it, or their *revolutionary* right to dismember, or overthrow it. I can not be ignorant of the fact that many worthy, and patriotic citizens are desirous of having the national constitution amended. While I make no recommendation of amendments, I fully recognize the rightful authority of the people over the whole subject, to be exercised in either of the modes prescribed in the instrument itself; and I should, under existing circumstances, favor, rather than oppose, a fair oppertunity being afforded the people to act upon it.

I will venture to add that, to me, the convention mode seems preferable, in that it allows amendments to originate with the people themselves, instead of only permitting them to take, or reject, propositions, originated by others, not especially chosen for the purpose, and which might not be precisely such, as they would wish to either accept or refuse. I understand a proposed amendment to the Constitution—which amendment, however, I have not seen, has passed Congress, to the effect that the federal government, shall never interfere with the domestic institutions of the States, including that of persons held to service.[8] To avoid misconstruction of what I have said, I depart from my purpose not to speak of particular amendments, so far as to say that, holding such a provision to now be implied constitutional law, I have no objection to its being made express, and irrevocable.

The Chief Magistrate derives all his authority from the people, and they have conferred none upon him to fix terms for the separation of the States. The people themselves can do this also if they choose; but the executive, as such, has nothing to do with it. His duty is to administer the present government, as it came to his hands, and to transmit it, unimpaired by him, to his successor.

Why should there not be a patient confidence in the ultimate justice of the people? Is there any better, or equal hope, in the world? In our present differences, is either party without faith of being in the right? If the Almighty Ruler of nations, with his eternal truth and justice, be on your side of the North, or on yours of the South, that truth, and that justice, will surely prevail, by the judgment of this great tribunal, the American people.

By the frame of the government under which we live, this same people have wisely given their public servants but little power for mischief; and have, with equal wisdom, provided for the return of that little to their own hands at very short intervals.

While the people retain their virtue, and vigilence, no administration, by any extreme of wickedness or folly, can very seriously injure the government, in the short space of four years.

My countrymen, one and all, think calmly and *well*, upon this whole subject. Nothing valuable can be lost by taking time. If there be an object to *hurry* any of you, in hot haste, to a step which you would never take *deliberately*, that object will be frustrated by taking time; but no good object can be frustrated by it. Such of you as are now dissatisfied, still have the old Constitution unimpaired, and, on the sensitive point, the laws of your own framing under it; while the new administration will have no immediate power, if it would, to change either. If it were admitted that you who are dissatisfied, hold the right side in the dispute, there still is no single good

---

[8] Shortly before Lincoln's inauguration, two-thirds majorities of the House and the Senate approved and sent to the states for ratification a proposed thirteenth amendment to the Constitution that guaranteed that the federal government would never interfere with slavery in the states. When the war began, the states ignored ratification. After four years of war, a very different thirteenth amendment, which abolished slavery, was ratified.

reason for precipitate action. Intelligence, patriotism, Christianity, and a firm reliance on Him, who has never yet forsaken this favored land, are still competent to adjust, in the best way, all our present difficulty.

In *your* hands, my dissatisfied fellow countrymen, and not in *mine*, is the momentous issue of civil war. The government will not assail you. You can have no conflict, without being yourselves the aggressors. *You* have no oath registered in Heaven to destroy the government, while *I* shall have the most solemn one to "preserve, protect and defend" it.

I am loth to close. We are not enemies, but friends. We must not be enemies. Though passion may have strained, it must not break our bonds of affection. The mystic chords of memory, stretching from every battlefield, and patriot grave, to every living heart and hearthstone, all over this broad land, will yet swell the chorus of the Union, when again touched, as surely they will be, by the better angels of our nature.

A WAR TO SAVE THE UNION

Lincoln encountered the military consequences of secession at Fort Sumter in the harbor of Charleston, South Carolina (see Map 1, pages xxii–xxiii). When Confederate batteries opened fire on the fort in the predawn darkness of April 12, 1861, the political controversies of secession became inextricably entangled in the military realities of civil war. After April 15, when Lincoln called for volunteers to suppress the secessionist rebels, four more slave states seceded—Tennessee, Arkansas, North Carolina, and Virginia. While Lincoln anxiously oversaw the organization of Union armies, he just as anxiously sought to prevent the slave states still in the Union—Maryland, Kentucky, Missouri, and Delaware—from joining the secession stampede. During his first year in office, Lincoln fashioned his military policies according to his views of the politics of secession, views he summarized in his addresses to Congress in July and December 1861 (Documents 16 and 17).

Lincoln considered himself to be the president of the entire United States, including the states that claimed to have seceded. He consistently refused to acknowledge that secession was an accomplished fact or that the Confederacy was a political entity separate from the Union. Instead, he declared secession an internal rebellion, an insurrection against the laws and Constitution of the United States. After the firing on Fort Sumter, Lincoln believed that war was necessary to suppress the insurrection and to prevent the Confederacy from achieving its goal of independence. In his view, the goal of the war was to prevent disunion, rather than to reunite two separate sovereignties.

Lincoln's concept of an indestructible Union shaped his military strategy. He believed secessionists were political insurgents—somewhat akin to an extremist political party—who had won elections in the slave states and had created governments and armies to pursue their separatist ambitions. But Lincoln suspected that secessionists did not command the loyalty of many southern citizens. Within the Confederacy, Lincoln claimed, hundreds of thousands of white southerners remained loyal to the Union. From the outset of the war, Lincoln sought to avoid offending these unionists within the seceding states by repeatedly affirming that their constitutional rights to property, including their slaves, would continue to be protected. By insisting on the distinction between disloyal southerners—who staffed and supported Confederate armies—and loyal southerners—who did neither—Lincoln hoped to awaken the sleeping giant of southern unionism, which would then cooperate with the federal government and work to defeat secessionists both militarily and politically. He also hoped that a war carefully targeted against disloyal secessionists would prevent the border slave states of Maryland, Delaware, Kentucky, and Missouri from joining the Confederacy by reassuring their residents that the goal of the war was to prevent disunion, not to undermine their right to own slaves. Lincoln's appeal to southern unionists in the Confederacy and in the loyal border states was the chief political component of his military strategy between the assault on Fort Sumter and his proclamation of emancipation on January 1, 1863 (Document 34).

By ordering the Confederate attack on Fort Sumter, Jefferson Davis inadvertently unified the North and aided Lincoln. The attack outraged almost all northerners and generated a tidal wave of patriotic fervor that swept through the free states, propelling men to volunteer to defend the nation and fight the rebels. Lincoln immediately called for 75,000 militia, and as the massive scale of the conflict began to come into focus, he soon asked for an additional 42,000 volunteers to serve for three years. By calling for troops, Lincoln exercised presidential powers explicitly authorized by the Constitution. He insisted that the Confederacy represented a domestic insurrection, not a foreign enemy. Although Lincoln needed and sought congressional support for the war, he directed the Union war effort with his constitutional powers as president and commander in chief.

While thousands of northern men hurriedly donned uniforms, organized companies and regiments, and said good-bye to friends and families, Lincoln declared a blockade of southern ports. Designed to strangle the Confederacy, the blockade was the centerpiece of what General Winfield Scott, the nation's chief military officer when Lincoln took office, termed the Anaconda strategy. Although it never eliminated Confederate maritime trade, the blockade greatly reduced the Confederacy's access to supplies from abroad and its ability to raise funds by selling cotton in foreign markets. By definition, a blockade is imposed by a nation on a foreign power, a policy in direct conflict with Lincoln's refusal to acknowledge Confederate sovereignty and his concept of the war as a domestic rebellion, as critics pointed out. Lincoln, however, shrugged off this contradiction and kept the blockade in place throughout the war.

Lincoln's most immediate concern following the attack on Fort Sumter was to secure the defense of Washington, D.C., which was surrounded by the slave states of Maryland and Virginia. Maryland secessionists quickly destroyed bridges and telegraph lines connecting Washington with the North. By April 25, enough soldiers had arrived in Washington to defend the capital, but the possibility still existed that Maryland would secede along with the rest of the slave states, a possibility that was militarily and politically unacceptable to Lincoln. The president watched developments in Maryland closely. Although Maryland remained in the Union, Lincoln authorized the suspension of the writ of habeas corpus, an action that allowed military officers to arrest and hold without a judicial hearing any person they believed to be aiding the Confederacy. Revoking the constitutional guarantee of habeas corpus—which requires release of any person whom a court determines to have been unlawfully arrested—signaled Lincoln's willingness to resort to extraordinary measures to protect Washington, the headquarters of the Union.

By July 4 when Congress assembled, Lincoln had not only exercised his authority as president and commander in chief, but he had also authorized the expenditure of vast sums to equip and supply the armed forces, a constitutional prerogative granted to Congress, not the president. In his message to the legislators, Lincoln reviewed the unprecedented crisis he had confronted when he became president, explaining what he had done and why.

16

Message to Congress in Special Session

July 4, 1861

Fellow-citizens of the Senate and House of Representatives:
Having been convened on an extraordinary occasion, as authorized by the Constitution, your attention is not called to any ordinary subject of legislation.

At the beginning of the present Presidential term, four months ago, the functions of the Federal Government were found to be generally suspended within the several States of South Carolina, Georgia, Alabama, Mississippi, Louisiana, and Florida, excepting only those of the Post Office Department.

Within these States, all the Forts, Arsenals, Dock-yards, Custom-houses, and the like, including the movable and stationary property in, and about them, had been seized, and were held in open hostility to this Government, excepting only Forts Pickens, Taylor, and Jefferson, on, and near the Florida coast, and Fort Sumter, in Charleston harbor, South Carolina. The Forts thus seized had been put in improved condition; new ones had been built; and armed forces had been organized, and were organizing, all avowedly with the same hostile purpose.

The Forts remaining in the possession of the Federal government, in, and near, these States, were either besieged or menaced by warlike preparations; and especially Fort Sumter was nearly surrounded by well-protected hostile batteries, with guns equal in quality to the best of its own, and outnumbering the latter as perhaps ten to one. A disproportionate share, of the Federal muskets and rifles, had somehow found their way into these States, and had been seized, to be used against the government. Accumulations of the public revenue, lying within them, had been seized for the same object. The Navy was scattered in distant seas; leaving but a very small part of it within the immediate reach of the government. Officers of the Federal Army and Navy, had resigned in great numbers; and, of those resigning, a large proportion had taken up arms against the government. Simultaneously, and in connection, with all this, the purpose to sever the Federal Union, was openly avowed. In accordance with this purpose, an ordinance had been adopted in each of these States, declaring the States, respectively, to be separated from the National Union. A formula for instituting a combined government of these states had been promulgated; and this illegal organization, in the character of confederate States was already invoking recognition, aid, and intervention, from Foreign Powers.

Finding this condition of things, and believing it to be an imperative duty upon the incoming Executive, to prevent, if possible, the consummation of such attempt to destroy the Federal Union, a choice of means to that end became indispensable. This choice was made; and was declared in the Inaugural address. The policy chosen looked to the exhaustion of all peaceful measures, before a resort to any stronger ones. It sought only to hold the public places and property, not already wrested from the Government, and to collect the revenue; relying for the rest, on time, discussion, and the ballot-box. It promised a continuance of the mails, at government expense, to the very people who were resisting the government; and it gave repeated pledges against any disturbance to any of the people, or any of their rights. Of all that which a president might constitutionally, and justifiably, do in such a case, everything was foreborne, without which, it was believed possible to keep the government on foot.

On the 5th of March, (the present incumbent's first full day in office) a letter of Major Anderson, commanding at Fort Sumter, written on the 28th of February, and received at the War Department on the 4th of March, was, by that Department, placed in his hands. This letter expressed the professional opinion of the writer, that reinforcements could not be thrown into that Fort within the time for his relief, rendered necessary by the limited supply of provisions, and with a view of holding possession of the same, with a force of less than twenty thousand good, and well-disciplined men. This opinion was concurred in by all the officers of his command. . . . The whole was immediately laid before Lieutenant General Scott, who at once concurred with Major Anderson in opinion. On reflection, however, he took full time, consulting with other officers, both of the Army and the Navy; and, at the end of four days, came reluctantly, but decidedly, to the same conclusion as before. He also stated at the same time that no such sufficient force was then at the control of the Government, or could be raised, and brought to the ground, within the time when the provisions in the Fort would be exhausted. In a purely military point of view, this reduced the duty of the administration, in the case, to the mere matter of getting the garrison safely out of the Fort.

It was believed, however, that to so abandon that position, under the circumstances, would be utterly ruinous; that the *necessity* under which it was to be done, would not be fully understood—that, by many, it would be construed as a part of a *voluntary* policy—that, at home, it would discourage the friends of the Union, embolden its adversaries, and go far to insure to the latter, a recognition abroad—that, in fact, it would be our national destruction consummated. This could not be allowed. Starvation was not yet upon the garrison; and ere it would be reached, *Fort Pickens* might be reinforced. This last, would be a clear indication of *policy*, and would better enable the country to accept the evacuation of Fort Sumter, as a military *necessity*. An order was at once directed to be sent for the landing of the troops from the Steam-ship Brooklyn, into Fort Pickens.

This order could not go by land, but must take the longer, and slower route by sea. The first return news from the order was received just one week before the fall of Fort Sumter. The news itself was, that . . . [t]o now re-inforce Fort Pickens, before a crisis would be reached at Fort Sumter[,] was impossible—rendered so by the near exhaustion of provisions in the latter-named Fort. In precaution against such a conjuncture, the government had, a few days before, commenced preparing an expedition, as well adapted as might be, to relieve Fort Sumter; which expedition was intended to be ultimately used, or not, according to circumstances. The strongest anticipated case, for using it, was now presented; and it was resolved to send it forward. As had been intended, in this contingency, it was also resolved to notify the Governor of South Carolina, that he might expect an attempt would be made to provision the Fort; and that, if the attempt should not be resisted, there would be no effort to throw in men, arms, or ammunition, without further notice, or in case of an attack upon the Fort. This notice was accordingly given; whereupon the Fort was attacked, and bombarded to its fall, without even awaiting the arrival of the provisioning expedition.

It is thus seen that the assault upon, and reduction of, Fort Sumter, was, in no sense, a matter of self defence on the part of the assailants. They well knew that the garrison in the Fort could, by no possibility, commit aggression upon them. They knew—they were expressly notified—that the giving of bread to the few brave and hungry men of the garrison, was all which would on that occasion be attempted, unless themselves, by resisting so much, should provoke more. They knew that this Government desired to keep the garrison in the Fort, not to assail them, but merely to maintain visible possession, and thus to preserve the Union from actual, and immediate dissolution—trusting, as herein-before stated, to time, discussion, and the ballot-box, for final adjustment; and they assailed, and reduced the Fort, for precisely the reverse object—to drive out the visible authority of the Federal Union, and thus force it to immediate dissolution.

That this was their object, the Executive well understood; and having said to them in the inaugural address, "You can have no conflict without being yourselves the aggressors," he took pains, not only to keep this declaration good, but also to keep the case so free from the power of ingenious sophistry, as that the world should not be able to misunderstand it. By the affair at Fort Sumter, with its surrounding circumstances, that point was reached. Then, and thereby, the assailants of the Government, began the conflict of arms, without a gun in sight, or in expectancy, to return their fire, save only the few in the Fort, sent to that harbor, years before, for their own protection, and still ready to give that protection, in whatever was lawful. In this act, discarding all else, they have forced upon the country, the distinct issue: "Immediate dissolution, or blood."

And this issue embraces more than the fate of these United States. It presents to the whole family of man, the question, whether a constitutional republic, or a democracy—a government of the people, by the same people—can, or cannot, maintain its territorial integrity, against its own domestic foes. It presents the question, whether discontented individuals, too few in numbers to control administration, according to organic law, in any case, can always, upon the pretences made in this case, or on any other pretences, or arbitrarily, without any pretence, break up their Government, and thus practically put an end to free government upon the earth. It forces us to ask: "Is there, in all republics, this inherent, and fatal weakness?" "Must a government, of necessity, be too *strong* for the liberties of its own people, or too *weak* to maintain its own existence?"

So viewing the issue, no choice was left but to call out the war power of the Government; and so to resist force, employed for its destruction, by force, for its preservation.

The call was made; and the response of the country was most gratifying; surpassing, in unanimity and spirit, the most sanguine expectation. Yet none of the States commonly called Slave-States, except Delaware, gave a Regiment through regular State organization. A few regiments have been organized within some others of those States, by individual enterprise, and received into the government service. Of course the seceded States, so called, (and to which Texas had been joined about the time of the inauguration,) gave no troops to the cause of the Union. The border States, so called, were not uniform in their actions; some of them being almost *for* the Union, while in others—as Virginia, North Carolina, Tennessee, and Arkansas—the Union sentiment was nearly repressed, and silenced. The course taken in Virginia was the most remarkable—perhaps the most important. A convention, elected by the people of that State, to consider this very question of disrupting the Federal Union, was in session at the capital of Virginia when Fort Sumter fell. To this body the people had chosen a large majority of *professed* Union men. Almost immediately after the fall of Sumter, many members of that majority went over to the original disunion minority, and, with them, adopted an ordinance for withdrawing the State from the Union. Whether this change was wrought by their great approval of the assault upon Sumter, or their great resentment at the government's resistance to that assault, is not definitely known. Although they submitted the ordinance, for ratification, to a vote of the people, to be taken on a day then somewhat more than a month distant, the convention, and the Legislature, (which was also in session at the same time and place) with leading men of the State, not members of either, immediately commenced acting, as if the State were already out of the Union. They pushed military preparations vigorously forward all over the state. They seized the United States Armory at Harper's Ferry, and the Navy-yard at Gosport, near Norfolk. They received—perhaps invited—into their state, large bodies of troops, with their warlike appointments, from the so-called seceded States. They formally entered into a treaty of temporary alliance, and co-operation with the so-called "Confederate States," and sent members to their Congress at Montgomery. And, finally, they permitted the insurrectionary government to be transferred to their capital at Richmond.[9]

The people of Virginia have thus allowed this giant insurrection to make its nest within her borders; and this government has no choice left but to deal with it, *where* it finds it. And it has the less regret, as the loyal citizens have, in due form, claimed its protection. Those loyal citizens, this government is bound to recognize, and protect, as being Virginia.

In the border States, so called—in fact, the middle states—there are those who favor a policy which they call "armed neutrality"—that is, an arming of those states to prevent the Union forces passing one way, or the disunion, the other, over their soil. This would be disunion completed. Figuratively speaking, it would be the building of an impassable wall along the line of separation. And yet, not quite an impassable one; for, under the guise of neutrality, it would tie the hands of the Union men, and freely pass supplies from among them, to the insurrectionists, which it could not do as an open enemy. At a stroke, it would take all the trouble off the hands of secession, except only what proceeds from the external blockade. It would do for the disunionists that which, of all things, they most desire—feed them well, and give them disunion without a struggle of their own. It recognizes no fidelity to the Constitution, no obligation to maintain the Union; and while very many who have favored it are, doubtless, loyal citizens, it is, nevertheless, treason in effect.

Recurring to the action of the government, it may be stated that, at first, a call was made for seventy-five thousand militia; and rapidly following this, a proclamation was issued for closing the ports of the insurrectionary districts by proceedings in the nature of Blockade. So far all was believed to be strictly legal. At this point the insurrectionists announced their purpose to enter upon the practice of privateering.

Other calls were made for volunteers, to serve three years, unless sooner discharged; and also for large additions to the regular Army and Navy. These measures, whether strictly legal or not, were ventured upon, under what appeared to be a popular demand, and a public necessity; trusting, then as now, that Congress would readily ratify them. It is believed that nothing has been done beyond the constitutional competency of Congress.

Soon after the first call for militia, it was considered a duty to authorize the Commanding General, in proper cases, according to his discretion, to

---

[9] The Confederate Congress agreed on May 21 to move its capital from Montgomery, Alabama, to Richmond, Virginia.

suspend the privilege of the writ of habeas corpus; or, in other words, to arrest, and detain, without resort to the ordinary processes and forms of law, such individuals as he might deem dangerous to the public safety. This authority has purposely been exercised but very sparingly. Nevertheless, the legality and propriety of what has been done under it are questioned; and the attention of the country has been called to the proposition that one who is sworn to "take care that the laws be faithfully executed," should not himself violate them.[10] Of course some consideration was given to the questions of power, and propriety, before this matter was acted upon. The whole of the laws which were required to be faithfully executed, were being resisted, and failing of execution, in nearly one-third of the States. Must they be allowed to finally fail of execution, even had it been perfectly clear, that by the use of the means necessary to their execution, some single law, made in such extreme tenderness of the citizen's liberty, that practically, it relieves more of the guilty, than of the innocent, should, to a very limited extent, be violated? To state the question more directly, are all the laws, *but one*, to go unexecuted, and the government itself go to pieces, lest that one be violated? Even in such a case, would not the official oath be broken, if the government should be overthrown, when it was believed that disregarding the single law, would tend to preserve it? But it was not believed that this question was presented. It was not believed that any law was violated. The provision of the Constitution that "The privilege of the writ of habeas corpus, shall not be suspended unless when, in cases of rebellion or invasion, the public safety may require it," is equivalent to a provision—is a provision—that such privilege may be suspended when, in cases of rebellion, or invasion, the public safety does require it. It was decided that we have a case of rebellion, and that the public safety does require the qualified suspension of the privilege of the writ which was authorized to be made. Now it is insisted that Congress, and not the Executive, is vested with this power. But the Constitution itself, is silent as to which, or who, is to exercise the power; and as the provision was plainly made for a dangerous emergency, it cannot be believed the framers of the instrument intended, that in every case, the danger should run its course, until Congress could be called together; the very assembling of which might be prevented, as was intended in this case, by the rebellion. . . .

The forbearance of this government had been so extraordinary, and so long continued, as to lead some foreign nations to shape their action as if they supposed the early destruction of our national Union was probable. While this, on discovery, gave the Executive some concern, he is now

---

[10] Lincoln is referring to the case of John Merryman, a rabid secessionist from Baltimore who was arrested and jailed at Fort McHenry. Merryman petitioned to be released under a writ of habeas corpus, and his plea was ultimately decided by Supreme Court chief justice Roger B. Taney on May 28. In *Ex parte Merryman*, Taney ruled that Lincoln had no constitutional power to suspend the writ of habeas corpus. Lincoln ignored Taney's decision and defended his actions in his address to Congress.

happy to say that the sovereignty, and rights of the United States, are now everywhere practically respected by foreign powers; and a general sympathy with the country is manifested throughout the world. . . .

It is now recommended that you give the legal means for making this contest a short, and a decisive one; that you place at the control of the government, for the work, at least four hundred thousand men, and four hundred millions of dollars. That number of men is about one tenth of those of proper ages within the regions where, apparently, *all* are willing to engage; and the sum is less than a twentythird part of the money value owned by the men who seem ready to devote the whole. A debt of six hundred millions of dollars *now*, is a less sum per head, than was the debt of our revolution, when we came out of that struggle; and the money value in the country now, bears even a greater proportion to what it was *then*, than does the population. Surely each man has as strong a motive *now*, to preserve our liberties, as each had *then*, to *establish* them.

A right result, at this time, will be worth more to the world, than ten times the men, and ten times the money. The evidence reaching us from the country, leaves no doubt, that the material for the work is abundant; and that it needs only the hand of legislation to give it legal sanction, and the hand of the Executive to give it practical shape and efficiency. One of the greatest perplexities of the government, is to avoid receiving troops faster than it can provide for them. In a word, the people will save their government, if the government itself, will do its part, only indifferently well.

It might seem, at first thought, to be of little difference whether the present movement at the South be called "secession" or "rebellion." The movers, however, well understand the difference. At the beginning, they knew they could never raise their treason to any respectable magnitude, by any name which implies *violation* of law. They knew their people possessed as much of moral sense, as much of devotion to law and order, and as much pride in, and reverence for, the history, and government, of their common country, as any other civilized, and patriotic people. They knew they could make no advancement directly in the teeth of these strong and noble sentiments. Accordingly they commenced by an insidious debauching of the public mind. They invented an ingenious sophism [plausible but fallacious argument], which, if conceded, was followed by perfectly logical steps, through all the incidents, to the complete destruction of the Union. The sophism itself is, that any state of the Union may, *consistently* with the national Constitution, and therefore *lawfully*, and *peacefully*, withdraw from the Union, without the consent of the Union, or of any other state. The little disguise that the supposed right is to be exercised only for just cause, themselves to be the sole judge of its justice, is too thin to merit any notice.

With rebellion thus sugar-coated, they have been drugging the public mind of their section for more than thirty years; and, until at length, they have brought many good men to a willingness to take up arms against the government the day *after* some assemblage of men have enacted the farcical pretence of taking their State out of the Union, who could have been brought to no such thing the day *before*.

This sophism derives much—perhaps the whole—of its currency, from the assumption, that there is some omnipotent, and sacred supremacy, pertaining to a *State*—to each State of our Federal Union. Our States have neither more, nor less power, than that reserved to them, in the Union, by the Constitution—no one of them ever having been a State *out* of the Union. The original ones passed into the Union even *before* they cast off their British colonial dependence; and the new ones each came into the Union directly from a condition of dependence, excepting Texas. And even Texas, in its temporary independence, was never designated a State. The new ones only took the designation of States, on coming into the Union, while that name was first adopted for the old ones, in, and by, the Declaration of Independence. Therein the "United Colonies" were declared to be "Free and Independent States"; but, even then, the object plainly was not to declare their independence of *one another*, or of the *Union*; but directly the contrary, as their mutual pledge, and their mutual action, before, at the time, and afterwards, abundantly show. The express plighting of faith, by each and all of the original thirteen, in the Articles of Confederation, two years later, that the Union shall be perpetual, is most conclusive. Having never been States, either in substance, or in name, *outside* of the Union, whence this magical omnipotence of "State rights," asserting a claim of power to lawfully destroy the Union itself? Much is said about the "sovereignty" of the States; but the word, even, is not in the national Constitution; nor, as is believed, in any of the State constitutions. What is a "sovereignty," in the political sense of the term? Would it be far wrong to define it "A political community, without a political superior"? Tested by this, no one of our States, except Texas, ever was a sovereignty. And even Texas gave up the character on coming into the Union; by which act, she acknowledged the Constitution of the United States, and the laws and treaties of the United States made in pursuance of the Constitution, to be, for her, the supreme law of the land. The States have their *status in* the Union, and they have no other *legal status*. If they break from this, they can only do so against law, and by revolution. The Union, and not themselves separately, procured their independence, and their liberty. By conquest, or purchase, the Union gave each of them, whatever of independence, and liberty, it has. The Union is older than any of the States; and, in fact, it created them as States. Originally, some dependent colonies made the Union; and, in turn, the Union threw off their old dependence, for them, and made them States, such as they are. Not one of them ever had a State constitution, independent of the Union. Of course, it is not forgotten that all the new States framed their constitutions, before they entered the

Union; nevertheless, dependent upon, and preparatory to, coming into the Union.

Unquestionably the States have the powers, and rights, reserved to them in, and by the National Constitution; but among these, surely, are not included all conceivable powers, however mischievous, or destructive; but, at most, such only, as were known in the world, at the time, as governmental powers; and certainly, a power to destroy the government itself, had never been known as a governmental—as a merely administrative power. This relative matter of National power, and State rights, as a principle, is no other than the principle of *generality*, and *locality*. Whatever concerns the whole, should be confided to the whole—to the general government; while, whatever concerns *only* the State, should be left exclusively, to the State. This is all there is of original principle about it. Whether the National Constitution, in defining boundaries between the two, has applied the principle with exact accuracy, is not to be questioned. We are all bound by that defining, without question.

What is now combatted, is the position that secession is *consistent* with the Constitution—is *lawful*, and *peaceful*. It is not contended that there is any express law for it; and nothing should ever be implied as law, which leads to unjust, or absurd consequences. The nation purchased, with money, the countries out of which several of these States were formed. Is it just that they shall go off without leave, and without refunding? The nation paid very large sums, (in the aggregate, I believe, nearly a hundred millions) to relieve Florida of the aboriginal tribes. Is it just that she shall now be off without consent, or without making any return? The nation is now in debt for money applied to the benefit of these so-called seceding States, in common with the rest. Is it just, either that creditors shall go unpaid, or the remaining States pay the whole? A part of the present national debt was contracted to pay the old debts of Texas. Is it just that she shall leave, and pay no part of this herself?

Again, if one State may secede, so may another; and when all shall have seceded, none is left to pay the debts. Is this quite just to creditors? Did we notify them of this sage view of ours, when we borrowed their money? If we now recognize this doctrine, by allowing the seceders to go in peace, it is difficult to see what we can do, if others choose to go, or to extort terms upon which they will promise to remain.

The seceders insist that our Constitution admits of secession. They have assumed to make a National Constitution of their own, in which, of necessity, they have either *discarded*, or *retained*, the right of secession, as they insist, it exists in ours. If they have discarded it, they thereby admit that, on principle, it ought not to be in ours. If they have retained it, by their own construction of ours they show that to be consistent they must secede from one another, whenever they shall find it the easiest way of settling their debts, or effecting any other selfish, or unjust object. The

principle itself is one of disintegration, and upon which no government
can possibly endure.

If all the States, save one, should assert the power to *drive* that one
out of the Union, it is presumed the whole class of seceder politicians
would at once deny the power, and denounce the act as the greatest out-
rage upon State rights. But suppose that precisely the same act, instead of
being called "driving the one out," should be called "the seceding of the
others from that one," it would be exactly what the seceders claim to do;
unless, indeed, they make the point, that the one, because it is a minority,
may rightfully do, what the others, because they are a majority, may not
rightfully do. These politicians are subtle, and profound, on the rights of
minorities. They are not partial to that power which made the Constitution, and speaks from the preamble, calling itself "We, the People."

It may well be questioned whether there is, to-day, a majority of the
legally qualified voters of any State, except perhaps South Carolina, in
favor of disunion. There is much reason to believe that the Union men are
the majority in many, if not in every other one, of the so-called seceded
States. The contrary has not been demonstrated in any one of them. It is
ventured to affirm this, even of Virginia and Tennessee; for the result of
an election, held in military camps, where the bayonets are all on one side
of the question voted upon, can scarcely be considered as demonstrating popular sentiment.[11] At such an election, all that large class who are,
at once, *for* the Union, and *against* coercion, would be coerced to vote
against the Union.

It may be affirmed, without extravagance, that the free institutions
we enjoy, have developed the powers, and improved the condition, of our
whole people, beyond any example in the world. Of this we now have a
striking, and an impressive illustration. So large an army as the government has now on foot, was never before known, without a soldier in it,
but who had taken his place there, of his own free choice. But more than
this: there are many single Regiments whose members, one and another,
possess full practical knowledge of all the arts, sciences, professions,
and whatever else, whether useful or elegant, is known in the world; and
there is scarcely one, from which there could not be selected, a President, a Cabinet, a Congress, and perhaps a Court, abundantly competent
to administer the government itself. Nor do I say this is not true, also,
in the army of our late friends, now adversaries, in this contest; but if it
is, so much better the reason why the government, which has conferred
such benefits on both them and us, should not be broken up. Whoever,
in any section, proposes to abandon such a government, would do well to
consider, in deference to what principle it is, that he does it—what better he is likely to get in its stead—whether the substitute will give, or be

[11] Lincoln is referring to the popular vote for secession in Virginia that took place on
May 23, weeks after Virginians had organized military units to support the Confederacy.

intended to give, so much of good to the people. There are some foreshadowings on this subject. Our adversaries have adopted some Declarations of Independence; in which, unlike the good old one, penned by Jefferson, they omit the words "all men are created equal." Why? They have adopted a temporary national constitution, in the preamble of which, unlike our good old one, signed by Washington, they omit "We, the People," and substitute "We, the deputies of the sovereign and independent States." Why? Why this deliberate pressing out of view, the rights of men, and the authority of the people?

This is essentially a People's contest. On the side of the Union, it is a struggle for maintaining in the world, that form, and substance of government, whose leading object is, to elevate the condition of men — to lift artificial weights from all shoulders — to clear the paths of laudable pursuit for all — to afford all, an unfettered start, and a fair chance, in the race of life. Yielding to partial, and temporary departures, from necessity, this is the leading object of the government for whose existence we contend.

I am most happy to believe that the plain people understand, and appreciate this. It is worthy of note, that while in this, the government's hour of trial, large numbers of those in the Army and Navy, who have been favored with the offices, have resigned, and proved false to the hand which had pampered them, not one common soldier, or common sailor is known to have deserted his flag.

Great honor is due to those officers who remain true, despite the example of their treacherous associates; but the greatest honor, and most important fact of all, is the unanimous firmness of the common soldiers, and common sailors. To the last man, so far as known, they have successfully resisted the traitorous efforts of those, whose commands, but an hour before, they obeyed as absolute law. This is the patriotic instinct of the plain people. They understand, without an argument, that destroying the government, which was made by Washington, means no good to them.

Our popular government has often been called an experiment. Two points in it, our people have already settled — the successful *establishing*, and the successful *administering* of it. One still remains — its successful *maintenance* against a formidable internal attempt to overthrow it. It is now for them to demonstrate to the world, that those who can fairly carry an election, can also suppress a rebellion — that ballots are the rightful, and peaceful, successors of bullets; and that when ballots have fairly, and constitutionally, decided, there can be no successful appeal, back to bullets; that there can be no successful appeal, except to ballots themselves, at succeeding elections. Such will be a great lesson of peace; teaching men that what they cannot take by an election, neither can they take it by a war — teaching all, the folly of being the beginners of a war.

Lest there be some uneasiness in the minds of candid men, as to what is to be the course of the government, towards the Southern States, *after* the rebellion shall have been suppressed, the Executive deems it proper to say, it will be his purpose then, as ever, to be guided by the Constitution, and the laws; and that he probably will have no different understanding of the powers, and duties of the Federal government, relatively to the rights of the States, and the people, under the Constitution, than that expressed in the inaugural address.

He desires to preserve the government, that it may be administered for all, as it was administered by the men who made it. Loyal citizens everywhere, have the right to claim this of their government; and the government has no right to withhold, or neglect it. It is not perceived that, in giving it, there is any coercion, any conquest, or any subjugation, in any just sense of those terms.

The Constitution provides, and all the States have accepted the provision, that "The United States shall guarantee to every State in this Union a republican form of government." But, if a State may lawfully go out of the Union, having done so, it may also discard the republican form of government; so that to prevent its going out, is an indispensable *means*, to the *end*, of maintaining the guaranty mentioned; and when an end is lawful and obligatory, the indispensable means to it, are also lawful, and obligatory.

It was with the deepest regret that the Executive found the duty of employing the war-power, in defence of the government, forced upon him. He could but perform this duty, or surrender the existence of the government. No compromise, by public servants, could, in this case, be a cure; not that compromises are not often proper, but that no popular government can long survive a marked precedent, that those who carry an election, can only save the government from immediate destruction, by giving up the main point, upon which the people gave the election. The people themselves, and not their servants, can safely reverse their own deliberate decisions. As a private citizen, the Executive could not have consented that these institutions shall perish; much less could he, in betrayal of so vast, and so sacred a trust, as these free people had confided to him. He felt that he had no moral right to shrink; nor even to count the chances of his own life, in what might follow. In full view of his great responsibility, he has, so far, done what he has deemed his duty. You will now, according to your own judgment, perform yours. He sincerely hopes that your views, and your action, may so accord with his, as to assure all faithful citizens, who have been disturbed in their rights, of a certain, and speedy restoration to them, under the Constitution, and the laws.

And having thus chosen our course, without guile, and with pure purpose, let us renew our trust in God, and go forward without fear, and with manly hearts.

ABRAHAM LINCOLN

WAR IN EARNEST

The first major collision of Union and Confederate armies occurred about twenty-five miles from Washington at Bull Run, a small river just north of Manassas, the junction of rail lines stretching west to the Shenandoah Valley and south toward Richmond (see Map 3). Under pressure from Lincoln to advance toward Richmond, General Irvin McDowell, who commanded the Union army in northeastern Virginia, attacked Confederate forces commanded by General Pierre G. T. Beauregard on July 21. After a long day of fighting, a Confederate counterattack forced Union soldiers to retreat. The retreat turned into a rout as officers lost control of their men, many of them near the end of their ninety-day enlistments, and the disorganized army rushed pell-mell back to Washington. The humiliating defeat at Bull Run convinced Lincoln and his advisers that the rapidly growing Union army needed to be much better trained, organized, and disciplined before undertaking a major campaign. The defeat also made clear that the war would require more soldiers and more time than anyone, including Lincoln, had anticipated. Within days, Lincoln authorized the recruitment of an additional one million men for three-year terms, and he replaced McDowell with General George B. McClellan, whom he charged to organize the newly formed Army of the Potomac into fighting trim.

In his first annual message to Congress, Lincoln summarized the few encouraging military developments of 1861, reiterated his intent to protect the property—including the slaves—of loyal citizens throughout the nation, and declared that the struggle to maintain the Union represented a defense of democratic government and free labor.

17

Annual Message to Congress
December 3, 1861

Fellow Citizens of the Senate and House of Representatives:
In the midst of unprecedented political troubles, we have cause of great gratitude to God for unusual good health, and most abundant harvests.

You will not be surprised to learn that, in the peculiar exigencies of the times, our intercourse with foreign nations has been attended with profound solicitude, chiefly turning upon our own domestic affairs.

A disloyal portion of the American people have, during the whole year, been engaged in an attempt to divide and destroy the Union. A nation which endures factious domestic division, is exposed to disrespect abroad; and one party, if not both, is sure, sooner or later, to invoke foreign intervention.

Nations [such as Britain and France] thus tempted to interfere, are not always able to resist the counsels of seeming expediency, and ungenerous ambition, although measures adopted under such influences seldom fail to be unfortunate and injurious to those adopting them.

The disloyal citizens of the United States who have offered the ruin of our country, in return for the aid and comfort which they have invoked abroad, have received less patronage and encouragement [from foreign powers] than they probably expected. If it were just to suppose, as the insurgents have seemed to assume, that foreign nations, in this case, discarding all moral, social, and treaty obligations, would act solely, and selfishly, for the most speedy restoration of commerce, including, especially, the acquisition of cotton, those nations appear, as yet, not to have seen their way to their object more directly, or clearly, through the destruction, than through the preservation, of the Union. If we could dare to believe that foreign nations are actuated by no higher principle than this, I am quite sure a sound argument could be made to show them that they can reach their aim more readily, and easily, by aiding to crush this rebellion, than by giving encouragement to it.

The principal lever relied on by the insurgents for exciting foreign nations to hostility against us, as already intimated, is the embarrassment of commerce. Those nations, however, not improbably, saw from the first, that it was the Union which made as well our foreign, as our domestic, commerce. They can scarcely have failed to perceive that the effort for disunion produces the existing difficulty; and that one strong nation promises more durable peace, and a more extensive, valuable and reliable commerce, than can the same nation broken into hostile fragments.

Opposite: **Map 3.** *Eastern Theater of the Civil War, 1861–1865*
The proximity of Washington, D.C., the Union capital, and Richmond, Virginia, the Confederate capital, concentrated armies, battles, and attention on killing fields within a 150-mile radius of Lincoln's office.

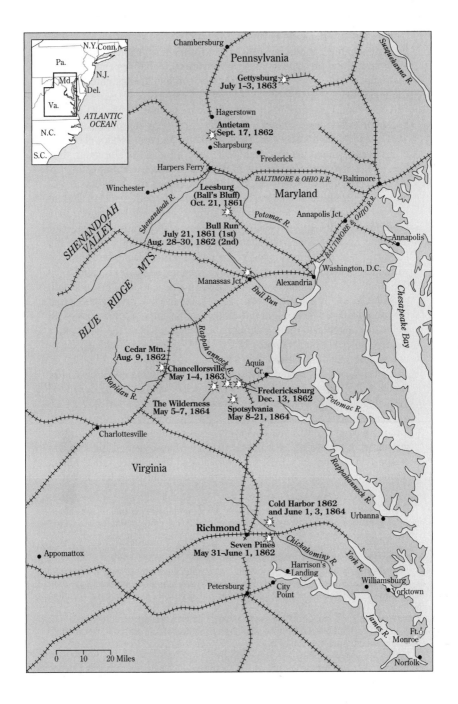

It is not my purpose to review our discussions with foreign states, because whatever might be their wishes, or dispositions, the integrity of our country, and the stability of our government, mainly depend, not upon them, but on the loyalty, virtue, patriotism, and intelligence of the American people. . . .

Under and by virtue of the act of Congress entitled "An act to confiscate property used for insurrectionary purposes," approved August 6, 1861, the legal claims of certain persons to the labor and service of certain other persons have become forfeited;[12] and numbers of the latter, thus liberated, are already dependent on the United States,[13] and must be provided for in some way. Besides this, it is not impossible that some of the States will pass similar enactments for their own benefit respectively, and by operation of which persons of the same class[14] will be thrown upon them for disposal. In such case I recommend that Congress provide for accepting such persons from such States, according to some mode of valuation, in lieu . . . of direct taxes, or upon some other plan to be agreed on with such States respectively; that such persons, on such acceptance by the general government, be at once deemed free; and that, in any event, steps be taken for colonizing both classes, (or the one first mentioned, if the other shall not be brought into existence,) at some place, or places, in a climate congenial to them.[15] It might be well to consider, too,—whether the free colored people already in the United States could not, so far as individuals may desire, be included in such colonization.

To carry out the plan of colonization may involve the acquiring of territory, and also the appropriation of money beyond that to be expended in the territorial acquisition. Having practiced the acquisition of territory for nearly sixty years, the question of constitutional power to do so is no longer an open one with us. The power was questioned at first by Mr. Jefferson, who, however, in the purchase of Louisiana, yielded his scruples on the plea of great expediency. If it be said that the only legitimate object of acquiring territory is to furnish homes for white men, this measure

[12] The First Confiscation Act provided that owners relinquished their claims to all property used in support of the rebellion, including slaves "employed in or upon any fort, navy yard, dock, armory, ship, entrenchment, or in the military or naval service." *The Statutes at Large, Treaties, and Proclamations, of the United States of America*, ed. George P. Sanger (Boston, 1863), XII, 389.

[13] Slaves ran away from their owners and into Union lines almost from the beginning of the war. Northern soldiers were under orders to return fugitive slaves to loyal owners unless the slaves had been employed to support the rebellion, in which case—under the terms of the First Confiscation Act—they no longer had owners and should not be returned. Hundreds, and later thousands, of such slaves were employed by the Union army, at first without official authorization. The evolution of Lincoln's policies about slavery is documented in chapter 5.

[14] That is, slaves.

[15] Lincoln's plans for colonization are documented in chapter 5, especially Document 30.

effects that object; for the emigration of colored men leaves additional room for white men remaining or coming here. Mr. Jefferson, however, placed the importance of procuring Louisiana more on political and commercial grounds than on providing room for population.

On this whole proposition,—including the appropriation of money with the acquisition of territory, does not the expediency amount to absolute necessity—that, without which the government itself cannot be perpetuated? The war continues. In considering the policy to be adopted for suppressing the insurrection, I have been anxious and careful that the inevitable conflict for this purpose shall not degenerate into a violent and remorseless revolutionary struggle. I have, therefore, in every case, thought it proper to keep the integrity of the Union prominent as the primary object of the contest on our part, leaving all questions which are not of vital military importance to the more deliberate action of the legislature.

In the exercise of my best discretion I have adhered to the blockade of the ports held by the insurgents, instead of putting in force, by proclamation, the law of Congress enacted at the late session, for closing those ports.[16]

So, also, obeying the dictates of prudence, as well as the obligations of law, instead of transcending, I have adhered to the act of Congress to confiscate property used for insurrectionary purposes. If a new law upon the same subject shall be proposed, its propriety will be duly considered.

The Union must be preserved, and hence, all indispensable means must be employed. We should not be in haste to determine that radical and extreme measures, which may reach the loyal as well as the disloyal, are indispensable.

The inaugural address at the beginning of the Administration, and the message to Congress at the late special session, were both mainly devoted to the domestic controversy out of which the insurrection and consequent war have sprung. Nothing now occurs to add or subtract, to or from, the principles or general purposes stated and expressed in those documents.

The last ray of hope for preserving the Union peaceably, expired at the assault upon Fort Sumter; and a general review of what has occurred since may not be unprofitable. What was painfully uncertain then, is much better defined and more distinct now; and the progress of events is plainly in the right direction. The insurgents confidently claimed a strong support from north of Mason and Dixon's line [separating free and slave states]; and the friends of the Union were not free from apprehension on the point.

---

[16] Lincoln believed that foreign governments were far less likely to contest a blockade than a closure of southern ports to commerce. The distinction between a blockade and a closure of ports is a legal technicality: A nation imposes a blockade on an enemy power; it can order a closure of its own ports. Lincoln was not troubled by this distinction.

This, however, was soon settled definitely and on the right side. South of the line, noble little Delaware led off right from the first. Maryland was made to *seem* against the Union. Our soldiers were assaulted, bridges were burned, and railroads torn up, within her limits; and we were many days, at one time, without the ability to bring a single regiment over her soil to the capital. Now, her bridges and railroads are repaired and open to the government; she already gives seven regiments to the cause of the Union and none to the enemy; and her people, at a regular election, have sustained the Union, by a larger majority, and a larger aggregate vote than they ever before gave to any candidate, or any question. Kentucky, too, for some time in doubt, is now decidedly, and, I think, unchangeably, ranged on the side of the Union. Missouri is comparatively quiet; and I believe cannot again be overrun by the insurrectionists. These three States of Maryland, Kentucky, and Missouri, neither of which would promise a single soldier at first, have now an aggregate of not less than forty thousand in the field, for the Union; while, of their citizens, certainly not more than a third of that number, and they of doubtful whereabouts, and doubtful existence, are in arms against it. After a somewhat bloody struggle of months, winter closes on the Union people of western Virginia, leaving them masters of their own country.[17]

An insurgent force of about fifteen hundred, for months dominating the narrow peninsular region, constituting the counties of Accomac and Northampton, and known as eastern shore of Virginia, together with some contiguous parts of Maryland, have laid down their arms; and the people there have renewed their allegiance to, and accepted the protection of, the old flag. This leaves no armed insurrectionist north of the Potomac, or east of the Chesapeake.

Also we have obtained a footing at each of the isolated points, on the southern coast, of Hatteras,[18] Port Royal,[19] Tybee Island, near Savannah, and Ship Island;[20] and we likewise have some general accounts of popular movements, in behalf of the Union, in North Carolina and Tennessee.

---

[17] Western Virginia overwhelmingly opposed secession. A provisional government in Wheeling declared the secession government in Richmond illegal; proclaimed that it represented the true, loyal state of Virginia; and sent senators and representatives to Congress. A prolonged military campaign finally pushed Confederate forces out of the region by mid-November 1861. The new state of West Virginia was admitted to the Union on June 20, 1863.

[18] On August 29, Union forces defeated the Confederate garrison at Hatteras Inlet, an opening through the barrier islands off the coast of North Carolina.

[19] On November 7, a Union fleet captured the Confederate stronghold at Port Royal, South Carolina, securing Union control of the best Atlantic harbor in Confederate territory. The Union navy subsequently captured Tybee Island, near the mouth of the Savannah River.

[20] After the Confederates abandoned Ship Island, in the Gulf of Mexico near the mouth of the Mississippi River, in September 1861, Union forces used it to supply ships enforcing the blockade along the Gulf Coast and to organize an assault on New Orleans.

These things demonstrate that the cause of the Union is advancing steadily and certainly southward.

Since your last adjournment, Lieutenant General Scott has retired from the head of the army. During his long life, the nation has not been unmindful of his merit; yet, on calling to mind how faithfully, ably and brilliantly he has served the country, from a time far back in our history, when few of the now living had been born, and thenceforward continually, I cannot but think we are still his debtors. I submit, therefore, for your consideration, what further mark of recognition is due to him, and to ourselves, as a grateful people.

With the retirement of General Scott came the executive duty of appointing, in his stead, a general-in-chief of the army. It is a fortunate circumstance that neither in council nor country was there, so far as I know, any difference of opinion as to the proper person to be selected. The retiring chief repeatedly expressed his judgment in favor of General McClellan for the position; and in this the nation seemed to give a unanimous concurrence.[21] The designation of General McClellan is therefore in considerable degree, the selection of the Country as well as of the Executive; and hence there is better reason to hope there will be given him, the confidence, and cordial support thus, by fair implication, promised, and without which, he cannot, with so full efficiency, serve the country.

It has been said that one bad general is better than two good ones; and the saying is true, if taken to mean no more than that an army is better directed by a single mind, though inferior, than by two superior ones, at variance, and cross-purposes with each other.

And the same is true, in all joint operations wherein those engaged, *can* have none but a common end in view, and *can* differ only as to the choice of means. In a storm at sea, no one on board *can* wish the ship to sink; and yet, not unfrequently, all go down together, because too many will direct, and no single mind can be allowed to control.

It continues to develop that the insurrection is largely, if not exclusively, a war upon the first principle of popular government—the rights of the people. Conclusive evidence of this is found in the most grave and maturely considered public documents, as well as in the general tone of the insurgents. In those documents we find the abridgement of the existing right of suffrage and the denial to the people of all right to participate in the selection of public officers, except the legislative boldly advocated, with labored arguments to prove that large control of the people in government, is the source of all political evil. Monarchy itself is sometimes hinted at as a possible refuge from the power of the people.

In my present position, I could scarcely be justified were I to omit raising a warning voice against this approach of returning despotism.

[21] General McClellan became general in chief of the army on November 1, 1861.

It is not needed, nor fitting here, that a general argument should be made in favor of popular institutions; but there is one point, with its connexions, not so hackneyed as most others, to which I ask a brief attention. It is the effort to place *capital* on an equal footing with, if not above *labor*, in the structure of government. It is assumed that labor is available only in connexion with capital; that nobody labors unless somebody else, owning capital, somehow by the use of it, induces him to labor. This assumed, it is next considered whether it is best that capital shall *hire* laborers, and thus induce them to work by their own consent, or *buy* them, and drive them to it without their consent. Having proceeded so far, it is naturally concluded that all laborers are either *hired* laborers, or what we call slaves. And further it is assumed that whoever is once a hired laborer, is fixed in that condition for life.

Now, there is no such relation between capital and labor as assumed; nor is there any such thing as a free man being fixed for life in the condition of a hired laborer. Both these assumptions are false, and all inferences from them are groundless.

Labor is prior to, and independent of, capital. Capital is only the fruit of labor, and could never have existed if labor had not first existed. Labor is the superior of capital, and deserves much the higher consideration. Capital has its rights, which are as worthy of protection as any other rights. Nor is it denied that there is, and probably always will be, a relation between labor and capital, producing mutual benefits. The error is in assuming that the whole labor of community exists within that relation [of labor and capital]. A few men own capital, and that few avoid labor themselves, and, with their capital, hire or buy another few to labor for them. A large majority belong to neither class—neither work for others, nor have others working for them. In most of the southern States, a majority of the whole people of all colors are neither slaves nor masters; while in the northern a large majority are neither hirers nor hired. Men with their families—wives, sons, and daughters—work for themselves, on their farms, in their houses, and in their shops, taking the whole product to themselves, and asking no favors of capital on the one hand, nor of hired laborers or slaves on the other. It is not forgotten that a considerable number of persons mingle their own labor with capital—that is, they labor with their own hands, and also buy or hire others to labor for them; but this is only a mixed, and not a distinct class. No principle stated is disturbed by the existence of this mixed class.

Again: as has already been said, there is not, of necessity, any such thing as the free hired laborer being fixed to that condition for life. Many independent men everywhere in these States, a few years back in their lives, were hired laborers. The prudent, penniless beginner in the world, labors for wages awhile, saves a surplus with which to buy tools or land for himself; then labors on his own account another while, and at length hires another new beginner to help him. This is the just, and generous, and prosperous system, which opens the way to all—gives hope to all, and consequent energy, and progress, and improvement of condition to all. No men living are more worthy to be trusted than those who toil up from poverty—none less inclined to take, or touch, aught which they have not honestly earned. Let them beware of surrendering a political power which they already possess, and which, if surrendered, will surely be used to close the door of advancement against such as they, and to fix new disabilities and burdens upon them, till all of liberty shall be lost.

From the first taking of our national census to the last are seventy years; and we find our population at the end of the period eight times as great as it was at the beginning. The increase of those other things which men deem desirable has been even greater. We thus have at one view, what the popular principle applied to government, through the machinery of the States and the Union, has produced in a given time; and also what, if firmly maintained, it promises for the future. There are already among us those, who, if the Union be preserved, will live to see it contain two hundred and fifty millions. The struggle of today, is not altogether for today—it is for a vast future also. With a reliance on Providence, all the more firm and earnest, let us proceed in the great task which events have devolved upon us.

ABRAHAM LINCOLN

4

Marching South

By the end of 1861, Lincoln had made little progress on his pledge to save the Union. Huge armies costing millions of dollars camped along the Mason-Dixon Line from Washington to Illinois, but they did not march forward to fight the Confederates. Jefferson Davis and his leading generals understood that their goal was to defend the Confederacy. They won if the Confederacy maintained its independence. Lincoln could not afford such a strategy. Defending the Union required attacking the Confederacy. But the humiliating defeat at Bull Run in July 1861 made most Union commanders cautious. They hesitated to attack until they believed their soldiers were sufficiently numerous, trained, and supplied. Eight months after the surrender of Fort Sumter, the Union army had yet to mount a significant invasion of Confederate territory, with the exception of the coastal forts Lincoln mentioned in his December 1861 congressional address (Document 17).

Republicans throughout the North criticized Lincoln and his generals and clamored for action. On December 20, 1861, Congress organized the Joint Committee on the Conduct of the War, providing a forum for Lincoln's critics and a powerful impetus for the military to do something, and soon. But few agreed on what the army should do. Antislavery leaders urged Lincoln to add freedom for slaves to the war aim of union, but he resisted for reasons that are documented in the next chapter. Lincoln himself could not even learn the plans of his general in chief, General George B. McClellan. McClellan had little regard for Lincoln—referring to him privately as an "idiot" and a "well meaning baboon"[1]—and simply refused to tell the president what he intended to do with his army. Lincoln was so discouraged in early January that he asked the army quartermaster general Montgomery C. Meigs, "General, what shall I

[1] Stephen W. Sears, ed., *The Civil War Papers of George B. McClellan* (New York, 1989), 85, 106.

do? The people are impatient. . . . The bottom is out of the tub. What shall I do?"[2]

Lincoln, in effect, answered his own question. Since his generals showed so little initiative, he assumed responsibility for the overall direction of military strategy. His own military experience was limited, as he said, to "charges upon the wild onions" and "a good many bloody struggles with the musquetoes" during the Black Hawk War thirty years earlier.[3] He tried to educate himself by checking out several books on military strategy from the Library of Congress in early January 1862. He began to outline a three-part offensive strategy. First, to boost morale and preserve political support for the war in the North, Union commanders must start to fight. Second, Union generals should coordinate their attacks to put maximum pressure on Confederate defenders and to prevent them from shifting reinforcements from one front to another. Third, Union officers should seek to punish and defeat Confederate armies. The Union would not be saved until the Confederacy could no longer field an effective army.

Lincoln advised, cajoled, and ordered his generals to follow his strategy, as the documents in this chapter illustrate. By the end of 1862, Union armies had won important victories and advanced deep into Confederate territory. Though bloodied, the Confederacy was far from defeated. The Union, too, was bloodied and seemingly stalled, making some in the North question whether the war should continue. Lincoln defended his leadership and refused to consider any peace that involved disunion. But he finally concluded that his military strategy could not succeed without a major new objective: emancipation, the subject of the next chapter.

"DELAY IS RUINING US"[4]

Lincoln peppered his commanders with questions and demanded that they take action. The following documents illustrate his efforts to direct military strategy. As commander in chief, Lincoln continually reminded his generals that their action—or inaction—had political as well as

---

[2] "General M. C. Meigs on the Conduct of the Civil War," *American Historical Review*, 26 (1920–1921), 292.

[3] Lincoln described his military service during the Black Hawk War in a speech to the House of Representatives, July 27, 1848. *CW*, I, 510.

[4] Lincoln to General Don C. Buell, January 7, 1862. *CW*, V, 93.

military consequences. In the West, Union armies achieved notable victories in the first half of 1862, while in the East, Lincoln became increasingly frustrated by McClellan, who, Lincoln told a friend, "has got the 'slows.'"[5]

Lincoln's plan for simultaneous attacks on Confederate armies made sense, but it was difficult to put into practice because of the complications of battles involving tens of thousands of men and animals on different battlefields, often separated by hundreds of miles. Lincoln acknowledged these practical difficulties but continued to insist that the general plan was sound. Impatient with the inaction of Union forces, Lincoln ordered his commanders to delay no longer. His principal objective for the simultaneous attacks was action.

[5] William E. Smith, *The Francis Preston Blair Family in Politics* (2 vols.; New York, 1933), II, 144–45.

18

President's General War Order No. 1

January 27, 1862

Executive Mansion
Washington

President's General War Order No. 1

Ordered that the 22nd. day of February 1862, be the day for a general movement of the Land and Naval forces of the United States against the insurgent forces. That especially —

The Army at & about, Fortress Monroe [Virginia].[6]

The Army of the Potomac.[7]

The Army of Western Virginia.[8]

The Army near Munfordsville, Ky.[9]

The Army and Flotilla at Cairo [Illinois].[10]

And a Naval force in the Gulf of Mexico,[11] be ready for a movement on that day.

[6] Commanded by General John E. Wool.
[7] Commanded by General George B. McClellan.
[8] Commanded by General William S. Rosecrans.
[9] Commanded by General Don Carlos Buell.
[10] Commanded by General Ulysses S. Grant and Flag Officer Andrew H. Foote.
[11] Commanded by Flag Officer David G. Farragut.

That all other forces, both Land and Naval, with their respective commanders, obey existing orders, for the time, and be ready to obey additional orders when duly given.

That the Heads of Departments, and especially the Secretaries of War and of the Navy, with all their subordinates; and the General-in-Chief,[12] with all other commanders and subordinates, of Land and Naval forces, will severally be held to their strict and full responsibilities, for the prompt execution of this order.

ABRAHAM LINCOLN

[12] McClellan.

THE PENINSULA CAMPAIGN

Lincoln eagerly sought to get McClellan's Army of the Potomac into combat. Stationed in and around Washington, this army drilled in the spotlight of public scrutiny. Lincoln firmly believed that McClellan should attack the Confederate forces closest to Washington, at Manassas. Three months earlier, McClellan had ventured an attack on Leesburg, Virginia, about thirty miles north of Manassas, and had suffered an embarrassing defeat at Ball's Bluff on October 21, 1861 (see Map 3, page 87). McClellan now had different plans about how best to deploy his army. Instead of attacking rebel positions near Washington, he proposed to take his men down the Potomac River and south on the Chesapeake Bay to the peninsula between the James and York rivers, southeast of Richmond. Lincoln expressed doubts about this peninsula campaign.

19

Letter to George B. McClellan

February 3, 1862

Executive Mansion
Washington

Major General McClellan
My dear Sir:
You and I have distinct, and different plans for a movement of the Army of the Potomac—yours to be down the Chesapeake, up the Rappahannock

to Urbana, and across land to the terminus of the Railroad[13] on the York River—, mine to move directly to a point on the Railroad South West of Manassas.

If you will give me satisfactory answers to the following questions, I shall gladly yield my plan to yours.

1st. Does not your plan involve a greatly larger expenditure of *time*, and *money* than mine?

2nd. Wherein is a victory *more certain* by your plan than mine?

3rd. Wherein is a victory *more valuable* by your plan than mine?

4th. In fact, would it not be *less* valuable, in this, that it would break no great line of the enemie's communications, while mine would?

5th. In case of disaster, would not a safe retreat be more difficult by your plan than by mine?

Yours truly
A. LINCOLN

[13] The railroad ran to Richmond.

In response to Lincoln's questions, McClellan argued that his plan "affords the shortest possible land routes to Richmond, & strikes directly at the enemy's power in the East. . . . This movement if successful gives us the capital, the commmunications, the supplies of the rebels; Norfolk would fall; all the waters of the Chesapeake would be ours; all Virginia would be in our power; & the enemy forced to abandon Tennessee & North Carolina." Confidently, McClellan lectured his commander in chief, "*I will stake my life, my reputation on the result—more than that, I will stake upon it the success of our cause. I hope but little from* [your plan for] *the attack on Manassas;—my judgment is against it.*"[14] Despite his deep misgivings, Lincoln permitted McClellan to test his confidence on the battlefield and to undertake his peninsula campaign. Within weeks, Lincoln's doubts proved well-founded.

[14] *CW*, V, 122, 124.

20

Letter to George B. McClellan

April 9, 1862

Washington

Major General McClellan
My dear Sir.

Your despatches[15] complaining that you are not properly sustained, while they do not offend me, do pain me very much. . . .

There is a curious mystery about the *number* of the troops now with you. When I telegraphed you on the 6th. saying you had over a hundred thousand with you, I had just obtained from the Secretary of War, a statement, taken as he said, from your own returns, making 108,000 then with you, and *en route* to you. You now say you will have but 85,000, when all *en route* to you shall have reached you. How can the discrepancy of 23,000 be accounted for? . . .

I suppose the whole force which has gone forward for you, is with you by this time; and if so, I think it is the precise time for you to strike a blow. By delay the enemy will relatively gain upon you—that is, he will gain faster, by *fortifications* and *re-inforcements*, than you can by re-inforcements alone.

And, once more let me tell you, it is indispensable to *you* that you strike a blow. *I* am powerless to help this. You will do me the justice to remember I always insisted, that going down the Bay in search of a field, instead of fighting at or near Mannassas, was only shifting, and not surmounting, a difficulty—that we would find the same enemy, and the same, or equal, intrenchments, at either place. The country will not fail to note—is now noting—that the present hesitation to move upon an intrenched enemy, is but the story of Manassas repeated.

I beg to assure you that I have never written you, or spoken to you, in greater kindness of feeling than now, nor with a fuller purpose to sustain you, so far as in my most anxious judgment, I consistently can. *But you must act.*

Yours very truly
A. LINCOLN

---

[15] In the past few days, Lincoln had received several telegrams from McClellan complaining that he was being deprived of soldiers and supplies. On April 5, McClellan had begun a siege of Yorktown, Virginia, about twenty miles up the peninsula from Fort Monroe, where he had landed his army.

By early May, Lincoln's plan of simultaneous, coordinated attacks seemed
to be working. After having been bogged down for a month in a siege,
McClellan finally took Yorktown on May 4 and began his long-delayed
advance toward Richmond. While McClellan's main force marched up
the peninsula, another contingent captured Norfolk on May 9, forcing
the rebels to evacuate, but not before they destroyed the *Merrimac*—the
ironclad ship the Confederates had captured and renamed the *Virginia*—
and other ships, weapons, and supplies about to fall into the Yankees'
hands.

McClellan's movement came on the heels of Union successes in the
West. General Grant, under General Henry W. Halleck's command, had
moved south along the Tennessee River heading for Corinth, Mississippi, the junction of the Confederacy's major north–south and east–
west railroads in the lower Mississippi Valley. Grant suffered a ferocious
surprise attack near Shiloh, Tennessee, on April 6 but regrouped his
men and, with reinforcements from General Buell, counterattacked the
next day and forced the rebel army to retreat to Corinth. About twenty
thousand men were killed or wounded at Shiloh, an omen of the bru-
tal, remorseless fighting that lay ahead. While Halleck's army licked
its wounds and began to inch toward Corinth, Flag Officer Farragut
captured New Orleans on April 25, securing Union control of the mouth
of the Mississippi.

Union successes in the West were not matched in the Virginia theater. In early May, Confederate general Thomas J. "Stonewall" Jackson
launched a surprise attack up the Shenandoah Valley that ultimately
forced the Union army under General Nathaniel Banks to retreat into
Maryland rather than reinforce McClellan's attempt to move up the peninsula toward Richmond. On June 25, McClellan attacked Confederate
defenses at Oak Grove, Virginia, initiating what became known as the
Seven Days' Battles. The next day, Confederate general Robert E. Lee
mounted a devastating counterattack against McClellan at Mechan-
icsville, just north of the Chickahominy River on the outskirts of
Richmond. McClellan complained to Secretary of War Edwin Stanton,
"I have lost this battle because my force was too small. . . . I know that
a few thousand more men would have changed this battle from a defeat
to a victory." McClellan concluded his message with two inflammatory
sentences that the telegraph officer simply deleted from the text he
knew Lincoln would read: "If I save this army now, I tell you plainly

that I owe no thanks to you or to any other persons in Washington. You have done your best to sacrifice this army."[16] Although Lincoln did not receive this insubordinant announcement, he nonetheless understood McClellan's desperate plight.

[16] *CW*, V, 290.

21

Letter to George B. McClellan

June 28, 1862

Washington City, D.C.

Major Gen. McClellan

Save your Army at all events. Will send re-inforcements as fast as we can. Of course they can not reach you to-day, to-morrow, or next day. I have not said you were ungenerous for saying you needed re-inforcement. I thought you were ungenerous in assuming that I did not send them as fast as I could. I feel any misfortune to you and your Army quite as keenly as you feel it yourself. If you have had a drawn battle, or a repulse, it is the price we pay for the enemy not being in Washington. We protected Washington, and the enemy concentrated on you; had we stripped Washington, he would have been upon us before the troops sent could have got to you. Less than a week ago you notified us that re-inforcements were leaving Richmond to come in front of us. It is the nature of the case, and neither you or the government that is to blame. Please tell at once the present condition and aspect of things. . . .

A. LINCOLN

Lee's attack and McClellan's retreat down the peninsula convinced Lincoln that the war was taking a disastrous turn and that the Union urgently needed more soldiers.

22

Letter to Secretary of State William H. Seward

June 28, 1862

Executive Mansion

Hon. W. H. Seward

My dear Sir

My view of the present condition of the War is about as follows:

The evacuation of Corinth,[17] and our delay by the flood in the Chicahominy,[18] has enabled the enemy to concentrate too much force in Richmond for McClellan to successfully attack. In fact there soon will be no substantial rebel force any where else. But if we send all the force from here to McClellan, the enemy will, before we can know of it, send a force from Richmond and take Washington. Or, if a large part of the Western Army be brought here to McClellan, they will let us have Richmond, and retake Tennessee, Kentucky, Missouri &c. What should be done is to hold what we have in the West, open the Mississippi,[19] and, take Chatanooga[20] & East Tennessee, without more—a reasonable force should, in every event, be kept about Washington for it's protection. Then let the country give us a hundred thousand new troops in the shortest possible time, which added to McClellan, directly or indirectly, will take Richmond, without endangering any other place which we now hold—and will substantially end the war. I expect to maintain this contest until successful, or till I die, or am conquered, or my term expires, or Congress or the country forsakes me; and I would publicly appeal to the country for this new force, were it not that I fear a general panic and stampede would follow—so hard is it to have a thing understood as it really is. I think the new force should be all, or nearly all infantry, principally because such can be raised most cheaply and quickly.

Yours very truly

A. LINCOLN

---

[17] Corinth, Mississippi, had been evacuated by its Confederate defenders on May 30.

[18] The flooded Chickahominy River delayed McClellan's attack on Richmond.

[19] Union forces had captured Baton Rouge, Louisiana, on May 12, and Memphis on June 6. But the Mississippi River remained under Confederate control from Port Hudson, Louisiana—about twenty-five miles upriver from Baton Rouge—to Vicksburg, Mississippi—about two hundred miles upriver from Port Hudson.

[20] Chattanooga, in the mountains of southeastern Tennessee, was an important railroad center, with lines stretching north into the Carolinas, south into Georgia, and west into Alabama.

On July 7, Lincoln left Washington to speak directly with McClellan and his officers at Harrison's Landing, Virginia, where McClellan's army was entrenched (see Map 3). Lincoln conferred with the generals and visited with other soldiers before returning to Washington on July 10. The next day, Lincoln signaled his loss of confidence in McClellan by naming Halleck—whose western armies had enjoyed such success in the past five months—general in chief, the position McClellan had held before beginning the peninsula campaign. But McClellan still commanded the Army of the Potomac, and Lincoln had not yet given up hope that something might be salvaged from McClellan's campaign.

Lincoln told Halleck that "he was satisfied McClellan would not fight [and] . . . that if by magic he could reinforce McClellan with 100,000 men today, he [McClellan] would be in ecstasy over it, thank him [Lincoln] for it, and tell him he would go to Richmond tomorrow; but that when tomorrow came, he would telegraph that he had certain information that the enemy had 400,000 men and that he could not advance without reinforcements."[21] Lincoln urged McClellan to use the soldiers he had, but McClellan did not renew his attack on Richmond. Instead, his failed peninsula campaign came to an end quietly on August 14, when, under orders from Halleck, he began to withdraw his army from Harrison's Landing for redeployment in northern Virginia.

THE SECOND BATTLE OF BULL RUN AND ANTIETAM

While the peninsula campaign was coming to an end, Union general John Pope led his new command, the Army of Virginia, south of Manassas, along the route to Richmond that Lincoln had long advocated. About fifty miles south of Manassas, Pope encountered Stonewall Jackson's army at Cedar Mountain, Virginia, on August 9 and was driven back. Pope slowly retreated northward along the rail line back to Manassas, awaiting reinforcement by McClellan. Before McClellan's men arrived, General Robert E. Lee reinforced Jackson, and the Confederates mauled Pope's army at the second battle of Bull Run between August 28 and 30 (see Map 3). Once again, defeated Union soldiers streamed into

---

[21] Theodore Calvin Pease and James G. Randall, eds., *The Diary of Orville Browning* (2 vols.; Springfield, 1925–1933), I, 563.

Washington, and victorious rebel armies camped within twenty miles of the White House.

After the second battle of Bull Run, Lincoln confided to his cabinet that "he felt almost ready to hang himself."[22] Victory over the Confederacy had seemed within reach in June, but now the Union cause appeared on the verge of defeat. Profoundly demoralized, Lincoln brooded about God's purpose in permitting the war to continue.

[22] *CW*, V, 486.

23

Meditation on Divine Will
September 2, 1862?[23]

The will of God prevails. In great contests each party claims to act in accordance with the will of God. Both *may* be, and one *must* be wrong. God can not be *for*, and *against* the same thing at the same time. In the present civil war it is quite possible that God's purpose is something different from the purpose of either party—and yet the human instrumentalities, working just as they do, are of the best adaptation to effect His purpose. I am almost ready to say this is probably true—that God wills this contest, and wills that it shall not end yet. By his mere quiet power, on the minds of the now contestants, He could have either *saved* or *destroyed* the Union without a human contest. Yet the contest began. And having begun He could give the final victory to either side any day. Yet the contest proceeds.

Fearing an imminent attack on Washington, Lincoln removed Pope from command on September 2 and replaced him with McClellan. Somebody was needed to organize the dispirited troops, and, Lincoln told his

[23] Although the original is not dated, the editors of Lincoln's papers agree that he wrote this note, essentially to himself, sometime in September 1862 and conjecture that he probably wrote it soon after the second battle of Bull Run, when he "seemed wrung by the bitterest anguish," according to one of his cabinet members. It is also possible, however, that he wrote this in late October when he met with Eliza P. Gurney, an English Quaker. *CW*, V, 404, 478.

secretary, "If he [McClellan] can't fight, he excels in making others ready to fight."[24] But McClellan had little time to organize.

Rather than marching methodically from Manassas to attack Washington, Lee set out to invade the North, crossing the Potomac River on September 5 and soon reaching Frederick, Maryland, about fifty miles northwest of Washington. Lincoln's frequent requests for news from McClellan reflected his awareness of the depth of the crisis. For once, McClellan moved quickly. In battles east of Frederick at Crampton's Gap and South Mountain on September 14, he pushed Lee back to Sharpsburg, Maryland, between the Potomac River and Antietam Creek, about ten miles north of Harpers Ferry (see Map 3). In the battle of Antietam on September 17, McClellan attacked Lee repeatedly in fighting that left twenty-three thousand killed and wounded, more casualties than in any other single day during the war. The next day, the two battered armies remained in place without fighting. That night, Lee quietly retreated across the Potomac into Virginia. McClellan had succeeded in turning back Lee's invasion of the North, but Lincoln and many other northerners were far from satisfied.

While McClellan's success at Antietam pleased Lincoln, he was deeply discouraged by Lee's escape with his army intact. McClellan "did not follow up his advantages after Antietam," Lincoln told a friend. "The army of the enemy should have been annihilated, but it was permitted to recross the Potomac without the loss of a man, and McClellan would not follow." Lincoln pointed out that he "coaxed, urged, and ordered" McClellan to pursue Lee, but to no avail. "At the expiration of two weeks after a peremptory order [to go after Lee, McClellan] . . . had only three-fourths of his army across the [Potomac] river and was six days doing that, whereas the rebel army . . . effected a crossing in one day."[25]

Lincoln continued to press McClellan to pursue Lee, who positioned his army south of Harpers Ferry near Winchester, Virginia (see Map 3). Confederate General J. E. B. Stuart exploited McClellan's passivity by leading a cavalry raid around McClellan's whole army between October 10 and 12, reaching as far north as Chambersburg, Pennsylvania, and returning almost entirely unscathed.

---

[24] Tyler Dennett, ed., *Lincoln and the Civil War in the Diaries and Letters of John Hay* (New York, 1939), 47.

[25] Pease and Randall, eds., *Diary of Orville Browning*, I, 589–90.

Figure 2. *Lincoln and McClellan at Antietam*

Taken on October 3, 1862, shortly after the battle of Antietam and Lincoln's announcement of the Preliminary Emancipation Proclamation, this photograph shows Lincoln on his visit to the army and General McClellan (the second man to the right of Lincoln).

Reproduced from the Collections of the Library of Congress.

24

Letter to George B. McClellan
October 13, 1862

Executive Mansion
Washington

Major General McClellan
My dear Sir

You remember my speaking to you of what I called your over-cautiousness. Are you not over-cautious when you assume that you can not do what the enemy is constantly doing? Should you not claim to be at least his equal in prowess, and act upon the claim?

As I understand, you telegraph Gen. Halleck that you can not subsist your army at Winchester unless the Railroad from Harper's Ferry to that point be put in working order. But the enemy does now subsist his army at Winchester at a distance nearly twice as great from railroad transportation as you would have to do without the railroad last named. He now wagons from Culpepper C.H.[26] which is just about twice as far as you would have to do from Harper's Ferry. He is certainly not more than half as well provided with wagons as you are. I certainly should be pleased for you to have the advantage of the Railroad from Harper's Ferry to Winchester, but it wastes all the remainder of autumn to give it to you; and, in fact ignores the question of *time*, which can not, and must not be ignored.

Again, one of the standard maxims of war, as you know, is "to operate upon the enemy's communications as much as possible without exposing your own." You seem to act as if this applies *against* you, but can not apply in your *favor*. Change positions with the enemy, and think you not he would break your communication with Richmond within the next twenty-four hours? You dread his going into Pennsylvania. But if he does so in full force, he gives up his communications to you absolutely, and you have nothing to do but to follow, and ruin him; if he does so with less than full force, fall upon, and beat what is left behind all the easier.

Exclusive of the water line, you are now nearer Richmond than the enemy is by the route that you *can*, and he *must* take. Why can you not reach there before him, unless you admit that he is more than your equal on a march. His route is the arc of a circle, while yours is the chord [a straight line connecting two points on a curve]. The roads are as good on yours as on his.

---

[26] Culpepper Courthouse stood about fifty miles south of Winchester.

You know I desired, but did not order, you to cross the Potomac below, instead of above the Shenandoah and Blue Ridge.[27] My idea was that this would at once menace the enemies' communications, which I would seize if he would permit. If he should move Northward I would follow him closely, holding his communications. If he should prevent our seizing his communications, and move towards Richmond, I would press closely to him, fight him if a favorable opportunity should present, and, at least, try to beat him to Richmond on the inside track. I say "try"; if we never try, we shall never succeed. If he make a stand at Winchester, moving neither North or South, I would fight him there, on the idea that if we can not beat him when he bears the wastage of coming to us, we never can when we bear the wastage of going to him. This proposition is a simple truth, and is too important to be lost sight of for a moment. In coming to us, he tenders us an advantage which we should not waive. We should not so operate as to merely drive him away. As we must beat him somewhere, or fail finally, we can do it, if at all, easier near to us, than far away. If we can not beat the enemy where he now is, we never can, he again being within the entrenchments of Richmond.

Recurring to the idea of going to Richmond on the inside track, the facility of supplying from the side away from the enemy is remarkable—as it were, by the different spokes of a wheel extending from the hub towards the rim—and this whether you move directly by the chord, or on the inside arc, hugging the Blue Ridge more closely. . . . I should think it preferable to take the route nearest the enemy, disabling him to make an important move without your knowledge, and compelling him to keep his forces together, for dread of you. The gaps [through the Blue Ridge] would enable you to attack if you should wish. For a great part of the way, you would be practically between the enemy and both Washington and Richmond, enabling us to spare you the greatest number of troops from here. When at length, running for Richmond ahead of him enables him to move this way; if he does so, turn and attack him in rear. But I think he should be engaged long before such point is reached. It is all easy if our troops march as well as the enemy; and it is unmanly to say they can not do it.

This letter is in no sense an order.

Yours truly
A. LINCOLN

---

[27] Lincoln wanted McClellan to cross the Potomac south of Harpers Ferry, in order to be positioned between Lee's army and Richmond.

Completely exasperated with the caution of McClellan, Lincoln finally removed him from his command in early November and replaced him with General Ambrose E. Burnside.

HOME-FRONT POLITICS

The long lists of casualties published by every newspaper across the North brought the costs of the war home to every family with a man in uniform. Lincoln's call for another 600,000 recruits in July and August 1862 made even more northern families scan those lists and wonder why Lincoln had a nearly insatiable need for soldiers. Although Lee's invasion of the North had been repulsed at the battle of Antietam in September, the Union army had made little progress toward defeating the Confederacy since the victories in the West in May and June. Many northern citizens criticized Lincoln's leadership and questioned his policies, especially after he announced the Preliminary Emancipation Proclamation on September 22, 1862 (Document 32). Resistance to fighting for black freedom coupled with resistance to fighting at all required Lincoln to send soldiers into Pennsylvania, Ohio, Indiana, and Wisconsin to enforce the recruitment of militia. Lincoln suspended the writ of habeas corpus throughout the nation, and hundreds of northerners were arrested and jailed, accused of resisting the militia draft or giving aid and comfort to the Confederacy. Many of the arrested dissidents were Democrats, an issue the party used in the fall elections—along with opposition to emancipation—with impressive success, boosting their congressional representation from forty-four to seventy-two.

Although the Republicans retained a majority in both houses of Congress, they, too, criticized Lincoln. On December 13, Burnside initiated yet another drive toward Richmond by attacking Lee's army at Fredericksburg, Virginia (see Map 3). In a deadly frontal assault on Confederate defenses, Burnside sustained a crushing defeat. A few days later, after Republican senators met with Lincoln and condemned the disastrous course of the war, Lincoln confessed to a friend, "They wish to get rid of me, and I am sometimes half disposed to gratify them. . . . We are now on the brink of destruction. It appears to me the Almighty is against us, and I can hardly see a ray of hope."[28]

[28] Pease and Randall, eds., *Diary of Orville Browning*, I, 600.

25

Proclamation Suspending the Writ of Habeas Corpus

September 24, 1862

**BY THE PRESIDENT OF THE
UNITED STATES OF AMERICA:
A PROCLAMATION.**

Whereas, it has become necessary to call into service not only volunteers but also portions of the militia of the States by draft in order to suppress the insurrection existing in the United States, and disloyal persons are not adequately restrained by the ordinary processes of law from hindering this measure and from giving aid and comfort in various ways to the insurrection;

Now, therefore, be it ordered, first, that during the existing insurrection and as a necessary measure for suppressing the same, all Rebels and Insurgents, their aiders and abettors within the United States, and all persons discouraging volunteer enlistments, resisting militia drafts, or guilty of any disloyal practice, affording aid and comfort to Rebels against the authority of the United States, shall be subject to martial law and liable to trial and punishment by Courts Martial or Military Commission:

Second. That the Writ of Habeas Corpus is suspended in respect to all persons arrested, or who are now, or hereafter during the rebellion shall be, imprisoned in any fort, camp, arsenal, military prison, or other place of confinement by any military authority or by the sentence of any Court Martial or Military Commission.[29]. . .

ABRAHAM LINCOLN

[29]The arrest of so many northern citizens engendered such a public opposition that most of them were released by late November, under orders from the War Department.

26

Letter to Carl Schurz

November 24, 1862

Executive Mansion
Washington

Gen. Carl Schurz[30]
My dear Sir

I have just received, and read, your letter of the 20th.[31] The purport of it is that we lost the late elections, and the administration is failing, because the war is unsuccessful; and that I must not flatter myself that I am not justly to blame for it. I certainly know that if the war fails, the administration fails, and that I *will* be blamed for it, whether I deserve it or not. And I ought to be blamed, if I could do better. You think I could do better; therefore you blame me already. I think I could not do better; therefore I blame you for blaming me. I understand you *now* to be willing to accept the help of men, who are not republicans, provided they have "heart in it." Agreed. I want no others. But who is to be the judge of hearts, or of "heart in it"? If I must discard my own judgment, and take yours, I must also take that of others; and by the time I should reject all I should be advised to reject, I should have none left, republicans, or others—not even yourself. For, be assured, my dear sir, there are men who have "heart in it" that think you are performing your part as poorly as you think I am performing mine.[32] I certainly have been dissatisfied with the slowness of Buell and McClellan; but before I relieved them[33] I had great fears I should not find successors to them, who would do better; and I am sorry to add, that I have seen little since to relieve those fears. I do not clearly see the prospect of any more rapid movements. I fear we shall at last find out that the difficulty is in our case, rather than in particular generals. I wish to disparage no one—certainly not those who sympathize with me; but I must say I need success more than I need sympathy, and that I have not seen the so much greater evidence of getting success from my sympathizers,

[30] Schurz, a German immigrant from Wisconsin, was an ardent Republican.
[31] In his letter, Schurz urged Lincoln to "indulge in no delusions as to the true causes of our defeat in the elections. . . . The people had sown confidence and reaped disaster and disappointment. . . . *The result of the elections was a most serious and severe reproof administered to the administration.*" Shurz accused Lincoln of putting "old democrats into high military positions" and continuing to support them "after they had been found failing . . . not only in a political but also a military sense." *CW*, V, 511.
[32] Schurz had commanded a division in the Union defeat at the second battle of Bull Run.
[33] Lincoln had removed Buell from command of the Army of the Cumberland in the western theater on October 30 and had replaced him with General William S. Rosecrans.

111

than from those who are denounced as the contrary. It does seem to me that in the field the two classes have been very much alike, in what they have done, and what they have failed to do. In sealing their faith with their blood, Baker,[34] an[d] Lyon,[35] and Bohlen,[36] and Richardson,[37] republicans, did all that men could do; but did they any more than Kearney,[38] and Stevens,[39] and Reno,[40] and Mansfield,[41] none of whom were republicans, and some, at least of whom, have been bitterly, and repeatedly, denounced to me as secession sympathizers? I will not perform the ungrateful task of comparing cases of failure. . . .

Very truly Your friend
A. LINCOLN

[34] Colonel Edward D. Baker, a friend of Lincoln's, was killed at Ball's Bluff, Virginia, October 21, 1861.

[35] General Nathaniel Lyon, a strong supporter of Lincoln's, was killed at Wilson's Creek, Missouri, August 10, 1861.

[36] General Henry Bohlen was killed at Freeman's Ford, Virginia, August 22, 1862.

[37] General Israel B. Richardson was wounded at South Mountain, September 14, 1862, and died of his wounds at Antietam, November 3, 1862.

[38] General Philip Kearney was killed at Chantilly, Virginia, September 1, 1862.

[39] General Isaac I. Stevens was killed at Chantilly, Virginia, September 1, 1862.

[40] General Jesse L. Reno was killed at South Mountain, September 14, 1862.

[41] General Joseph F. K. Mansfield was mortally wounded at Antietam, September 17, 1862, and died the next day.

5

Toward Emancipation

Before Lincoln became president, he pledged to protect slavery where it existed and to prevent its expansion into federal territories. As he had explained in speech after speech since the passage of the Kansas-Nebraska Act in 1854, he believed that slavery was morally wrong but that the Constitution gave the federal government no power to abolish it. Legally, slaves were a form of property protected by the Constitution. Only states had the power to decide whether they would permit or prohibit slavery.

Lincoln's prepresidential speeches also made clear that widespread belief in white supremacy throughout the North limited the popular appeal of eliminating slavery because it immediately raised the question of whether free blacks should be equal to whites—a question to which most white northerners would unhesitatingly answer no. Lincoln himself did not fully share these white supremacist views. As he outlined in his speeches, he did not believe that whites and blacks were equal in all ways, but he insisted that they had equal claims to the fruits of their labor and to the basic human right of liberty. Lincoln knew that many white citizens did not agree with him and that, in a representative democracy of white men, their views mattered, even though he thought they were wrong.

In sum, Lincoln's ideas about the immorality of slavery were constrained by his overriding faith in the morality of democracy. When he became president, he believed that what he could do about slavery was limited legally by the Constitution and socially and politically by the ideology of white supremacy. The war changed his thinking about slavery in three fundamental ways, as the documents in this chapter demonstrate.

First, as commander in chief in wartime, he possessed the constitutional authority to undertake otherwise unconstitutional actions—

including those against slavery—demanded by military necessity. Second, his strategy to end disunion and win the war determined how he exercised his powers as commander in chief. From the beginning of the war through the middle of 1862, Lincoln believed that protecting slavery would appeal to loyal unionists within the Confederacy and would cement the loyalty of the border slave states of Maryland, Delaware, Kentucky, and Missouri. Discouraging news from the battlefield during the second half of 1862, the certainty that the border states would not join the Confederacy, and the failure of unionists in the seceded states to assert themselves to oppose the rebels led Lincoln to believe that ending, rather than protecting, slavery was the way to win the war.

Third, Lincoln perceived that the war had changed northern public opinion about slavery. Union soldiers who carried out Lincoln's policies while fighting in the South came to believe that by protecting slavery, they aided the enemy, who benefited from slave labor. When slaves began to flee from their masters and flock toward Union lines, many Union soldiers concluded that the army should protect them, not the slaveholders. Most white northerners began to agree, especially after the military reverses of 1862. The war created political momentum in the North in favor of ending slavery as a way to defeat the rebellion.

Lincoln's movement toward emancipation also reflected a shift in his thinking about the most important parts of his political constituency. In the North, he became less focused on loyal slaveholders in the border states and more concerned about maintaining support for the war, especially among Republicans. In the South, his search for potential allies against the rebels shifted away from loyal unionists and toward slaves. By January 1863, both shifts identified Lincoln and the Republican party with war and black freedom to a degree unthinkable when Lincoln became president—unthinkable, that is, except by the secessionists, whose actions ultimately propelled Lincoln to become "the Great Emancipator." In the final analysis, secessionist slaveholders were their own worst enemies.

REASSURING LOYAL SOUTHERNERS

During the first year of the war, Lincoln tried to end disunion by combating secessionist rebels and reassuring loyal southerners that their rights as U.S. citizens, including their right to own slaves, would not be impaired. This conciliatory appeal to southern unionists aroused the ire of antislavery Republicans, who believed that the war should be against both slavery and secession.

When slaves escaped to Union lines, Lincoln's promise to protect loyal slaveholders' rights to slave property turned many Union soldiers into slave catchers, an experience few enjoyed and many abhorred. In May 1861, General Benjamin F. Butler declared the slaves who came to his garrison at Fortress Monroe, Virginia, "contraband of war," and he put them to work for his army. "Contraband"—confiscated property—became a synonym for fugitive slaves throughout the North. Lincoln acceded to Butler's contraband policy, but he did not adopt it as general practice for the Union army. Instead, Lincoln insisted that soldiers return slaves who belonged to loyal masters. The First Confiscation Act, passed by Congress on August 6, 1861, provided that any slaves who worked to support the Confederate military effort could be seized from their masters. But the act did not otherwise alter the distinction Lincoln maintained between loyal and disloyal slaveholders. In August 1861, General John C. Frémont, commander of Union forces in Missouri, unilaterally declared that the slaves of disloyal owners were free, prompting Lincoln to overrule him and to assert the president's primacy in determining policies about slavery, as he explained in the following letter.

27

Letter to Orville H. Browning

September 22, 1861

Private & confidential.

Executive Mansion
Washington

Hon. O. H. Browning[1]
My dear Sir
. . . Genl. Fremont's proclamation, as to confiscation of property, and the liberation of slaves, is *purely political*, and not within the range of *military* law, or necessity. If a commanding General finds a necessity to seize the

---

[1] Orville H. Browning, a Republican, was a U.S. senator from Illinois and a friend of Lincoln's.

Figure 3. *Virginia Contraband*
This carefully posed photograph—taken in the spring of 1862 near Yorktown, Virginia, during McClellan's peninsula campaign—portrays four Virginia slaves, perhaps members of one family, doing laundry and chopping wood for Union soldiers at the large encampment in the background.

Massachusetts Commandery of the Military Order of the Loyal Legion and the U.S. Army Military History Institute.

farm of a private owner, for a pasture, an encampment, or a fortification, he has the right to do so, and to so hold it, as long as the necessity lasts; and this is within military law, because within military necessity. But to say the farm shall no longer belong to the owner, or his heirs forever; and this as well when the farm is not needed for military purposes as when it is, is purely political, without the savor of military law about it. And the same is true of slaves. If the General needs them, he can seize them, and use them; but when the need is past, it is not for him to fix their permanent future condition. That must be settled according to laws made by law-makers, and not by military proclamations. The proclamation [of Frémont] in the point in question, is simply "dictatorship." It assumes that the general may do *anything* he pleases—confiscate the lands and free the slaves of *loyal* people, as well as of disloyal ones. And going the whole figure I have no doubt would be more popular with some thoughtless people, than that which has been done! But I cannot assume this reckless position; nor allow others to assume it on my responsibility. You speak of it as being the only means of *saving* the government. On the contrary it is itself the surrender of the government. Can it be pretended that it is any longer the government of the U.S.—any government of Constitution and laws,—wherein a General, or a President, may make permanent rules of property by proclamation?

I do not say Congress might not with propriety pass a law, on the point, just such as General Fremont proclaimed. I do not say I might not, as a member of Congress, vote for it. What I object to, is, that I as President, shall expressly or impliedly seize and exercise the permanent legislative functions of the government.

So much as to principle. Now as to policy. No doubt the thing was popular in some quarters, and would have been more so if it had been a general declaration of emancipation. The Kentucky Legislature would not budge till that proclamation was modified;[2] and Gen. Anderson[3] telegraphed me that on the news of Gen. Fremont having actually issued deeds of manumission, a whole company of our Volunteers threw down their arms and disbanded. I was so assured, as to think it probable, that the very arms we had furnished Kentucky would be turned against us. I think to lose Kentucky is nearly the same as to lose the whole game. Kentucky gone, we can not hold Missouri, nor, as I think, Maryland. These all against us, and the job on our hands is too large for us. We would as well

[2] In other words, the Kentucky legislature insisted that Frémont's proclamation be nullified. Lincoln's old Kentucky friend Joshua Speed wrote him that "so fixed is public sentiment in this state against freeing negroes . . . that you had as well attack the freedom of worship in the North or the right of a parent to teach his child to read, as to wage war in a slave state on such a principle." Victor B. Howard, *Black Liberation in Kentucky: Emancipation and Freedom, 1862–1884* (Lexington, Ky., 1983), 6.

[3] General Robert Anderson, of Fort Sumter fame, now commanded the Department of Kentucky.

consent to separation at once, including the surrender of this capitol. On the contrary, if you will give up your restlessness for new positions, and back me manfully on the grounds upon which you and other kind friends gave me the election, and have approved in my public documents, we shall go through triumphantly.

You must not understand I took my course on the proclamation *because* of Kentucky. I took the same ground in a private letter to General Fremont before I heard from Kentucky.

You think I am inconsistent because I did not also forbid Gen. Fremont to shoot men under the proclamation. I understand that part to be within military law; but I also think, and so privately wrote Gen. Fremont, that it is impolitic in this, that our adversaries have the power, and will certainly exercise it, to shoot as many of our men as we shoot of theirs. I did not say this in the public letter, because it is a subject I prefer not to discuss in the hearing of our enemies.

There has been no thought of removing Gen. Fremont on any ground connected with his proclamation. . . .

Your friend as ever
A. LINCOLN

Instead of threatening the rights of slaveholders, Lincoln asked Congress to approve his plan for gradual, compensated emancipation. Such a plan, he argued, honored the constitutional limits of federal power while strengthening the Union. Lincoln's plan also included a threat, only partially veiled, that emancipation could come about in a way that slaveholders and other Americans would find less palatable.

28

Message to Congress

March 6, 1862

Fellow-citizens of the Senate, and House of Representatives:
I recommend the adoption of a Joint Resolution by your honorable bodies which shall be substantially as follows:

"Resolved that the United States ought to co-operate with any state which may adopt gradual abolishment of slavery, giving to such state pecuniary aid, to be used by such state in it's discretion, to compensate for the inconveniences public and private, produced by such change of system."

If the proposition contained in the resolution does not meet the approval of Congress and the country, there is the end; but if it does command such approval, I deem it of importance that the states and people immediately interested, should be at once distinctly notified of the fact, so that they may begin to consider whether to accept or reject it. The federal government would find it's highest interest in such a measure, as one of the most efficient means of self-preservation. The leaders of the existing insurrection entertain the hope that this government will ultimately be forced to acknowledge the independence of some part of the disaffected region, and that all the slave states North of such part will then say "the Union, for which we have struggled, being already gone, we now choose to go with the Southern section." To deprive them of this hope, substantially ends the rebellion; and the initiation of emancipation completely deprives them of it, as to all the states initiating it. The point is not that *all* the states tolerating slavery would very soon, if at all, initiate emancipation; but that, while the offer is equally made to all, the more Northern shall, by such initiation, make it certain to the more Southern, that in no event, will the former ever join the latter, in their proposed confederacy. I say "initiation" because, in my judgment, gradual, and not sudden emancipation, is better for all. In the mere financial, or pecuniary view, any member of Congress, with the census-tables and Treasury-reports before him, can readily see for himself how very soon the current expenditures of this war would purchase, at fair valuation, all the slaves in any named State. Such a proposition, on the part of the general government, sets up no claim of a right, by federal authority, to interfere with slavery within state limits, referring, as it does, the absolute control of the subject, in each case, to the state and it's people, immediately interested. It is proposed as a matter of perfectly free choice with them.

In the annual message last December, I thought fit to say "The Union must be preserved; and hence all indispensable means must be employed." I said this, not hastily, but deliberately. War has been made, and continues to be, an indispensable means to this end. A practical re-acknowledgment of the national authority would render the war unnecessary, and it would at once cease. If, however, resistance continues, the war must also continue; and it is impossible to foresee all the incidents, which may attend and all the ruin which may follow it. Such as may seem indispensable, or may obviously promise great efficiency towards ending the struggle, must and will come.

The proposition now made, though an offer only, I hope it may be esteemed no offence to ask whether the pecuniary consideration tendered would not be of more value to the States and private persons concerned, than are the institution, and property in it, in the present aspect of affairs.

While it is true that the adoption of the proposed resolution would be merely initiatory, and not within itself a practical measure, it is recommended in the hope that it would soon lead to important practical results. In full view of my great responsibility to my God, and to my country, I earnestly beg the attention of Congress and the people to the subject.

ABRAHAM LINCOLN

On March 10, 1862, Lincoln met with a delegation of border-state congressmen to encourage them to support his plan. According to Maryland congressman John W. Crisfield, Lincoln said that

we were engaged in a terrible, wasting, and tedious war; immense armies were in the field, and must continue on the field as long as the war lasts; that these armies must, of necessity, be brought into contact with slaves in the [border] states we represented and in other states as they advanced; that slaves would come to the camps and continual irritation was kept up; that he was constantly annoyed by conflicting and antagonistic complaints; on the one side, a certain class complained if the slave was not protected by the army; persons were frequently found who, participating in these views, acted in a way unfriendly to the slaveholder; on the other hand, slaveholders complained that their rights were interfered with, their slaves induced to abscond and protected within the lines; these complaints were numerous, loud, and deep, were a serious annoyance to him and embarrassing to the progress of the war; that it kept alive a spirit hostile to the government in the states we represented; strengthened the hopes of the Confederates that at some day the border states would unite with them and thus tend to prolong the war; and he was of the opinion, if this resolution should be adopted by Congress and accepted by our [border] states, these causes of irritation and these hopes would be removed and more would be accomplished towards shortening the war than could be hoped from the greatest victory achieved by the Union armies.[4]

While Congress deliberated on Lincoln's proposal, it adopted an article of war on March 13 that prohibited any Union soldier or sailor from returning fugitive slaves to their masters. Slave owners who claimed to be loyal could still come within Union lines to retrieve their slaves, but military personnel were forbidden to aid them.

A few weeks later, on April 10, Congress adopted Lincoln's plan for gradual, compensated emancipation. The congressional vote was an omen

[4] Edward McPherson, *The Political History of the United States of America, during the Great Rebellion* (Washington, D.C., 1864), 210.

of the limited appeal of the plan to border-state slaveholders. Almost all Democrats and border-state unionists voted against the plan; Republicans united in its support.

Soon afterward, on April 16, Congress took the lead and abolished slavery in the District of Columbia, providing funds to compensate slave owners and to colonize freed slaves someplace outside the United States. Lincoln told a friend that "he regretted the bill had been passed in its present form; that it should have been for gradual emancipation; that now families would at once be deprived of cooks, stable boys, etc., and they [the former slaves] of their protectors without any provision for them."[5] Nonetheless, Lincoln approved the bill, announcing, "I have never doubted the constitutional authority of congress to abolish slavery in this District; and I have ever desired to see the national capital freed from the institution in some satisfactory way. Hence there has never been, in my mind, any question upon the subject, except the one of expediency, arising in view of all the circumstances."[6]

In the South, circumstances did not favor emancipation, Lincoln believed. In early May, General David Hunter, commander of Union forces occupying coastal enclaves along the South Carolina and Georgia coasts, decided to declare that the tens of thousands of slaves in his region were free. Claiming military necessity, Hunter issued his declaration without consulting or informing the president. Lincoln responded quickly, revoking Hunter's declaration. After the failure of McClellan's peninsula campaign, Lincoln invited senators and representatives from the loyal slave states to meet with him. He appealed again for their support for gradual compensated emancipation.

[5] Theodore Calvin Pease and James G. Randall, eds., *The Diary of Orville Hickman Browning* (2 vols.; Springfield, 1925–1933), I, 541.

[6] "Message to Congress," April 16, 1862, *CW*, V, 192.

29

Appeal to Border-State Representatives to Favor Compensated Emancipation

July 12, 1862

Gentlemen. After the adjournment of Congress, now very near, I shall have no opportunity of seeing you for several months. Believing that you of the border-states hold more power for good than any other equal number of members, I feel it a duty which I can not justifiably waive, to make this appeal to you. I intend no reproach or complaint when I assure you that in my opinion, if you all had voted for the resolution in the gradual emancipation message of last March, the war would now be substantially ended. And the plan therein proposed is yet one of the most potent, and swift means of ending it. Let the states which are in rebellion see, definitely and certainly, that, in no event, will the states you represent ever join their proposed Confederacy, and they can not, much longer maintain the contest. But you can not divest them of their hope to ultimately have you with them so long as you show a determination to perpetuate the institution within your own states. Beat them at elections, as you have overwhelmingly done, and, nothing daunted, they still claim you as their own. You and I know what the lever of their power is. Break that lever before their faces, and they can shake you no more forever.

Most of you have treated me with kindness and consideration; and I trust you will not now think I improperly touch what is exclusively your own, when, for the sake of the whole country I ask "Can you, for your states, do better than to take the course I urge?" Discarding *punctillio*,[7] and maxims adapted to more manageable times, and looking only to the unprecedentedly stern facts of our case, can you do better in any possible event? You prefer that the constitutional relation of the states to the nation shall be practically restored, without disturbance of the institution; and if this were done, my whole duty, in this respect, under the constitution, and my oath of office, would be performed. But it is not done, and we are trying to accomplish it by war. The incidents of the war can not be avoided. If the war continue long, as it must, if the object be not sooner attained, the institution in your states will be extinguished by mere friction and abrasion—by the mere incidents of the war. It will be gone, and you will have nothing valuable in lieu of it. Much of it's value is gone already. How much better for you, and for your people, to take the step which, at once, shortens the war, and secures substantial compensation for that which is sure to be wholly lost in any other event. How much better to thus save

[7] Setting aside fine points of formal doctrines, such as states' rights to govern slavery.

the money which else we sink forever in the war. How much better to do it while we can, lest the war ere long render us pecuniarily unable to do it. How much better for you, as seller, and the nation as buyer, to sell out, and buy out, that without which the war could never have been, than to sink both the thing to be sold, and the price of it, in cutting one another's throats.

I do not speak of emancipation *at once,* but of a *decision* at once to emancipate *gradually.* Room in South America for colonization can be obtained cheaply, and in abundance; and when numbers shall be large enough to be company and encouragement for one another, the freed people will not be so reluctant to go.

I am pressed with a difficulty not yet mentioned — one which threatens division among those who, united are none too strong. An instance of it is known to you. Gen. Hunter is an honest man. He was, and I hope, still is, my friend. I valued him none the less for his agreeing with me in the general wish that all men everywhere, could be free. He proclaimed all men free within certain states, and I repudiated the proclamation. He expected more good, and less harm from the measure, than I could believe would follow. Yet in repudiating it, I gave dissatisfaction, if not offence, to many whose support the country can not afford to lose. And this is not the end of it. The pressure, in this direction, is still upon me, and is increasing. By conceding what I now ask, you can relieve me, and much more, can relieve the country, in this important point. Upon these considerations I have again begged your attention to the message of March last. Before leaving the Capital, consider and discuss it among yourselves. You are patriots and statesmen; and, as such, I pray you, consider this proposition; and, at the least, commend it to the consideration of your states and people. As you would perpetuate popular government for the best people in the world, I beseech you that you do in no wise omit this. Our common country is in great peril, demanding the loftiest views, and boldest action to bring it speedy relief. Once relieved, it's form of government is saved to the world; it's beloved history, and cherished memories, are vindicated; and it's happy future fully assured, and rendered inconceivably grand. To you, more than to any others, the previlege is given, to assure that happiness, and swell that grandeur, and to link your own names therewith forever.

Lincoln's arguments failed to persuade most of the border-state representatives. Eight of them agreed with Lincoln, but a majority of twenty replied that the federal government could not afford to compensate slaveholders and that in any case Lincoln's plan would strengthen rebellion in the Confederacy and in the loyal border states while not reducing the political pressure to take the unconstitutional step of emancipating slaves by proclamation.

Disappointed by border-state recalcitrance and demoralized by Union military reverses, Lincoln concluded, as he told two of his cabinet members privately on June 13, 1862, "We must free the slaves or be ourselves subdued."[8] While Lincoln contemplated emancipation, Congress passed the Second Confiscation Act on July 17, 1862. This law reflected the desire of Congress to move beyond Lincoln's policy of conciliation toward the South. The act declared the slaves of disloyal masters to be free and delegated to federal courts the task of determining the loyalty of slave owners. Since federal courts, after all, were not operating in the Confederacy, the act provided that slaves who came to Union lines were captives of war and that no Union official could surrender them to any person who claimed them. In effect, the Second Confiscation Act made Union army lines a haven of freedom for fugitive slaves. Once within Union lines, slaves were protected from the ownership claims of any master, and if their master was disloyal, slaves had congressional sanction for their freedom. The act also authorized Lincoln to employ "persons of African descent" in "any war service for which they may be found competent."[9]

After discussing his plan to issue a proclamation of emancipation with his cabinet on July 22, Lincoln accepted the advice of Secretary of State William H. Seward to delay a public announcement. Seward pointed out, Lincoln recalled later, that "the depression of the public mind, consequent upon our repeated [military] reverses, is so great I fear the effect of so important a step. It may be viewed as the last measure of an exhausted government—a cry for help—the government stretching forth its hands to Ethiopia, instead of Ethiopia stretching forth her hands to the government." Seward suggested, according to Lincoln, that "you postpone its issue until you can give it to the country supported by military success, instead of issuing it, as would be the case now, upon the greatest disasters of the war"—namely, the failure of McClellan's peninsula campaign.[10]

[8] Howard K. Beale, ed., *Diary of Gideon Welles, Secretary of the Navy under Lincoln and Johnson* (3 vols.; New York, 1960), I, 70.

[9] *The Statutes at Large, Treaties, and Proclamations, of the United States of America,* ed. George P. Sanger (Boston, 1863), XII, 589–92.

[10] Francis B. Carpenter, *Six Months at the White House with Abraham Lincoln: The Story of a Picture* (New York, 1866), 20–24.

While Lincoln awaited a victory on the battlefield, he invited a delegation of African Americans to the White House to hear his arguments in favor of colonization—that is, of sending black Americans to Africa, the Caribbean, or South America. Lincoln not only hoped black Americans would see what he believed was the wisdom of colonization, which he had long supported. He also sought to make clear to white Americans that, in his view, emancipation did not need to increase the number of free black people in American society. Instead, blacks could be sent away to some foreign land. The following transcript of Lincoln's meeting was published in the *New York Tribune* and other newspapers.

30

Address on Colonization to a Delegation of Black Americans

August 14, 1862

This afternoon the President of the United States gave audience to a Committee of colored men at the White House. They were introduced by the Rev. J. Mitchell, Commissioner of Emigration.[11] E. M. Thomas,[12] the Chairman, remarked that they were there by invitation to hear what the Executive had to say to them. Having all been seated, the President, after a few preliminary observations, informed them that a sum of money had been appropriated by Congress, and placed at his disposition for the purpose of aiding the colonization in some country of the people, or a portion of them, of African descent, thereby making it his duty, as it had for a long time been his inclination, to favor that cause; and why, he asked, should the people of your race be colonized, and where? Why should they leave this country? This is, perhaps, the first question for proper consideration. You and we are different races. We have between us a broader difference than exists between almost any other two races. Whether it is right or wrong I need not discuss, but this physical difference is a great disadvantage to us both, as I think your race suffer very greatly, many of them by living among us, while ours suffer from your presence. In a word

---

[11] Reverend James Mitchell of Indiana worked as an emigration agent in support of congressional authorization of $100,000 for colonization in the bill abolishing slavery in the District of Columbia and another $500,000 in an act that granted funds to colonize freed slaves who were in the custody of the Union army.

[12] Edward M. Thomas was the president of the Anglo-African Institute for the Encouragement of Industry and Art.

we suffer on each side. If this is admitted, it affords a reason at least why we should be separated. You here are freemen I suppose.

A Voice: Yes, sir.

The President—Perhaps you have long been free, or all your lives. Your race are suffering, in my judgment, the greatest wrong inflicted on any people. But even when you cease to be slaves, you are yet far removed from being placed on an equality with the white race. You are cut off from many of the advantages which the other race enjoy. The aspiration of men is to enjoy equality with the best when free, but on this broad continent, not a single man of your race is made the equal of a single man of ours. Go where you are treated the best, and the ban is still upon you.

I do not propose to discuss this, but to present it as a fact with which we have to deal. I cannot alter it if I would. It is a fact, about which we all think and feel alike, I and you. We look to our condition, owing to the existence of the two races on this continent. I need not recount to you the effects upon white men, growing out of the institution of Slavery. I believe in its general evil effects on the white race. See our present condition—the country engaged in war!—our white men cutting one another's throats, none knowing how far it will extend; and then consider what we know to be the truth. But for your race among us there could not be war, although many men engaged on either side do not care for you one way or the other. Nevertheless, I repeat, without the institution of Slavery and the colored race as a basis, the war could not have an existence.

It is better for us both, therefore, to be separated. I know that there are free men among you, who even if they could better their condition are not as much inclined to go out of the country as those, who being slaves could obtain their freedom on this condition. I suppose one of the principal difficulties in the way of colonization is that the free colored man cannot see that his comfort would be advanced by it. You may believe you can live in Washington or elsewhere in the United States the remainder of your life [as easily], perhaps more so than you can in any foreign country, and hence you may come to the conclusion that you have nothing to do with the idea of going to a foreign country. This is (I speak in no unkind sense) an extremely selfish view of the case.

But you ought to do something to help those who are not so fortunate as yourselves. There is an unwillingness on the part of our people, harsh as it may be, for you free colored people to remain with us. Now, if you could give a start to white people, you would open a wide door for many to be made free. If we deal with those who are not free at the beginning, and whose intellects are clouded by Slavery, we have very poor materials to start with. If intelligent colored men, such as are before me, would move in this matter, much might be accomplished. It is exceedingly important that we have men at the beginning capable of thinking as white men, and not those who have been systematically oppressed.

There is much to encourage you. For the sake of your race you should sacrifice something of your present comfort for the purpose of being as grand in that respect as the white people. It is a cheering thought throughout life that something can be done to ameliorate the condition of those who have been subject to the hard usage of the world. It is difficult to make a man miserable while he feels he is worthy of himself, and claims kindred to the great God who made him. In the American Revolutionary war sacrifices were made by men engaged in it; but they were cheered by the future. Gen. Washington himself endured greater physical hardships than if he had remained a British subject. Yet he was a happy man, because he was engaged in benefiting his race—something for the children of his neighbors, having none of his own.

The colony of Liberia has been in existence a long time. In a certain sense it is a success. The old President of Liberia, Roberts,[13] has just been with me—the first time I ever saw him. He says they have within the bounds of that colony between 300,000 and 400,000 people, or more than in some of our old States, such as Rhode Island or Delaware, or in some of our newer States, and less than in some of our larger ones. They are not all American colonists, or their descendants. Something less than 12,000 have been sent thither from this country. Many of the original settlers have died, yet, like people elsewhere, their offspring outnumber those deceased.

The question is if the colored people are persuaded to go anywhere, why not there? One reason for an unwillingness to do so is that some of you would rather remain within reach of the country of your nativity. I do not know how much attachment you may have toward our race. It does not strike me that you have the greatest reason to love them. But still you are attached to them at all events.

The place I am thinking about having for a colony is in Central America.[14] It is nearer to us than Liberia—not much more than one-fourth as far as Liberia, and within seven days' run by steamers. Unlike Liberia it is on a great line of travel—it is a highway. The country is a very excellent one for any people, and with great natural resources and advantages, and especially because of the similarity of climate with your native land—thus being suited to your physical condition.

The particular place I have in view is to be a great highway from the Atlantic or Caribbean Sea to the Pacific Ocean, and this particular place

[13] Joseph Jenkins Roberts served as president of Liberia, a colony on the coast of West Africa, from 1847 to 1856. Born free in Norfolk, Virginia, in 1809, he emigrated to Liberia in 1829.

[14] Lincoln had in mind land in northern Panama on the Chiriquí Lagoon. The Chiriquí Improvement Company, owned by Ambrose W. Thompson, a Philadelphian, purchased hundreds of thousands of acres of land in the region in 1855 and proposed in August 1861 to sell coal to the U.S. Navy at Chiriquí Lagoon for about half the prevailing price.

has all the advantages for a colony. On both sides there are harbors among the finest in the world. Again, there is evidence of very rich coal mines. A certain amount of coal is valuable in any country, and there may be more than enough for the wants of the country. Why I attach so much importance to coal is, it will afford an opportunity to the inhabitants for immediate employment till they get ready to settle permanently in their homes.[15]

If you take colonists where there is no good landing, there is a bad show; and so where there is nothing to cultivate, and of which to make a farm. But if something is started so that you can get your daily bread as soon as you reach there, it is a great advantage. Coal land is the best thing I know of with which to commence an enterprise.

To return, you have been talked to upon this subject, and told that a speculation is intended by gentlemen, who have an interest in the country, including the coal mines.[16] We have been mistaken all our lives if we do not know whites as well as blacks look to their self-interest. Unless among those deficient of intellect everybody you trade with makes something. You meet with these things here as elsewhere.

If such persons have what will be an advantage to them, the question is whether it cannot be made of advantage to you. You are intelligent, and know that success does not as much depend on external help as on self-reliance. Much, therefore, depends upon yourselves. As to the coal mines, I think I see the means available for your self-reliance.

I shall, if I get a sufficient number of you engaged, have provisions made that you shall not be wronged. If you will engage in the enterprise I will spend some of the money intrusted to me. I am not sure you will succeed. The Government may lose the money, but we cannot succeed unless we try; but we think, with care, we can succeed.

The political affairs in Central America are not in quite as satisfactory condition as I wish. There are contending factions in that quarter; but it is true all the factions are agreed alike on the subject of colonization, and want it, and are more generous than we are here. To your colored race they have no objection. Besides, I would endeavor to have you made equals, and have the best assurance that you should be the equals of the best.

The practical thing I want to ascertain is whether I can get a number of able-bodied men, with their wives and children, who are willing to go, when I present evidence of encouragement and protection. Could I get a

---

[15] In other words, Lincoln proposed that black colonists mine and load coal for the Chiriqui Improvement Company, from which they would purchase land, and the Navy would buy the coal. A provisional contract to this effect between the U.S. government and the Chiriqui Improvement Company was signed on September 12, 1862. *CW*, IV, 561; V, 2–3, 371, 414, 418–19.

[16] Lincoln is referring to Ambrose Thompson.

hundred tolerably intelligent men, with their wives and children, to "cut their own fodder" [work for their future benefit], so to speak? Can I have fifty? If I could find twenty-five able-bodied men, with a mixture of women and children, good things in the family relation, I think I could make a successful commencement.

I want you to let me know whether this can be done or not. This is the practical part of my wish to see you. These are subjects of very great importance, worthy of a month's study, [instead] of a speech delivered in an hour. I ask you then to consider seriously not pertaining to yourselves merely, nor for your race, and ours, for the present time, but as one of the things, if successfully managed, for the good of mankind—not confined to the present generation, but as

> "From age to age descends the lay [song],
> To millions yet to be,
> Till far its echoes roll away,
> Into eternity."

The above is merely given as the substance of the President's remarks.

The Chairman of the delegation briefly replied that "they would hold a consultation and in a short time give an answer."[17] The President said, "Take your full time—no hurry at all."

The delegation then withdrew.

[17] Most black Americans remained hostile toward colonization.

Although Lincoln had resolved privately to issue an emancipation proclamation, in public he continued to insist that his goal was to save the Union without necessarily doing anything about slavery. In a letter published on August 19, 1862, in the *New York Tribune*, the prominent Republican editor Horace Greeley criticized Lincoln for "the policy you seem to be pursuing with regard to the slaves of Rebels." Greeley raised nine objections, including, "We think you are strangely and disastrously remiss . . . with regard to the emancipating provisions of the new Confiscation Act."[18] Lincoln responded to Greeley with the following public letter, quickly reprinted in newspapers across the North, which announced that his policy toward slavery would depend on what was necessary to save the Union, a public hint of his private decision.

[18] *CW*, V, 389.

31

Letter to Horace Greeley

August 22, 1862

Executive Mansion
Washington

Hon. Horace Greely
Dear Sir
I have just read yours of the 19th. addressed to myself through the New-York Tribune. If there be in it any statements, or assumptions of fact, which I may know to be erroneous, I do not, now and here, controvert them. If there be in it any inferences which I may believe to be falsely drawn, I do not now and here, argue against them. If there be perceptable in it an impatient and dictatorial tone, I waive it in deference to an old friend, whose heart I have always supposed to be right.

As to the policy I "seem to be pursuing" as you say, I have not meant to leave any one in doubt.

I would save the Union. I would save it the shortest way under the Constitution. The sooner the national authority can be restored; the nearer the Union will be "the Union as it was." If there be those who would not save the Union, unless they could at the same time *save* slavery, I do not agree with them. If there be those who would not save the Union unless they could at the same time *destroy* slavery, I do not agree with them. My paramount object in this struggle *is* to save the Union, and is *not* either to save or to destroy slavery. If I could save the Union without freeing *any* slave I would do it, and if I could save it by freeing *all* the slaves I would do it; and if I could save it by freeing some and leaving others alone I would also do that. What I do about slavery, and the colored race, I do because I believe it helps to save the Union; and what I forbear, I forbear because I do *not* believe it would help to save the Union. I shall do *less* whenever I shall believe what I am doing hurts the cause, and I shall do *more* whenever I shall believe doing more will help the cause. I shall try to correct errors when shown to be errors; and I shall adopt new views so fast as they shall appear to be true views.

I have here stated my purpose according to my view of *official* duty; and I intend no modification of my oft-expressed *personal* wish that all men every where could be free.

Yours,
A. LINCOLN

ANNOUNCING EMANCIPATION

Union success at the battle of Antietam gave Lincoln enough of a victory to make his emancipation plan public. Five days later, on September 22, 1862, he convened his cabinet and told them what he had decided to do. Before reading the proclamation to them, Lincoln explained, as Treasury Secretary Salmon P. Chase recorded in his diary,

> I have, as you are aware, thought a great deal about the relation of this war to slavery; and you all remember that, several weeks ago, I read to you an order I had prepared on this subject, which, on account of objections made by some of you, was not issued. Ever since then, my mind has been much occupied with this subject, and I have thought all along that the time for acting on it might very probably come. I think the time has come now. I wish it were a better time. I wish that we were in a better condition. The action of the army against the rebels has not been quite what I should have best liked. But they have been driven out of Maryland, and Pennsylvania is no longer in danger of invasion. When the rebel army was at Frederick, I determined, as soon as it should be driven out of Maryland, to issue a proclamation of emancipation such as I thought most likely to be useful. I said nothing to anyone; but I made the promise to myself and [hesitating a little] to my Maker. The rebel army is now driven out, and I am going to fulfill that promise. I have got you together to hear what I have written down. I do not wish your advice about the main matter; for that I have determined for myself.[19]

[19] John Niven et al., eds., *The Salmon P. Chase Papers*, Volume I, *Journals, 1829–1872* (Kent, Ohio, 1993), 393–94.

32

Preliminary Emancipation Proclamation

September 22, 1862

BY THE PRESIDENT OF THE UNITED STATES OF AMERICA: A PROCLAMATION.

I, Abraham Lincoln, President of the United States of America, and Commander-in-chief of the Army and Navy thereof, do hereby proclaim and declare that hereafter, as heretofore, the war will be prossecuted for the object of practically restoring the constitutional relation between the United States, and each of the states, and the people thereof, in which states that relation is, or may be suspended, or disturbed.

That it is my purpose, upon the next meeting of Congress to again recommend the adoption of a practical measure tendering pecuniary aid to the free acceptance or rejection of all slave-states, so called, the people whereof may not then be in rebellion against the United States, and which states, may then have voluntarily adopted, or thereafter may voluntarily adopt, immediate, or gradual abolishment of slavery within their respective limits; and that the effort to colonize persons of African descent, with their consent, upon this continent, or elsewhere, with the previously obtained consent of the Governments existing there, will be continued.

That on the first day of January in the year of our Lord, one thousand eight hundred and sixty-three, all persons held as slaves within any state, or designated part of a state, the people whereof shall then be in rebellion against the United States shall be then, thenceforward, and forever free; and the executive government of the United States, including the military and naval authority thereof, will recognize and maintain the freedom of such persons, and will do no act or acts to repress such persons, or any of them, in any efforts they may make for their actual freedom.

That the executive will, on the first day of January aforesaid, by proclamation, designate the States, and parts of states, if any, in which the people thereof respectively, shall then be in rebellion against the United States; and the fact that any state, or the people thereof shall, on that day be, in good faith represented in the Congress of the United States, by members chosen thereto, at elections wherein a majority of the qualified voters of such state shall have participated, shall, in the absence of strong countervailing testimony, be deemed conclusive evidence that such state and the people thereof, are not then in rebellion against the United States.

That attention is hereby called to an act of Congress entitled "An act to make an additional Article of War" approved March 13, 1862, and which act is in the words and figure following:

Be it enacted by the Senate and House of Representatives of the United States of America in Congress assembled, That hereafter the following shall be promulgated as an additional article of war for the government of the army of the United States, and shall be obeyed and observed as such:

Article——. All officers or persons in the military or naval service of the United States are prohibited from employing any of the forces under their respective commands for the purpose of returning fugitives from service or labor, who may have escaped from any persons to whom such service or labor is claimed to be due, and any officer who shall be found guilty by a court-martial of violating this article shall be dismissed from the service.

Sec. 2. *And be it further enacted,* That this act shall take effect from and after its passage.

Also to the ninth and tenth sections of an act entitled "An Act to suppress Insurrection, to punish Treason and Rebellion, to seize and confiscate property of rebels, and for other purposes," approved July 17, 1862, and which sections are in the words and figures following:

Sec. 9. *And be it further enacted*, That all slaves of persons who shall hereafter be engaged in rebellion against the government of the United States, or who shall in any way give aid or comfort thereto, escaping from such persons and taking refuge within the lines of the army; and all slaves captured from such persons or deserted by them and coming under the control of the government of the United States; and all slaves of such persons found *on* (or) being within any place occupied by rebel forces and afterwards occupied by the forces of the United States, shall be deemed captives of war, and shall be forever free of their servitude and not again held as slaves.

Sec. 10. *And be it further enacted*, That no slave escaping into any State, Territory, or the District of Columbia, from any other State, shall be delivered up, or in any way impeded or hindered of his liberty, except for crime, or some offence against the laws, unless the person claiming said fugitive shall first make oath that the person to whom the labor or service of such fugitive is alleged to be due is his lawful owner, and has not borne arms against the United States in the present rebellion, nor in any way given aid and comfort thereto; and no person engaged in the military or naval service of the United States shall, under any pretence whatever, assume to decide on the validity of the claim of any person to the service or labor of any other person, or surrender up any such person to the claimant, on pain of being dismissed from the service.

And I do hereby enjoin upon and order all persons engaged in the military and naval service of the United States to observe, obey, and enforce, within their respective spheres of service, the act, and sections above recited.

And the executive will in due time recommend that all citizens of the United States who shall have remained loyal thereto throughout the rebellion, shall (upon the restoration of the constitutional relation between the United States, and their respective states, and people, if that relation shall have been suspended or disturbed) be compensated for all losses by acts of the United States, including the loss of slaves. . . .

ABRAHAM LINCOLN

One month before the Emancipation Proclamation was to take effect, Lincoln presented Congress a detailed proposal for the form of gradual, compensated emancipation he preferred. Unlike the Emancipation Proclamation, which applied only to the states in rebellion, Lincoln's proposed scheme for gradual emancipation was designed to eliminate slavery—eventually—throughout the United States.

33

Annual Message to Congress

December 1, 1862

Fellow-citizens of the Senate and House of Representatives:
Since your last annual assembling another year of health and bountiful harvests has passed. And while it has not pleased the Almighty to bless us with a return of peace, we can but press on, guided by the best light He gives us, trusting that in His own good time, and wise way, all will yet be well. . . .

Applications have been made to me by many free Americans of African descent to favor their emigration, with a view to such colonization as was contemplated in recent acts of Congress. Other parties, at home and abroad—some from interested motives, others upon patriotic considerations, and still others influenced by philanthropic sentiments—have suggested similar measures; while, on the other hand, several of the Spanish-American republics have protested against the sending of such colonies to their respective territories.[20] Under these circumstances, I have declined to move any such colony to any state, without first obtaining the consent of its government, with an agreement on its part to receive and protect such emigrants in all the rights of freemen; and I have, at the same time, offered to the several states situated within the tropics, or having colonies there, to negotiate with them, subject to the advice and consent of the Senate, to favor the voluntary emigration of persons of that class to their respective territories, upon conditions which shall be equal, just, and humane. Liberia and Hayti are, as yet, the only countries to which colonists of African descent from here, could go with certainty of being received and adopted as citizens; and I regret to say such persons, contemplating colonization, do not seem so willing to migrate to those countries, as to some others, nor so willing as I think their interest demands. I believe, however, opinion among them, in this respect, is improving; and that, ere long, there will be an augmented, and considerable migration to both these countries, from the United States. . . .

[20] The governments of Honduras, Nicaragua, and Costa Rica objected to Lincoln's colonization plan for Chiriquí Lagoon, and it was ultimately abandoned.

On the twenty-second day of September last a proclamation was issued
by the Executive. . . .
. . . I now respectfully recall your attention to what may be called "compensated emancipation." . . .
Our national strife springs not from our permanent part; not from the
land we inhabit; not from our national homestead. There is no possible
severing of this, but would multiply, and not mitigate, evils among us. In
all its adaptations and aptitudes, it demands union, and abhors separation.
In fact, it would, ere long, force reunion, however much of blood and trea-
sure the separation might have cost.
Our strife pertains to ourselves—to the passing generations of men;
and it can, without convulsion, be hushed forever with the passing of one
generation.
In this view, I recommend the adoption of the following resolution and
articles amendatory to the Constitution of the United States:

> *Resolved by the Senate and House of Representatives of the United
> States of America in Congress assembled,* (two thirds of both houses
> concurring,) That the following articles be proposed to the legisla-
> tures (or conventions) of the several States as amendments to the
> Constitution of the United States, all or any of which articles when
> ratified by three-fourths of the said legislatures (or conventions) to
> be valid as part or parts of the said Constitution, viz:
> Article——.
> Every State, wherein slavery now exists, which shall abolish the
> same therein, at any time, or times, before the first day of January, in
> the year of our Lord one thousand and nine hundred, shall receive
> compensation from the United States as follows, to wit:
> The President of the United States shall deliver to every such
> State, bonds of the United States, bearing interest at the rate of
> ＿＿＿ per cent, per annum, to an amount equal to the aggregate sum
> of ＿＿＿ for each slave shown to have been therein, by the eighth
> census of the United States, said bonds to be delivered to such State
> by instalments, or in one parcel, at the completion of the abolish-
> ment, accordingly as the same shall have been gradual, or at one
> time, within such State; and interest shall begin to run upon any such
> bond, only from the proper time of its delivery as aforesaid. Any State
> having received bonds as aforesaid, and afterwards reintroducing or
> tolerating slavery therein, shall refund to the United States the bonds
> so received, or the value thereof, and all interest paid thereon.
> Article——.
> All slaves who shall have enjoyed actual freedom by the chances
> of the war, at any time before the end of the rebellion, shall be forever
> free; but all owners of such, who shall not have been disloyal, shall
> be compensated for them, at the same rates as is provided for States

adopting abolishment of slavery, but in such way, that no slave shall be twice accounted for.

Article———.

Congress may appropriate money, and otherwise provide, for colonizing free colored persons, with their own consent, at any place or places without the United States.

I beg indulgence to discuss these proposed articles at some length. Without slavery the rebellion could never have existed; without slavery it could not continue.

Among the friends of the Union there is great diversity, of sentiment, and of policy, in regard to slavery, and the African race amongst us. Some would perpetuate slavery; some would abolish it suddenly, and without compensation; some would abolish it gradually, and with compensation; some would remove the freed people from us, and some would retain them with us; and there are yet other minor diversities. Because of these diversities, we waste much strength in struggles among ourselves. By mutual concession we should harmonize, and act together. This would be compromise; but it would be compromise among the friends, and not with the enemies of the Union. These articles are intended to embody a plan of such mutual concessions. If the plan shall be adopted, it is assumed that emancipation will follow, at least, in several of the States.

As to the first article, the main points are: first, the emancipation; secondly, the length of time for consummating it—thirty-seven years; and thirdly, the compensation.

The emancipation will be unsatisfactory to the advocates of perpetual slavery; but the length of time should greatly mitigate their dissatisfaction. The time spares both races from the evils of sudden derangement—in fact, from the necessity of any derangement—while most of those whose habitual course of thought will be disturbed by the measure will have passed away before its consummation. They will never see it. Another class will hail the prospect of emancipation, but will deprecate the length of time. They will feel that it gives too little to the now living slaves. But it really gives them much. It saves them from the vagrant destitution which must largely attend immediate emancipation in localities where their numbers are very great; and it gives the inspiring assurance that their posterity shall be free forever. The plan leaves to each State, choosing to act under it, to abolish slavery now, or at the end of the century, or at any intermediate time, or by degrees, extending over the whole or any part of the period; and it obliges no two states to proceed alike. It also provides for compensation, and generally the mode of making it. This, it would seem, must further mitigate the dissatisfaction of those who favor perpetual slavery, and especially of those who are to receive the compensation. Doubtless some of those who are to pay, and not to receive will object. Yet the measure is both just and economical. In a certain sense the liberation of slaves is the destruction of property—property acquired by descent, or by purchase, the same as any other property. It is no less true for having been often said, that the people of the south are not more responsible for the original introduction of this property, than are the people of the north; and when it is remembered how unhesitatingly we all use cotton and sugar, and share the profits of dealing in them, it may not be quite safe to say, that the south has been more responsible than the north for its continuance. If then, for a common object, this property is to be sacrificed is it not just that it be done at a common charge?

And if, with less money, or money more easily paid, we can preserve the benefits of the Union by this means, than we can by the war alone, is it not also economical to do it? Let us consider it then. Let us ascertain the sum we have expended in the war since compensated emancipation was proposed last March, and consider whether, if that measure had been promptly accepted, by even some of the slave States, the same sum would not have done more to close the war, than has been otherwise done. If so the measure would save money, and, in that view, would be a prudent and economical measure. Certainly it is not so easy to pay *something* as it is to pay *nothing*; but it is easier to pay a *large* sum than it is to pay a larger one. And it is easier to pay any sum *when* we are able, than it is to pay it *before* we are able. The war requires large sums, and requires them at once. The aggregate sum necessary for compensated emancipation, of course, would be large. But it would require no ready cash; nor the bonds even, any faster than the emancipation progresses. This might not, and probably would not, close before the end of the thirty-seven years. At that time we shall probably have a hundred millions of people to share the burden, instead of thirty one millions, as now. . . .

The proposed emancipation would shorten the war, perpetuate peace, insure this increase of population, and proportionately the wealth of the country. . . .

As to the second article, I think it would be impracticable to return to bondage the class of persons therein contemplated. Some of them, doubtless, in the property sense, belong to loyal owners; and hence, provision is made in this article for compensating such.

The third article relates to the future of the freed people. It does not oblige, but merely authorizes, Congress to aid in colonizing such as may consent. This ought not to be regarded as objectionable, on the one hand, or on the other, in so much as it comes to nothing, unless by the mutual consent of the people to be deported, and the American voters, through their representatives in Congress.

I cannot make it better known than it already is, that I strongly favor colonization. And yet I wish to say there is an objection urged against free colored persons remaining in the country, which is largely imaginary, if not sometimes malicious.

It is insisted that their presence would injure, and displace white labor and white laborers. If there ever could be a proper time for mere catch arguments, that time surely is not now. In times like the present, men should utter nothing for which they would not willingly be responsible through time and in eternity. Is it true, then, that colored people can displace any more white labor, by being free, than by remaining slaves? If they stay in their old places, they jostle no white laborers; if they leave their old places, they leave them open to white laborers. Logically, there is neither more nor less of it. Emancipation, even without deportation, would probably enhance the wages of white labor, and, very surely, would not reduce them. Thus, the customary amount of labor would still have to be performed; the freed people would surely not do more than their old proportion of it, and very probably, for a time, would do less, leaving an increased part to white laborers, bringing their labor into greater demand, and, consequently, enhancing the wages of it. With deportation, even to a limited extent, enhanced wages to white labor is mathematically certain. Labor is like any other commodity in the market—increase the demand for it, and you increase the price of it. Reduce the supply of black labor, by colonizing the black laborer out of the country, and, by precisely so much, you increase the demand for, and wages of, white labor.

But it is dreaded that the freed people will swarm forth, and cover the whole land? Are they not already in the land? Will liberation make them any more numerous? Equally distributed among the whites of the whole country, and there would be but one colored to seven whites. Could the one, in any way, greatly disturb the seven? There are many communities now, having more than one free colored person, to seven whites; and this, without any apparent consciousness of evil from it. The District of Columbia, and the States of Maryland and Delaware, are all in this condition. The District has more than one free colored to six whites; and yet, in its frequent petitions to Congress, I believe it has never presented the presence of free colored persons as one of its grievances. But why should emancipation south, send the free people north? People, of any color, seldom run, unless there be something to run from. *Heretofore* colored people, to some extent, have fled north from bondage; and *now*, perhaps, from both bondage and destitution. But if gradual emancipation and deportation be adopted, they will have neither to flee from. Their old masters will give them wages at least until new laborers can be procured; and the freed men, in turn, will gladly give their labor for the wages, till new homes can be found for them, in congenial climes, and with people of their own blood and race. This proposition can be trusted on the mutual interests involved. And, in any event, cannot the north decide for itself, whether to receive them?

Again, as practice proves more than theory, in any case, has there been any irruption of colored people northward, because of the abolishment of slavery in this District last spring?

What I have said of the proportion of free colored persons to the whites, in the District, is from the census of 1860, having no reference to persons called contrabands, nor to those made free by the act of Congress abolishing slavery here. . . .

This plan is recommended as a means, not in exclusion of, but additional to, all others for restoring and preserving the national authority throughout the Union. The subject is presented exclusively in its economical aspect. The plan would, I am confident, secure peace more speedily, and maintain it more permanently, than can be done by force alone; while all it would cost, considering amounts, and manner of payment, and times of payment, would be easier paid than will be the additional cost of the war, if we rely solely upon force. It is much—very much—that it would cost no blood at all.

The plan is proposed as permanent constitutional law. It cannot become such without the concurrence of, first, two-thirds of Congress, and, afterwards, three-fourths of the States. The requisite three-fourths of the States will necessarily include seven of the Slave states. Their concurrence, if obtained, will give assurance of their severally adopting emancipation, at no very distant day, upon the new constitutional terms. This assurance would end the struggle now, and save the Union forever.

I do not forget the gravity which should characterize a paper addressed to the Congress of the nation by the Chief Magistrate of the nation. Nor do I forget that some of you are my seniors, nor that many of you have more experience than I, in the conduct of public affairs. Yet I trust that in view of the great responsibility resting upon me, you will perceive no want of respect to yourselves, in any undue earnestness I may seem to display.

Is it doubted, then, that the plan I propose, if adopted, would shorten the war, and thus lessen its expenditure of money and of blood? Is it doubted that it would restore the national authority and national prosperity, and perpetuate both indefinitely? Is it doubted that we here—Congress and Executive—can secure its adoption? Will not the good people respond to a united, and earnest appeal from us? Can we, can they, by any other means, so certainly, or so speedily, assure these vital objects? We can succeed only by concert. It is not "can *any* of us *imagine* better?" but "can we *all* do better?" Object whatsoever is possible, still the question recurs "can we do better?" The dogmas of the quiet past, are inadequate to the stormy present. The occasion is piled high with difficulty, and we must rise with the occasion. As our case is new, so we must think anew, and act anew. We must disenthrall our selves, and then we shall save our country.

Fellow-citizens, *we* cannot escape history. We of this Congress and this administration, will be remembered in spite of ourselves. No personal significance, or insignificance, can spare one or another of us. The fiery trial through which we pass, will light us down, in honor or dishonor, to the latest generation. We *say* we are for the Union. The world will not forget that we say this. We know how to save the Union. The world knows we do know how to save it. We—even *we here*—hold the power, and bear the responsibility. In *giving* freedom to the *slave*, we *assure* freedom to the *free*—honorable alike in what we give, and what we preserve. We shall nobly save, or meanly lose, the last best, hope of earth. Other means may succeed; this could not fail. The way is plain, peaceful, generous, just—a way which, if followed, the world will forever applaud, and God must forever bless.

ABRAHAM LINCOLN

On January 1, 1863, after shaking hands with hundreds of white well-wishers at the White House New Year's Day reception, Lincoln signed the Emancipation Proclamation, remarking, "I never in my life felt more certain that I was doing right than I do in signing this paper."[21] Carefully crafted to exert his limited constitutional authority as commander in chief, the proclamation did not emancipate slaves in areas under Union control, where conventional constitutional restraints remained in force. In other words, Lincoln emancipated slaves in rebel states where he claimed constitutional authority as commander in chief, but he did not emancipate slaves in regions where he lacked constitutional authority as commander in chief. More than a decree of emancipation, the proclamation also announced that blacks would now be allowed to serve in Union armed forces.

[21] Frederick W. Seward, *Seward at Washington, as Senator and Secretary of State: A Memoir of His Life with Selections from His Letters, 1861–1872* (New York, 1891), 151.

34

Emancipation Proclamation

January 1, 1863

BY THE PRESIDENT OF THE
UNITED STATES OF AMERICA:
A PROCLAMATION.

Whereas, on the twentysecond day of September, in the year of our Lord one thousand eight hundred and sixty two, a proclamation was issued by the President of the United States, containing, among other things, the following, towit:

That on the first day of January, in the year of our Lord one thousand eight hundred and sixty-three, all persons held as slaves within any State or designated part of a State, the people whereof shall then be in rebellion against the United States, shall be then, thenceforward, and forever free; and the Executive Government of the United States, including the military and naval authority thereof, will recognize and maintain the freedom of such persons, and will do no act or acts to repress such persons, or any of them, in any efforts they may make for their actual freedom.

That the Executive will, on the first day of January aforesaid, by proclamation, designate the States and parts of States, if any, in which the people thereof, respectively, shall then be in rebellion against the United States; and the fact that any State, or the people thereof, shall on that day be, in good faith, represented in the Congress of the United States by members chosen thereto at elections wherein a majority of the qualified voters of such State shall have participated, shall, in the absence of strong countervailing testimony, be deemed conclusive evidence that such State, and the people thereof, are not then in rebellion against the United States.

Now, therefore I, Abraham Lincoln, President of the United States, by virtue of the power in me vested as Commander-in-Chief, of the Army and Navy of the United States in time of actual armed rebellion against authority and government of the United States, and as a fit and necessary war measure for suppressing said rebellion, do, on this first day of January, in the year of our Lord one thousand eight hundred and sixty three, and in accordance with my purpose so to do publicly proclaimed for the full period of one hundred days, from the day first above mentioned, order and designate as the States and parts of States wherein the people thereof respectively, are this day in rebellion against the United States, the following, towit:

Arkansas, Texas, Louisiana, (except the Parishes of St. Bernard, Plaquemines, Jefferson, St. Johns, St. Charles, St. James[,] Ascension, Assumption, Terrebonne, Lafourche, St. Mary, St. Martin, and Orleans, including the City of New-Orleans), Mississippi, Alabama, Florida, Georgia, South-Carolina, North-Carolina, and Virginia, (except the fortyeight counties designated as West Virginia, and also the counties of Berkley, Accomac, Northampton, Elizabeth-City, York, Princess Ann, and Norfolk, including the cities of Norfolk & Portsmouth[)]; and which excepted parts are, for the present, left precisely as if this proclamation were not issued.

And by virtue of the power, and for the purpose aforesaid, I do order and declare that all persons held as slaves within said designated States, and parts of States, are, and henceforward shall be free; and that the Executive government of the United States, including the military and naval authorities thereof, will recognize and maintain the freedom of said persons.

And I hereby enjoin upon the people so declared to be free to abstain from all violence, unless in necessary self-defence; and I recommend to them that, in all cases when allowed, they labor faithfully for reasonable wages.

And I further declare and make known, that such persons of suitable condition, will be received into the armed service of the United States to garrison forts, positions, stations, and other places, and to man vessels of all sorts in said service.

And upon this act, sincerely believed to be an act of justice, warranted by the Constitution, upon military necessity, I invoke the considerate judgment of mankind, and the gracious favor of Almighty God. . . .

ABRAHAM LINCOLN

6

A War for Freedom and Union

The Emancipation Proclamation of January 1, 1863, signaled Lincoln's conclusion that a war to save the Union could not be won without ending slavery in the Confederacy. In addition to announcing a new war aim, the Emancipation Proclamation declared a new meaning for the Union, a meaning Lincoln explained in his Gettysburg Address (Document 42).

Without Union victories on the battlefield, the Emancipation Proclamation remained just words on paper. Unless Confederate armies could be defeated, northern superiority in manpower and other military resources would do nothing to free the slaves or save the Union. Only hard, relentless fighting could prevent the Confederacy from maintaining its independence. Lincoln understood better than any other northern leader the enormous sacrifice required for military success.

In December 1862, after Union attackers in the gruesome defeat at Fredericksburg suffered more than twice as many casualties as Confederate defenders, Lincoln explained to William O. Stoddard, one of his clerks, why the loss was not as bad as it seemed. Stoddard wrote later that Lincoln proposed an "awful arithmetic" that would turn costly losses like Fredericksburg into ultimate victory. According to Stoddard, Lincoln said that if the battle of Fredericksburg "were to be fought over again, every day, through a week of days, with the same relative results, the army under Lee would be wiped out to its last man, the [Union] Army of the Potomac would still be a mighty host, the war would be over, the Confederacy gone, and peace would be won at a smaller cost of life than it will be if the week of lost battles must be dragged out through yet another year of camps, marches, and of deaths in hospitals, rather than upon the field. No general yet found can face the arithmetic, but the end of the war will be at hand when he shall be discovered."[1]

[1] William O. Stoddard, *Inside the White House in War Times* (New York, 1890), 179.

143

During 1863, Lincoln continued to search for a general who grasped this awful arithmetic. He had difficulty finding generals who fully realized that victory required the destruction of Confederate armies. As commander in chief, he constantly urged his generals not just to win battles but to destroy the enemy. Even after the exhilarating victory at Gettysburg, Pennsylvania, in early July 1863, the defeated Confederates slipped away to regroup and fight again. But the thrilling capture of Vicksburg, Mississippi, in July, followed by the occupation of Chattanooga and Knoxville, Tennessee, later in the year, made clear that General Ulysses S. Grant shared Lincoln's vision of victory and how to achieve it. By the end of the year, Lincoln had found his general.

As the following documents reveal, Lincoln's determination to fight an aggressive war for freedom and Union engendered intense political controversy in the North. It also prompted initiatives to take greater advantage of African Americans' contributions to the military effort.

EMANCIPATION AND BLACK SOLDIERS

The Emancipation Proclamation authorized African American men to serve in the armed forces. Aware of the army's pressing need for manpower, Lincoln encouraged army officials to recruit black regiments from the thousands of contrabands streaming into Union camps. Black recruitment went slowly, partly because of doubts among army commanders about whether former slaves would make good soldiers. Lincoln refused to retreat from the new war aim of freedom, but he was well aware that many white northerners—both soldiers and civilians—considered his policy unwise, or worse.

35

Letter to Ulysses S. Grant

August 9, 1863

Executive Mansion
Washington

My dear General Grant:[2]
... Gen. Thomas has gone again to the Mississippi Valley, with the view of raising colored troops.[3] I have no reason to doubt that you are doing what you reasonably can upon the same subject. I believe it is a resource which, if vigorously applied now, will soon close the contest. It works doubly, weakening the enemy and strengthening us. We were not fully ripe for it until the river was opened.[4] Now, I think at least a hundred thousand can, and ought to be rapidly organized along it's shores, relieving all the white troops to serve elsewhere.

Mr. Dana[5] understands you as believing that the emancipation proclamation has helped some in your military operations. I am very glad if this is so.[6] ...

Yours very truly
A. LINCOLN

[2] Just a month earlier, Grant had captured Vicksburg. When he received this letter, he was in Cairo, Illinois.

[3] General Lorenzo Thomas was put in charge of the recruitment of African American soldiers in the Mississippi Valley. By the end of 1863, he had enlisted nearly twenty thousand black men.

[4] The Union did not control the entire length of the Mississippi River until July 1863, with the capture of Vicksburg and Port Hudson, Louisiana.

[5] Charles A. Dana, assistant secretary of war and former editor of the *New York Tribune*, was with Grant's army during the Vicksburg campaign.

[6] Grant replied, "I have given the subject of arming the negro my hearty support. This, with emancipation ... is the heavyest blow yet given the Confederacy. ... Gen. Thomas is now with me and you may rely on it I will give him all the aid in my power." *CW*, VI, 375.

Black soldiers fought valiantly in a number of engagements—including battles at Port Hudson, Louisiana, in May 1863; at Milliken's Bend, near Vicksburg, in June 1863; and at Fort Wagner, near Charleston, South Carolina, in July 1863. The Confederacy considered black soldiers to be insurrectionists and refused to treat them as prisoners of war when they were captured. Instead, rebel soldiers often summarily executed black captives or sold them into slavery. Lincoln proclaimed that the Union would retaliate against such outrages.

36

Order of Retaliation

July 30, 1863

Executive Mansion
Washington D.C.

It is the duty of every government to give protection to its citizens, of whatever class, color, or condition, and especially to those who are duly organized as soldiers in the public service. The law of nations and the usages and customs of war as carried on by civilized powers, permit no distinction as to color in the treatment of prisoners of war as public enemies. To sell or enslave any captured person, on account of his color, and for no offence against the laws of war, is a relapse into barbarism and a crime against the civilization of the age.

The government of the United States will give the same protection to all its soldiers, and if the enemy shall sell or enslave anyone because of his color, the offense shall be punished by retaliation upon the enemy's prisoners in our possession.

It is therefore ordered that for every soldier of the United States killed in violation of the laws of war, a rebel soldier shall be executed; and for every one enslaved by the enemy or sold into slavery, a rebel soldier shall be placed at hard labor on the public works and continued at such labor until the other shall be released and receive the treatment due to a prisoner of war.[7]

ABRAHAM LINCOLN

---

[7] In practice, the Union enforced this policy haphazardly, fearing that the Confederacy would counter by punishing white Union prisoners similarly. For the remainder of the war, black soldiers captured by the Confederacy were routinely executed, returned to their masters, or sold into slavery. When the Confederacy refused to exchange black prisoners of war for captured Confederates, the Union stopped all prisoner exchanges.

Figure 4. *Wartime President*
This photograph taken in 1863, unlike the many formal presidential portraits of Lincoln, captures the president in a more casual pose that may better reflect the canny, shrewd, confident, and cordial man visitors encountered when they met him.

From the Lincoln Financial Foundation Collection, courtesy of the Indiana State Museum.

Thousands of slaves liberated by the Emancipation Proclamation—especially women, children, and elderly men—crowded into contraband camps near Union lines in the Mississippi Valley. Lincoln proposed that they be put to work on abandoned plantations.

The Emancipation Proclamation did not apply to the loyal slave states of Maryland, Delaware, Kentucky, or Missouri. Although Lincoln continued to hope that these border states would adopt some plan for gradual emancipation, he believed that the Constitution still protected slavery within the Union. Lincoln resisted pressure to extend the Emancipation Proclamation to regions of the Confederacy exempted because they were under Union control. Since he believed that the Constitution permitted emancipation only as a military necessity, he held that Union initiatives based on any other considerations violated the Constitution and created grave political risks for both the Republican party and the eventual abolition of slavery.

37

Letter to Salmon P. Chase

September 2, 1863

Executive Mansion
Washington

Hon. S. P. Chase[8]
My dear Sir:
Knowing your great anxiety that the emancipation proclamation shall now be applied to certain parts of Virginia and Louisiana which were exempted from it last January, I state briefly what appear to me to be difficulties in the way of such a step. The original proclamation has no constitutional or legal justification, except as a military measure. The exemptions were made because the military necessity did not apply to the exempted localities. Nor does that necessity apply to them now any more than it did then. If I take the step[9] must I not do so, without the argument of military

---

[8] An ambitious antislavery Republican from Ohio, Salmon P. Chase served as Lincoln's secretary of the Treasury until he was appointed chief justice of the Supreme Court in October 1864.
[9] Applying the Emancipation Proclamation to the exempted areas.

necessity, and so, without any argument, except the one that I think the measure politically expedient, and morally right? Would I not thus give up all footing upon constitution or law? Would I not thus be in the boundless field of absolutism? Could this pass unnoticed, or unresisted? Could it fail to be perceived that without any further stretch, I might do the same in Delaware, Maryland, Kentucky, Tennessee, and Missouri; and even change any law in any state? Would not many of our own friends shrink away appalled? Would it not lose us the elections, and with them, the very cause we seek to advance?

THE DECISIVE SUMMER OF 1863

The lack of military progress in the Virginia theater by January 1863 caused Lincoln to replace General Ambrose Burnside, commander of the Army of the Potomac, with General Joseph Hooker. A West Point graduate, "Fighting Joe" Hooker had gained a reputation as an aggressive general since the beginning of the war. Lincoln made clear that he expected Hooker to fight and win battles.

38

Letter to Joseph Hooker
January 26, 1863

Executive Mansion
Washington

Major General Hooker
General.

I have placed you at the head of the Army of the Potomac. Of course I have done this upon what appear to me to be sufficient reasons. And yet I think it best for you to know that there are some things in regard to which, I am not quite satisfied with you. I believe you to be a brave and a skilful soldier, which, of course, I like. I also believe you do not mix politics with your profession, in which you are right. You have confidence in yourself, which is a valuable, if not an indispensable quality. You are ambitious, which, within reasonable bounds, does good rather than harm. But I think that during Gen. Burnside's command of the Army, you have taken counsel of your ambition, and thwarted him as much as you could, in which you did a great wrong to the country, and to a most meritorious and honorable brother officer. I have heard, in such way as to believe it, of your recently saying that both the Army and the Government needed a Dictator. Of course it was not *for* this, but in spite of it, that I have given you the command. Only those generals who gain successes, can set up dictators. What I now ask of you is military success, and I will risk the dictatorship. The government will support you to the utmost of it's ability, which is neither more nor less than it has done and will do for all commanders. I much fear that the spirit which you have aided to infuse into the Army, of criticising their Commander, and withholding confidence from him, will now turn upon you. I shall assist you as far as I can, to put it down. Neither you, nor Napoleon, if he were alive again, could get any good out of an army, while such a spirit prevails in it.

And now, beware of rashness. Beware of rashness, but with energy, and sleepless vigilance, go forward, and give us victories.

Yours very truly
A. LINCOLN

By the end of April 1863, the Union armies seemed stalled on every front. In the West, Grant's months-long campaign to assault Vicksburg remained stymied by the city's defenses and the marshy terrain along the Mississippi River. In the East, Hooker still faced Lee's army stretched along the Rappahannock River near Fredericksburg. Within the next three months, a series of ferocious battles in both the East and the West decisively improved the prospects of the Union and lifted Lincoln's spirits. In early May, however, Lincoln had few omens of the good fortune that lay ahead.

During the first week of May, Hooker finally launched an attack on Lee's defenses near Chancellorsville. Although Hooker's men outnumbered the Confederates nearly two to one, Lee's soldiers outmaneuvered, outsmarted, and outfought the Yankees, inflicting another humiliating and costly defeat on the Army of the Potomac and forcing Hooker to retreat back to the northern side of the Rappahannock (see Map 3, page 87).

In mid-May, Lee formulated a bold plan to capitalize on his victory at Chancellorsville and the fighting prowess of his men by racing up the Shenandoah Valley and invading Pennsylvania. Marching into the northern heartland would allow his army to forage supplies from Yankee civilians; to embarrass Lincoln, the Republican party, and the Union army; to encourage Democratic opponents of the war in the North; and maybe even to force Lincoln to concede defeat and recognize the independence of the Confederacy.

As Lee's movement toward the North became clear, Lincoln sensed a great opportunity. If Union commanders would attack Lee while his army was separated from secure supplies and easy reinforcements, the Army of Northern Virginia might finally be defeated. Lacking confidence that Hooker would take action, Lincoln replaced him with General George G. Meade in late June. In just a few days, Meade's army collided repeatedly with Lee's invaders at Gettysburg, Pennsylvania. In pivotal, deadly battles on July 1–3 that featured heroics on both sides, Union troops finally forced Lee's army to retreat from the battlefield and to abandon the northern invasion. For Lincoln, the Union triumph at Gettysburg was tempered by frustration that Lee's army escaped destruction.

Celebrations of the great victory at Gettysburg were still under way when word reached Lincoln that Grant, in a campaign Lincoln termed "one of the most brilliant in the world,"[10] had captured Vicksburg (see Map 4). The heavily defended city sat atop high bluffs on the east bank of the Mississippi River. After making a fruitless effort to circumvent the city during the winter of 1862–1863 by cutting a way through the tangled swamps west of the river, Grant marched his soldiers in April along the western bank of the river across a neck of land that jutted toward Vicksburg. Under cover of darkness in mid-April, Grant ran a fleet of troop transports and gunboats down the river, directly past Vicksburg's artillery batteries, which fired on but failed to destroy the Union flotilla. By the end of April, Grant's soldiers rendezvoused with the boats about thirty miles south of Vicksburg. Instead of continuing down the river to link up with the Union army under General Nathaniel Banks, which was attempting to capture the southernmost Confederate stronghold on the river at Port Hudson, Louisiana, Grant adopted a far bolder strategy, against the advice of his subordinate commanders. To divert Confederate defenders, he sent General William T. Sherman's men up the Yazoo River north of Vicksburg. Then Grant ferried his soldiers across the Mississippi unopposed to capture Port Gibson and Grand Gulf on

[10] Lincoln to Isaac N. Arnold, May 26, 1863, *CW*, VI, 230.

Map 4. *Grant's Vicksburg Campaign, April–July 1863*

Grant's bold campaign converted what seemed to be Vicksburg's impregnable position on the Mississippi River into an inescapable trap for Confederate defenders.

Battle Cry of Freedom: The Era of the Civil War by McPherson (1988). Map "The Vicksburg Campaign April–July 1863," p. 632, © 1988 by Oxford University Press, Inc. By permission of Oxford University Press, Inc.

May 1 and 2. Rather than then crossing the Big Black River and marching north directly to Vicksburg, Grant abandoned his source of supplies on the Mississippi and headed east toward Jackson, Mississippi, where a large Confederate army menaced the rear of any Union attack on Vicksburg. In a series of major engagements in mid-May, Grant's army defeated Confederate forces at Jackson and destroyed much of the city, then pushed west toward Vicksburg, defeating rebel defenders at Champion's Hill on May 16 and Big Black River on May 17 to bring Vicksburg under siege. The siege was finally broken when the Confederates surrendered the city on July 4. Grant's Vicksburg campaign was the most brilliantly executed military strategy of the war, and unlike Lee's invasion of the North, Grant's campaign achieved its objective. For a brief time, Lincoln believed that the end of the war was near.

39

Letter to Ulysses S. Grant

July 13, 1863

Executive Mansion
Washington

Major General Grant
My dear General
I do not remember that you and I ever met personally. I write this now as a grateful acknowledgment for the almost inestimable service you have done the country. I wish to say a word further. When you first reached the vicinity of Vicksburg, I thought you should do, what you finally did— march the troops across the neck, run the batteries with the transports, and thus go below; and I never had any faith, except a general hope that you knew better than I, that the Yazoo Pass expedition, and the like, could succeed. When you got below, and took Port-Gibson, Grand Gulf, and vicinity, I thought you should go down the river and join Gen. Banks; and when you turned Northward East of the Big Black, I feared it was a mistake. I now wish to make the personal acknowledgment that you were right, and I was wrong.

Yours very truly
A. LINCOLN

Lincoln remained frustrated that Meade, the commander of the Army of the Potomac, failed to show the relentless will to engage and attempt to destroy the enemy that Grant had exhibited. He expressed his frustration in the following letter, which he decided not to send in order to avoid offending Meade.

40

Letter to George G. Meade

July 14, 1863

Executive Mansion
Washington

Major General Meade

I have just seen your despatch to Gen. Halleck, asking to be relieved of your command, because of a supposed censure of mine.[11] I am very—*very*—grateful to you for the magnificient success you gave the cause of the country at Gettysburg; and I am sorry now to be the author of the slightest pain to you. But I was in such deep distress myself that I could not restrain some expression of it. I had been oppressed nearly ever since the battles at Gettysburg, by what appeared to be evidences that . . . [you] were not seeking a collision with the enemy, but were trying to get him across the [Potomac] river without another battle. What these evidences were, if you please, I hope to tell you at some time, when we shall both feel better. The case, summarily stated is this. You fought and beat the enemy at Gettysburg; and, of course, to say the least, his loss was as great as yours. He retreated; and you did not, as it seemed to me, pressingly pursue him; but a flood in the river detained him, till, by slow degrees, you were again upon him. You had at least twenty thousand veteran troops directly with you, and as many more raw ones within supporting distance, all in addition to those who fought with you at Gettysburg; while it was not possible that he had received a single recruit; and yet you stood and let the flood run down, bridges be built, and the enemy move away at his leisure, without attacking him. . . . Again, my dear general, I do not believe you appreciate the magnitude of the misfortune involved in Lee's escape.

---

[11] Meade had offered his resignation in response to Halleck's message urging him to pursue and attack Lee after the battle of Gettysburg. Halleck explained that "the escape of Lee's army without another battle created great dissatisfaction in the mind of the President, and it will require an active and energetic pursuit on your part to remove the impression that it has not been sufficiently active heretofore." *CW*, VI, 328.

He was within your easy grasp, and to have closed upon him would, in connection with our other late successes, have ended the war. As it is, the war will be prolonged indefinitely. If you could not safely attack Lee last monday, how can you possibly do so South of the [Potomac] river, when you can take with you very few more than two thirds of the force you then had in hand? It would be unreasonable to expect, and I do not expect you can now effect much. Your golden opportunity is gone, and I am distressed immeasureably because of it.

I beg you will not consider this a prossecution, or persecution of yourself. As you had learned that I was dissatisfied, I have thought it best to kindly tell you why.

POLITICS OF WAR AND FREEDOM

To replenish the army's manpower, Congress passed the nation's first draft law on March 3, 1863, bringing the war to the doorstep of nearly every household in the North. Each congressional district was required to supply a certain number of recruits, based on its population of men between twenty and forty-five years old. Since volunteers counted toward a district's quota, many places offered bounties to men who would enlist and thereby reduce the number of men subject to the draft. To supplement the draft, Lincoln declared an amnesty for soldiers who were absent without leave and called on northern citizens to help enforce enlistments.

Resistance to the draft broke out in communities across the North, especially where Democratic politicians denounced the war and emancipation. In New York City, resistance exploded into a full-scale riot on July 13, just as men were to be called for the draft. The rioters, many of them Irish laborers, pummeled any black person they could find, burned homes in black neighborhoods, and lynched several African Americans from lampposts. The riots continued for four days until order was restored by several regiments of Union soldiers who dashed from Pennsylvania, where they had fought at Gettysburg, to turn their weapons on fellow northerners. In all, more than one hundred people, mostly black Americans, died in the riots, and several hundred others suffered wounds. Above all else, the New York riots illustrated that the draft could ignite a powder keg of political unrest, especially because drafted men would be fighting not just to restore the Union but also to free black slaves.

The Emancipation Proclamation, the draft law passed by Congress in March 1863, the halting progress of northern armies until the summer of 1863, the seemingly endless lists of dead and wounded published in newspapers throughout the Union, and Lincoln's continued willingness to suspend the writ of habeas corpus combined to strengthen a desire to end the war, especially among northern Democrats. Growing peace sentiment in the North threatened to undermine the recruitment of soldiers and to subvert Lincoln's dual war goals of union and freedom. Even the many Democratic politicians who supported the war often intensely opposed emancipation both because they considered black people inferior to whites and because the abolition of slavery fundamentally changed the character of the Union. Newly elected Democratic legislators in Illinois and Indiana, for example, passed resolutions calling for a cease-fire and a peace conference to restore the Union as it was—that is, with slavery. The seriousness of Democratic opposition to the war caused Lincoln, as he explained to a Republican senator in January 1863, to fear " 'the fire in the rear'—meaning the Democracy . . .— more than our military chances."[12]

Lincoln responded to Democratic criticisms in two ways. First, he defended his legal and constitutional authority to enforce the draft, to suspend the writ of habeas corpus, and to issue the Emancipation Proclamation. Second, he explained his views of the historical significance of the war not just for the United States, but for the cause of democracy and freedom throughout the world. Lincoln took advantage of an invitation to address a Republican rally in Springfield, Illinois, to send a public letter that mounted a spirited defense of his policies.

---

[12] Charles Sumner to Francis Lieber, January 17, 1863, in Edward L. Pierce, ed., *Memoir and Letters of Charles Sumner* (4 vols.; Boston, 1877–1893), IV, 114.

41

Letter to James C. Conkling

August 26, 1863

Executive Mansion
Washington

Hon. James C. Conkling[13]

My Dear Sir.

Your letter inviting me to attend a mass-meeting of unconditional Union-men, to be held at the Capital of Illinois, on the 3d day of September, has been received.

It would be very agreeable to me, to thus meet my old friends, at my own home; but I can not, just now, be absent from here, so long as a visit there, would require.

The meeting is to be of all those who maintain unconditional devotion to the Union; and I am sure my old political friends will thank me for tendering, as I do, the nation's gratitude to those other noble men, whom no partizan malice, or partizan hope, can make false to the nation's life.

There are those who are dissatisfied with me. To such I would say: You desire peace; and you blame me that we do not have it. But how can we attain it? There are but three conceivable ways. First, to suppress the rebellion by force of arms. This, I am trying to do. Are you for it? If you are, so far we are agreed. If you are not for it, a second way is, to give up the Union. I am against this. Are you for it? If you are, you should say so plainly. If you are not for *force*, nor yet for *dissolution*, there only remains some imaginable *compromise*. I do not believe any compromise, embracing the maintenance of the Union, is now possible. All I learn, leads to a directly opposite belief. The strength of the rebellion, is its military—its army. That army dominates all the country, and all the people, within its range. Any offer of terms made by any man or men within that range, in opposition to that army, is simply nothing for the present; because such man or men, have no power whatever to enforce their side of a compromise, if one were made with them. To illustrate—Suppose refugees from the South, and peace men of the North, get together in convention, and frame and proclaim a compromise embracing a restoration of the Union; in what way can that compromise be used to keep Lee's army out of Pennsylvania? Meade's army can keep Lee's army out of Pennsylvania; and, I think, can ultimately drive it out of existence. But no paper compromise,

---

[13] Conkling, a lawyer and ardent Republican in Springfield, Illinois, had been Lincoln's friend for many years.

to which the controllers of Lee's army are not agreed, can, at all, affect that army. In an effort at such compromise we should waste time, which the enemy would improve to our disadvantage; and that would be all. A compromise, to be effective, must be made either with those who control the rebel army, or with the people first liberated from the domination of that army, by the success of our own army. Now allow me to assure you, that no word or intimation, from that rebel army, or from any of the men controlling it, in relation to any peace compromise, has ever come to my knowledge or belief. All charges and insinuations to the contrary, are deceptive and groundless. And I promise you, that if any such proposition shall hereafter come, it shall not be rejected, and kept a secret from you. I freely acknowledge myself the servant of the people, according to the bond of service—the United States constitution; and that, as such, I am responsible to them.

But, to be plain, you[14] are dissatisfied with me about the negro. Quite likely there is a difference of opinion between you and myself upon that subject. I certainly wish that all men could be free, while I suppose you do not. Yet I have neither adopted, nor proposed any measure, which is not consistent with even your view, provided you are for the Union. I suggested compensated emancipation, to which you replied you wished not to be taxed to buy negroes. But I had not asked you to be taxed to buy negroes, except in such way, as to save you from greater taxation to save the Union exclusively by other means.

You dislike the emancipation proclamation; and, perhaps, would have it retracted. You say it is unconstitutional—I think differently. I think the constitution invests its commander-in-chief, with the law of war, in time of war. The most that can be said, if so much, is, that slaves are property. Is there—has there ever been—any question that by the law of war, property, both of enemies and friends, may be taken when needed? And is it not needed when ever taking it, helps us, or hurts the enemy? Armies, the world over, destroy enemies' property when they can not use it; and even destroy their own to keep it from the enemy. Civilized belligerents do all in their power to help themselves, or hurt the enemy, except a few things regarded as barbarous or cruel. Among the exceptions are the massacre of vanquished foes, and non-combatants, male and female.

But the proclamation, as law, either is valid, or is not valid. If it is not valid, it needs no retraction. If it is valid, it can not be retracted, any more than the dead can be brought to life. Some of you profess to think its retraction would operate favorably for the Union. Why better *after* the retraction, than *before* the issue? There was more than a year and a half of trial to suppress the rebellion before the proclamation issued, the last

---

[14] Here and subsequently Lincon is referring to those who oppose his policies.

one hundred days of which passed under an explicit notice[15] that it was coming, unless averted by those in revolt, returning to their allegiance. The war has certainly progressed as favorably for us, since the issue of the proclamation as before. I know as fully as one can know the opinions of others, that some of the commanders of our armies in the field who have given us our most important successes, believe the emancipation policy, and the use of colored troops, constitute the heaviest blow yet dealt to the rebellion; and that, at least one of those important successes [at Milliken's Bend during Grant's attack on Vicksburg] could not have been achieved when it was, but for the aid of black soldiers. Among the commanders holding these views are some who have never had any affinity with what is called abolitionism, or with republican party politics; but who hold them purely as military opinions. I submit these opinions as being entitled to some weight against the objections, often urged, that emancipation, and arming the blacks, are unwise as military measures, and were not adopted, as such, in good faith.

You say you will not fight to free negroes. Some of them seem willing to fight for you; but, no matter. Fight you, then, exclusively to save the Union. I issued the proclamation on purpose to aid you in saving the Union. Whenever you shall have conquered all resistance to the Union, if I shall urge you to continue fighting, it will be an apt time, then, for you to declare you will not fight to free negroes.

I thought that in your struggle for the Union, to whatever extent the negroes should cease helping the enemy, to that extent it weakened the enemy in his resistance to you. Do you think differently? I thought that whatever negroes can be got to do as soldiers, leaves just so much less for white soldiers to do, in saving the Union. Does it appear otherwise to you? But negroes, like other people, act upon motives. Why should they do any thing for us, if we will do nothing for them? If they stake their lives for us, they must be prompted by the strongest motive—even the promise of freedom. And the promise being made, must be kept.

The signs look better. The Father of Waters[16] again goes unvexed to the sea. Thanks to the great North-West for it. Nor yet wholly to them. Three hundred miles up, they met New-England, Empire, Key-Stone, and Jersey, hewing their way right and left.[17] The Sunny South too, in more colors than one, also lent a hand. On the spot, their part of the history was jotted down in black and white. The job was a great national one; and let none be banned who bore an honorable part in it. And while those who have cleared the great river may well be proud, even that is not all. It is

---

[15] The Preliminary Emanicipation Proclamation, issued September 22, 1862 (Document 32).

[16] The Mississippi River.

[17] Lincoln is referring to Union regiments from different regions and states responsible for the great victories during the summer.

hard to say that anything has been more bravely, and well done, than at Antietam, Murfreesboro, Gettysburg, and on many fields of lesser note. Nor must Uncle Sam's Web-feet[18] be forgotten. At all the watery margins they have been present. Not only on the deep sea, the broad bay, and the rapid river, but also up the narrow muddy bayou, and wherever the ground was a little damp, they have been, and made their tracks. Thanks to all. For the great republic—for the principle it lives by, and keeps alive—for man's vast future,—thanks to all.

Peace does not appear so distant as it did. I hope it will come soon, and come to stay; and so come as to be worth the keeping in all future time. It will then have been proved that, among free men, there can be no successful appeal from the ballot to the bullet; and that they who take such appeal are sure to lose their case, and pay the cost. And then, there will be some black men who can remember that, with silent tongue, and clenched teeth, and steady eye, and well-poised bayonet, they have helped mankind on to this great consummation; while, I fear, there will be some white ones, unable to forget that, with malignant heart, and deceitful speech, they have strove to hinder it.

Still let us not be over-sanguine of a speedy final triumph. Let us be quite sober. Let us diligently apply the means, never doubting that a just God, in his own good time, will give us the rightful result.

Yours very truly
A. LINCOLN

[18] The Union navy.

Lincoln crystallized his thoughts about the historical significance of the war in his brief speech at the dedication of the massive military cemetery at Gettysburg. Eventually recognized as the most eloquent speech ever given by an American president, the Gettysburg Address explained Lincoln's view of why the war must go on, despite the horrendous sacrifices of life and limb. Without mentioning slavery, the address answered those who were tired of the war and were opposed to emancipation by proclaiming that the soldiers at Gettysburg had died to defend democracy and preserve the Union. Lincoln ennobled the Union cause by attaching the profession of human equality in the Declaration of Independence to both the Union and the war. The address fused his war goals of union and freedom with equality.

42

The Gettysburg Address

November 19, 1863

Four score and seven years ago our fathers brought forth on this continent, a new nation, conceived in Liberty, and dedicated to the proposition that all men are created equal.

Now we are engaged in a great civil war, testing whether that nation, or any nation so conceived and so dedicated, can long endure. We are met on a great battle-field of that war. We have come to dedicate a portion of that field, as a final resting place for those who here gave their lives that that nation might live. It is altogether fitting and proper that we should do this.

But, in a larger sense, we can not dedicate—we can not consecrate—we can not hallow—this ground. The brave men, living and dead, who struggled here, have consecrated it, far above our poor power to add or detract. The world will little note, nor long remember what we say here, but it can never forget what they did here. It is for us the living, rather, to be dedicated here to the unfinished work which they who fought here have thus far so nobly advanced. It is rather for us to be here dedicated to the great task remaining before us—that from these honored dead we take increased devotion to that cause for which they gave the last full measure of devotion—that we here highly resolve that these dead shall not have died in vain—that this nation, under God, shall have a new birth of freedom—and that government of the people, by the people, for the people, shall not perish from the earth.

ABRAHAM LINCOLN

7

Defending a New Birth of Freedom

For Lincoln, defending the nation's new birth of freedom required action on three closely related fronts. First, the Union army had to make progress on the battlefield. But the army could not be reinforced with the necessary men and supplies unless the increasingly war-weary people of the North supported Lincoln's determination to fight to restore the Union without slavery. In regions of the Confederacy occupied by the Union army, a second front demanded attention. Some pathway needed to be marked out for bringing seceded states back into the Union without empowering the rebels—thereby undermining rather than reuniting the nation—or violating the pledge of freedom to millions of slaves. Any plan for reconstruction of the Union consistent with a new birth of freedom depended, of course, on the success of Union armies and the willingness of northern citizens to insist that reunion could only be achieved without slavery. The third front lay along the partisan divide within the northern electorate. Lincoln had to defend his Republican vision of reunion by defeating Confederate armies against some Democrats' promise to stop the war and restore the Union as it was, with slavery. Unless the Union achieved military victory by Election Day in November 1864, a new birth of freedom for the nation depended on Lincoln's re-election to a second term. Lincoln had to match his generals' military strategy with his own adroit maneuvers through dangerous political terrain.

WAR WITHOUT END

Even after the failure of General Robert E. Lee's invasion of the North in the summer of 1863, the military strategy of the Confederacy focused ultimately on peace sentiment in the North. If Confederate armies could continue to inflict heavy casualties on Union forces and prolong the war, northern citizens might decide that it was preferable to stop fighting and to recognize Confederate independence. Confederate armies did not necessarily need to win battles to contribute to this strategy. They had to stay intact, adopt a largely defensive posture, and maintain their ability to send potent political messages northward in the reports of Union men killed and wounded. Essentially, the Confederacy gambled that the "awful arithmetic" that heartened Lincoln (see the introduction to chapter 6) would demoralize the northern people.

Lincoln understood that time favored the Confederate strategy, especially if Union armies could not make readily visible progress in capturing rebel strongholds and destroying southern armies. The North's superior resources of manpower and supplies would not matter if northerners decided that the war was not worth fighting, that they had had enough of sacrificing their men to a war with no end in sight. Lincoln needed victories now to reassure northern families that the war would end soon, before they were willing to accept peace at the price of Confederate independence.

After his spectacular success at Vicksburg, General Ulysses S. Grant took command of Union forces in eastern Tennessee and, in a series of complex and hard-fought engagements, succeeded in driving Confederate defenders from Chattanooga and Knoxville. Grant's multiple victories earned him fame throughout the North and made him an obvious choice to become commander of all Union armies. In February, Congress revived the rank of lieutenant general, last held by George Washington, and in early March Lincoln promoted Grant to that rank and made him general in chief, second in command only to the president. Grant quickly moved his headquarters from the West to the Virginia theater and prepared for a campaign to replicate his western successes in the East. Lincoln's confidence in Grant—in contrast, for example, to his previous doubts about Generals McClellan and Hooker—could hardly have been expressed more forthrightly than in the following letter, written shortly before the start of Grant's eastern campaign.

43

Letter to Ulysses S. Grant

April 30, 1864

Executive Mansion
Washington

Lieutenant General Grant.

Not expecting to see you again before the Spring campaign opens, I wish to express, in this way, my entire satisfaction with what you have done up to this time, so far as I understand it. The particulars of your plans I neither know, or seek to know. You are vigilant and self-reliant; and, pleased with this, I wish not to obtrude any constraints or restraints upon you. While I am very anxious that any great disaster, or the capture of our men in great numbers, shall be avoided, I know these points are less likely to escape your attention than they would be mine. If there is anything wanting which is within my power to give, do not fail to let me know it.

And now with a brave Army, and a just cause, may God sustain you.

Yours very truly
A. LINCOLN

Grant's plan called for an attack by all Union armies to begin on May 5. A simultaneous assault across the entire line from Virginia to Mississippi was intended to immobilize Confederate defenders and to prevent reinforcements from being shifted to repulse major Union offensives. When Grant explained his plan, Lincoln—who had advocated the concept for a long time—declared, "As we say out West, if a man can't skin he must hold a leg while somebody else does."[1] The Confederate armies, however, did not hold still to be skinned; they fought back fiercely.

Grant, like other commanders before him in the Virginia theater, became bogged down. Between May 5 and 7 the ferocity and skill of Confederate defenders turned back Yankee attacks in the Wilderness—a heavily wooded region about fifteen miles west of Fredericksburg—and between May 8 and 21 at Spotsylvania—about ten miles southeast of the Wilderness (see Map 3, page 87). During these battles, Grant

[1] Ulysses S. Grant, *Personal Memoirs of U. S. Grant* (2 vols.; New York, 1885–1886), II, 143.

Figure 5. *General Grant at City Point, Virginia*

This photograph, taken during the siege of Petersburg, Virginia, between mid-June 1864 and early April 1865, shows Grant wearing the insignia of his rank but obviously not concerned with a spit-and-polish image. It conveys Grant's relentless focus and composure, so admired by Lincoln.

Reproduced from the Collections of the Library of Congress.

suffered more than thirty thousand casualties. But unlike other commanders in the East, Grant did not retreat. He continued to engage Lee's army, relentlessly moving southeast toward Richmond. In early June at Cold Harbor, about ten miles outside the city, Lee inflicted another bloody defeat on Grant's men. Grant then moved most of his army south of Richmond to attack Petersburg. After the failure of his initial assaults on Petersburg's defenses, Grant settled into a siege by June 18. For the next ten months, Grant besieged the city, largely immobilizing both Lee's army and his own. By mid-August, with the November presidential election on the horizon, the discouraging reports from the battlefield and the continuing draft created great unease in the North.

PLANNING RECONSTRUCTION

Union military successes in the Mississippi Valley during the summer of 1863 presented Lincoln with an opportunity to design a plan for bringing rebel states back into the Union—a plan he continued to promote for the remainder of his presidency. In theory, any such plan contradicted Lincoln's refusal to recognize secession as a reality. In practice, however, Lincoln knew that he could not permit rebel states that had been conquered by the Union army to come back into the Union as if nothing had happened and to continue to fight politically for what they had lost on the battlefield. Lincoln proposed that, as a prerequisite for the restoration of a rebel state to the Union, a small core of loyal unionists would adopt a new state constitution that recognized emancipation. Lincoln was willing to allow the reconstructed states a great deal of latitude in defining the new status of former slaves. By setting a relatively low and minimally punitive threshold for readmission, Lincoln hoped to show Confederates that, if they stopped fighting, it would be fairly easy and painless for them to regain their former status in the Union. Lincoln was also fully aware that if new state governments were formed by unionists, the elected officials from those states would likely be Republicans, who—not coincidentally—would support his policies and his re-election to a second term. Lincoln's plan for reconstruction would both restore the Union and strengthen Republican control of the federal government by supplementing northern Republicans with newly hatched southern Republicans. Designing such a plan, however, proved easier than implementing it.

44

Letter to Nathaniel P. Banks

August 5, 1863

Executive Mansion
Washington

My dear General Banks[2]

Being a poor correspondent is the only apology I offer for not having sooner tendered my thanks for your very successful, and very valuable military operations this year. The final stroke in opening the Mississippi never should, and I think never will, be forgotten. . . .

Governor Boutwell[3] read me to-day that part of your letter to him, which relates to Louisiana affairs. While I very well know what I would be glad for Louisiana to do, it is quite a different thing for me to assume direction of the matter. I would be glad for her to make a new Constitution recognizing the emancipation proclamation, and adopting emancipation in those parts of the state to which the proclamation does not apply.[4] And while she is at it, I think it would not be objectionable for her to adopt some practical system by which the two races could gradually live themselves out of their old relation to each other, and both come out better prepared for the new. Education for young blacks should be included in the plan. After all, the power, or element, of "contract" may be sufficient for this probationary period; and, by it's simplicity, and flexibility, may be the better.[5]

As an anti-slavery man I have a motive to desire emancipation, which pro-slavery men do not have; but even they have strong enough reason to thus place themselves again under the shield of the Union; and to thus perpetually hedge against the recurrence of the scenes through which we are now passing.

---

[2] Banks, a former governor of Massachusetts and a prominent Republican, had commanded the Union force that had captured Port Hudson, Louisiana, on July 9, 1863, finally eliminating the last Confederate choke point on the Mississippi River. He currently commanded the Department of the Gulf, which included Louisiana.

[3] George S. Boutwell, former governor of Massachusetts and a fervently antislavery Republican, was elected to Congress in 1863.

[4] The Emancipation Proclamation did not apply to those parts of Louisiana under the control of the Union army on January 1, 1863, which included New Orleans and the surrounding parishes.

[5] Lincoln is suggesting that former slaves may enter into contracts to work for white people. In theory, the legal limits of written contracts, mutually agreed upon, would replace the almost limitless coercions of slavery.

Gov. Shepley[6] has informed me that Mr. Durant[7] is now taking a registry, with a view to the election of a Constitutional convention in Louisiana. This, to me, appears proper. If such convention were to ask my views, I could present little else than what I now say to you. I think the thing should be pushed forward, so that if possible, it's mature work may reach here by the meeting of Congress.

For my own part I think I shall not, in any event, retract the emancipation proclamation; nor, as executive, ever return to slavery any person who is free by the terms of that proclamation, or by any of the acts of Congress.

If Louisiana shall send members to Congress, their admission to seats will depend, as you know, upon the respective Houses, and not upon the President.

If these views can be of any advantage in giving shape, and impetus, to action there, I shall be glad for you to use them prudently for that object. Of course you will confer with intelligent and trusty citizens of the State. . . . Still it is perhaps better to not make the letter generally public.

Yours very truly
A. LINCOLN

[6] George F. Shepley, a Union general who had been a well-known lawyer in Maine, had been appointed military governor of Louisiana by Lincoln in June 1862.
[7] Thomas J. Durant was attorney general of Louisiana. Lincoln was informed that Durant was registering voters who would participate in electing delegates to a state constitutional convention.

In his annual address to Congress in December 1863, Lincoln reviewed military and political developments during the last year and publicly outlined his plans for reconstruction. He explained that he believed rebels should be required to take an oath to uphold both the federal constitution and emancipation and that such a requirement was within his constitutional authority.

45

Annual Message to Congress

December 8, 1863

. . . When Congress assembled a year ago the war had already lasted nearly twenty months, and there had been many conflicts on both land and sea, with varying results.

The rebellion had been pressed back into reduced limits; yet the tone of public feeling and opinion, at home and abroad, was not satisfactory. With other signs, the popular elections, then just past, indicated uneasiness among ourselves, while amid much that was cold and menacing the kindest words coming from Europe were uttered in accents of pity, that we were too blind to surrender a hopeless cause. Our commerce was suffering greatly by a few armed vessels built upon and furnished from foreign shores, and we were threatened with such additions from the same quarter as would sweep our trade from the sea and raise our blockade. We had failed to elicit from European governments anything hopeful upon this subject. The preliminary emancipation proclamation, issued in September, was running its assigned period to the beginning of the new year. A month later the final proclamation came, including the announcement that colored men of suitable condition would be received into the war service. The policy of emancipation, and of employing black soldiers, gave to the future a new aspect, about which hope, and fear, and doubt contended in uncertain conflict. According to our political system, as a matter of civil administration, the general government had no lawful power to effect emancipation in any State, and for a long time it had been hoped that the rebellion could be suppressed without resorting to it as a military measure. It was all the while deemed possible that the necessity for it might come, and that if it should, the crisis of the contest would then be presented. It came, and as was anticipated, it was followed by dark and doubtful days. Eleven months having now passed, we are permitted to take another review. The rebel borders are pressed still further back, and by the complete opening of the Mississippi the country dominated by the rebellion is divided into distinct parts, with no practical communication between them. Tennessee and Arkansas have been substantially cleared of insurgent control, and influential citizens in each, owners of slaves and advocates of slavery at the beginning of the rebellion, now declare openly for emancipation in their respective States. Of those States not included in the emancipation proclamation, Maryland, and Missouri, neither of which three years ago would tolerate any restraint upon the extension of slavery into new territories, only dispute now as to the best mode of removing it within their own limits.

Of those who were slaves at the beginning of the rebellion, full one hundred thousand are now in the United States military service, about one-half of which number actually bear arms in the ranks; thus giving the double advantage of taking so much labor from the insurgent cause, and supplying the places which otherwise must be filled with so many white men. So far as tested, it is difficult to say they are not as good soldiers as any. No servile insurrection, or tendency to violence or cruelty, has marked the measures of emancipation and arming the blacks. These measures have been much discussed in foreign countries, and contemporary with such discussion the tone of public sentiment there is much improved. At home the same measures have been fully discussed, supported, criticised, and denounced, and the annual elections following are highly encouraging to those whose official duty it is to bear the country through this great trial. Thus we have the new reckoning. The crisis which threatened to divide the friends of the Union is past.

Looking now to the present and future, and with reference to a resumption of the national authority within the States wherein that authority has been suspended, I have thought fit to issue a proclamation, a copy of which is herewith transmitted [Document 46]. On examination of this proclamation it will appear, as is believed, that nothing is attempted beyond what is amply justified by the Constitution. True, the form of an oath is given, but no man is coerced to take it. The man is only promised a pardon in case he voluntarily takes the oath. The Constitution authorizes the Executive to grant or withhold the pardon at his own absolute discretion; and this includes the power to grant on terms, as is fully established by judicial and other authorities.

It is also proffered that if, in any of the States named, a State government shall be, in the mode prescribed, set up, such government shall be recognized and guarantied by the United States, and that under it the State shall, on the constitutional conditions, be protected against invasion and domestic violence. The constitutional obligation of the United States to guaranty to every State in the Union a republican form of government, and to protect the State, in the cases stated, is explicit and full. But why tender the benefits of this provision only to a State government set up in this particular way? This section of the Constitution contemplates a case wherein the element within a State, favorable to republican government, in the Union, may be too feeble for an opposite and hostile element external to, or even within the State; and such are precisely the cases with which we are now dealing.

An attempt to guaranty and protect a revived State government, constructed in whole, or in preponderating part, from the very element against whose hostility and violence it is to be protected, is simply absurd. There must be a test by which to separate the opposing elements, so as to build only from the sound; and that test is a sufficiently liberal one, which accepts as sound whoever will make a sworn recantation of his former unsoundness.

But if it be proper to require, as a test of admission to the political body, an oath of allegiance to the Constitution of the United States, and to the Union under it, why also to the laws and proclamations in regard to slavery? Those laws and proclamations were enacted and put forth for the purpose of aiding in the suppression of the rebellion. To give them their fullest effect, there had to be a pledge for their maintenance. In my judgment they have aided, and will further aid, the cause for which they were intended. To now abandon them would be not only to relinquish a lever of power, but would also be a cruel and an astounding breach of faith. I may add at this point, that while I remain in my present position I shall not attempt to retract or modify the emancipation proclamation; nor shall I return to slavery any person who is free by the terms of that proclamation, or by any of the acts of Congress. For these and other reasons it is thought best that support of these measures shall be included in the oath; and it is believed the Executive may lawfully claim it in return for pardon and restoration of forfeited rights, which he has clear constitutional power to withhold altogether, or grant upon the terms which he shall deem wisest for the public interest. It should be observed, also, that this part of the oath is subject to the modifying and abrogating power of legislation and supreme judicial decision.

The proposed acquiescence of the national Executive in any reasonable temporary State arrangement for the freed people is made with the view of possibly modifying the confusion and destitution which must, at best, attend all classes by a total revolution of labor throughout whole States. It is hoped that the already deeply afflicted people in those States may be somewhat more ready to give up the cause of their affliction, if, to this extent, this vital matter be left to themselves; while no power of the national Executive to prevent an abuse is abridged by the proposition.

The suggestion in the proclamation as to maintaining the political framework of the States on what is called reconstruction, is made in the hope that it may do good without danger of harm. It will save labor and avoid great confusion.

But why any proclamation now upon this subject? This question is beset with the conflicting views that the step might be delayed too long or be taken too soon. In some States the elements for resumption seem ready for action, but remain inactive, apparently for want of a rallying point—a plan of action. Why shall A adopt the plan of B, rather than B that of A? And if A and B should agree, how can they know but that the general government here will reject their plan? By the proclamation a plan is presented which may be accepted by them as a rallying point, and which they are assured in advance will not be rejected here. This may bring them to act sooner than they otherwise would.

The objections to a premature presentation of a plan by the national Executive consists in the danger of committals on points which could be more safely left to further developments. Care has been taken to so shape the document as to avoid embarrassments from this source. Saying that, on certain terms, certain classes will be pardoned, with rights restored, it is not said that other classes, or other terms, will never be included. Saying that reconstruction will be accepted if presented in a specified way, it is not said it will never be accepted in any other way.

The movements, by State action, for emancipation in several of the States, not included in the emancipation proclamation, are matters of profound gratulation. And while I do not repeat in detail what I have heretofore so earnestly urged upon this subject, my general views and feelings remain unchanged; and I trust that Congress will omit no fair opportunity of aiding these important steps to a great consummation.

In the midst of other cares, however important, we must not lose sight of the fact that the war power is still our main reliance. To that power alone can we look, yet for a time, to give confidence to the people in the contested regions, that the insurgent power will not again overrun them. Until that confidence shall be established, little can be done anywhere for what is called reconstruction. Hence our chiefest care must still be directed to the army and navy, who have thus far borne their harder part so nobly and well. And it may be esteemed fortunate that in giving the greatest efficiency to these indispensable arms, we do also honorably recognize the gallant men, from commander to sentinel, who compose them, and to whom, more than to others, the world must stand indebted for the home of freedom disenthralled, regenerated, enlarged, and perpetuated.

ABRAHAM LINCOLN

46

Proclamation of Amnesty and Reconstruction
December 8, 1863

BY THE PRESIDENT OF THE UNITED STATES OF AMERICA: A PROCLAMATION.

Whereas, in and by the Constitution of the United States, it is provided that the President "shall have power to grant reprieves and pardons for offences against the United States, except in cases of impeachment"; and

Whereas a rebellion now exists whereby the loyal State governments of several States have for a long time been subverted, and many persons have committed and are now guilty of treason against the United States; and

Whereas, with reference to said rebellion and treason, laws have been enacted by Congress declaring forfeitures and confiscation of property and liberation of slaves, all upon terms and conditions therein stated, and also declaring that the President was thereby authorized at any time thereafter, by proclamation, to extend to persons who may have participated in the existing rebellion, . . . pardon and amnesty,[8] with such exceptions

---

[8] A pardon is an exemption from punishment for a crime (in this case, treason) for which a person has already been convicted. An amnesty is an exemption from prosecution for a criminal act (again, treason).

and at such times and on such conditions as he may deem expedient for the public welfare; and . . .

Whereas, with reference to said rebellion, the President of the United States has issued several proclamations, with provisions in regard to the liberation of slaves; and

Whereas it is now desired by some persons heretofore engaged in said rebellion to resume their allegiance to the United States, and to reinaugurate loyal State governments within and for their respective States; therefore,

I, Abraham Lincoln, President of the United States, do proclaim, declare, and make known to all persons who have, directly or by implication, participated in the existing rebellion, except as hereinafter excepted, that a full pardon is hereby granted to them and each of them, with restoration of all rights of property, except as to slaves, . . . and upon the condition that every such person shall take and subscribe an oath, and thenceforward keep and maintain said oath inviolate; and which oath shall be registered for permanent preservation, and shall be of the tenor and effect following, to wit:

I, ———, do solemnly swear, in presence of Almighty God, that I will henceforth faithfully support, protect and defend the Constitution of the United States, and the union of the States thereunder; and that I will, in like manner, abide by and faithfully support all acts of Congress passed during the existing rebellion with reference to slaves, so long and so far as not repealed, modified or held void by Congress, or by decision of the Supreme Court; and that I will, in like manner, abide by and faithfully support all proclamations of the President made during the existing rebellion having reference to slaves, so long and so far as not modified or declared void by decision of the Supreme Court. So help me God.

The persons excepted from the benefits of the foregoing provisions are all who are, or shall have been, civil or diplomatic officers or agents of the so-called confederate government; all who have left judicial stations under the United States to aid the rebellion; all who are, or shall have been, military or naval officers of said so-called confederate government above the rank of colonel in the army, or of lieutenant in the navy; all who left seats in the United States Congress to aid the rebellion; all who resigned commissions in the army or navy of the United States, and afterwards aided the rebellion; and all who have engaged in any way in treating colored persons or white persons, in charge of such, otherwise than lawfully as prisoners of war, and which persons may have been found in the United States service, as soldiers, seamen, or in any other capacity.

And I do further proclaim, declare, and make known, that whenever, in any of the States of Arkansas, Texas, Louisiana, Mississippi, Tennessee, Alabama, Georgia, Florida, South Carolina, and North Carolina, a number of persons, not less than one-tenth in number of the votes cast in such State at the Presidential election of the year of our Lord one thousand eight hundred and sixty, each having taken the oath aforesaid and not having since violated it, and being a qualified voter by the election law of the State existing immediately before the so-called act of secession, and excluding all others, shall re-establish a State government which shall be republican, and in no wise contravening said oath, such shall be recognized as the true government of the State, and the State shall receive thereunder the benefits of the constitutional provision which declares that "The United States shall guaranty to every State in this union a republican form of government, and shall protect each of them against invasion; and, on application of the legislature, or the executive, (when the legislature cannot be convened,) against domestic violence."

And I do further proclaim, declare, and make known that any provision which may be adopted by such State government in relation to the freed people of such State, which shall recognize and declare their permanent freedom, provide for their education, and may yet be consistent, as a temporary arrangement, with their present condition as a laboring, landless, and homeless class, will not be objected to by the national Executive. And it is suggested as not improper, that, in constructing a loyal State government in any State, the name of the State, the boundary, the subdivisions, the constitution, and the general code of laws, as before the rebellion, be maintained, subject only to the modifications made necessary by the conditions hereinbefore stated. . . .

To avoid misunderstanding, it may be proper to say that this proclamation, so far as it relates to State governments, has no reference to States wherein loyal State governments have all the while been maintained. And for the same reason, it may be proper to further say that whether members sent to Congress from any State shall be admitted to seats, constitutionally rests exclusively with the respective Houses, and not to any extent with the Executive. And still further, that this proclamation is intended to present the people of the States wherein the national authority has been suspended, and loyal State governments have been subverted, a mode in and by which the national authority and loyal State governments may be re-established within said States, or in any of them; and, while the mode presented is the best the Executive can suggest, with his present impressions, it must not be understood that no other possible mode would be acceptable. . . .

ABRAHAM LINCOLN

47

Letter to Michael Hahn
March 13, 1864

Private

Executive Mansion
Washington

Hon. Michael Hahn[9]

My dear Sir:

I congratulate you on having fixed your name in history as the first-free-state Governor of Louisiana. Now you are about to have a Convention which, among other things, will probably define the elective franchise. I barely suggest for your private consideration, whether some of the colored people may not be let in—as, for instance, the very intelligent, and especially those who have fought gallantly in our ranks. They would probably help, in some trying time to come, to keep the jewel of liberty within the family of freedom. But this is only a suggestion, not to the public, but to you alone.[10]

Yours truly
A. LINCOLN

[9] Hahn was a New Orleans unionist who was supported by General Banks and was elected governor of Louisiana on February 22, 1864, winning the support of the majority of the eleven thousand voters who met the requirements of Lincoln's Proclamation of Amnesty and Reconstruction.

[10] In fact, the new state constitution adopted in September 1864 did not allow African Americans to vote.

Many Republicans in Congress believed that Lincoln's reconstruction plan was far too generous toward Confederates who were, after all, killing and maiming thousands of Union soldiers. On July 2, 1864, only a few days before adjournment, Congress passed a more demanding formula for reconstruction. The Wade-Davis bill—named for Benjamin F. Wade, the Ohio abolitionist who chaired the Senate committee that sponsored the bill, and Henry Winter Davis, the Maryland Republican who headed the House committee—required the abolition of slavery by an electorate composed of 50 percent of voters in the 1860 presidential election (as opposed to 10 percent in Lincoln's plan) who swore an oath that they had never aided the rebellion or voluntarily borne arms against the Union (an "ironclad oath" compared to the oath of future loyalty under Lincoln's plan). In addition to the more stringent criteria for readmission, the Wade-Davis bill asserted congressional rather than presidential power over reconstruction. Rather than veto the bill, Lincoln simply refused to sign it, reasserting both his authority and the general outline of his plan for reconstruction.

THE POLITICAL CAMPAIGN FOR UNION, FREEDOM, AND WAR

Beset by Republican critics for his caution and by Democratic foes for his refusal to stop the war and to abandon emancipation, Lincoln used the bully pulpit of the presidency to declare again and again his conviction that war was absolutely necessary to achieve the inseparable goals of Union and freedom. Without explicitly saying so, Lincoln was at the same time campaigning for re-election. Discouraging news from the battlefield made many northerners receptive to the idea of peace. Lincoln firmly believed that without military victory, the Union's new birth of freedom would be sacrificed to war weariness and the revitalization of slavery.

Although women could not vote, Lincoln had no doubts about their political influence. He seized opportunities to praise their contributions to the war effort and to solicit their continued support. Throughout the North, women organized local voluntary associations to send soldiers clothing, bandages, medicines, food, and other items. In June 1861, local groups coalesced into the United States Sanitary Commission, which, with Lincoln's approval, funneled goods purchased with private funds into the hands of soldiers at the front. The Sanitary Commission held fairs in many northern cities, selling homemade goods to raise money to aid soldiers. Lincoln praised women's efforts in his address to a Sanitary Commission fair in March 1864.

48

Remarks at Closing of Sanitary Fair, Washington, D.C.

March 18, 1864

Ladies and Gentlemen: I appear to say but a word. This extraordinary war in which we are engaged falls heavily upon all classes of people, but the most heavily upon the soldier. For it has been said, all that a man hath will he give for his life; and while all contribute of their substance the soldier puts his life at stake, and often yields it up in his country's cause. The highest merit, then, is due to the soldier. [Cheers.]

In this extraordinary war extraordinary developments have manifested themselves, such as have not been seen in former wars; and amongst these manifestations nothing has been more remarkable than these fairs for the relief of suffering soldiers and their families. And the chief agents in these fairs are the women of America. [Cheers.]

I am not accustomed to the use of the language of eulogy; I have never studied the art of paying compliments to women; but I must say that if all that has been said by orators and poets since the creation of the world in praise of woman were applied to the women of America, it would not do them justice for their conduct during this war. I will close by saying God bless the women of America! [Great applause.]

When a delegation from Kentucky met with Lincoln to express the dissatisfaction in their state about the enlistment of slaves in the Federal army, Lincoln explained why he had concluded that the Union could not be saved without the black soldiers made available by emancipation. In a widely reprinted letter, Lincoln summarized his argument for the absolute necessity of emancipation, thereby undercutting claims made by many northern Democrats that the Union could be restored without further bloodshed by negotiating a peace settlement that did not demand emancipation.

49

Letter to Albert G. Hodges

April 4, 1864

Executive Mansion
Washington

A. G. Hodges, Esq.[11]
Frankfort, Ky.

My dear Sir:
You ask me to put in writing the substance of what I verbally said the other day, in your presence, to Governor Bramlette[12] and Senator Dixon.[13] It was about as follows:

> I am naturally anti-slavery. If slavery is not wrong, nothing is wrong. I can not remember when I did not so think, and feel. And yet I have never understood that the Presidency conferred upon me an unrestricted right to act officially upon this judgment and feeling. It was in the oath I took that I would, to the best of my ability, preserve, protect, and defend the Constitution of the United States. I could not take the office without taking the oath. Nor was it my view that I might take an oath to get power, and break the oath in using the power. I understood, too, that in ordinary civil administration this oath even forbade me to practically indulge my primary abstract judgment on the moral question of slavery. I had publicly declared this many times, and in many ways. And I aver that, to this day, I have done no official act in mere deference to my abstract judgment and feeling on slavery. I did understand however, that my oath to preserve the constitution to the best of my ability, imposed upon me the duty of preserving, by every indispensable means, that government—that nation—of which that constitution was the organic law. Was it possible to lose the nation, and yet preserve the constitution? By general law life *and* limb must be protected; yet often a limb must be amputated to save a life; but a life is never wisely given to save a limb. I felt that measures, otherwise unconstitutional, might become lawful, by becoming indispensable to the preservation of the constitution, through the preservation of the nation. Right or wrong, I assumed this ground, and now avow it. I could not feel that, to the best of my ability, I had even tried to preserve the constitution, if, to save

---

[11] Hodges was the editor of the *Frankfort (Kentucky) Commonwealth*.
[12] Thomas E. Bramlette was governor of Kentucky.
[13] Archibald Dixon was a former U.S. senator from Kentucky.

slavery, or any minor matter, I should permit the wreck of government, country, and Constitution all together. When, early in the war, Gen. Fremont attempted military emancipation, I forbade it, because I did not then think it an indispensable necessity. When a little later, Gen. Cameron,[14] then Secretary of War, suggested the arming of blacks, I objected, because I did not yet think it an indispensable necessity. When, still later, Gen. Hunter attempted military emancipation, I again forbade it, because I did not yet think the indispensable necessity had come. When, in March, and May, and July 1862 I made earnest, and successive appeals to the border states to favor compensated emancipation, I believed the indispensable necessity for military emancipation, and arming the blacks would come, unless averted by that measure. They declined the proposition; and I was, in my best judgment, driven to the alternative of either surrendering the Union, and with it, the Constitution, or of laying strong hand upon the colored element. I chose the latter. In choosing it, I hoped for greater gain than loss; but of this, I was not entirely confident. More than a year of trial now shows no loss by it in our foreign relations, none in our home popular sentiment, none in our white military force,—no loss by it any how or any where. On the contrary, it shows a gain of quite a hundred and thirty thousand soldiers, seamen, and laborers. These are palpable facts, about which, as facts, there can be no cavilling. We have the men; and we could not have had them, without the measure.

And now let any Union man who complains of the measure, test himself by writing down in one line that he is for subduing the rebellion by force of arms; and in the next, that he is for taking these hundred and thirty thousand men from the Union side, and placing them where they would be but for the measure he condemns. If he can not face his case so stated, it is only because he can not face the truth.

I add a word which was not in the verbal conversation. In telling this tale I attempt no compliment to my own sagacity. I claim not to have controlled events, but confess plainly that events have controlled me. Now, at the end of three years struggle the nation's condition is not what either party, or any man devised, or expected. God alone can claim it. Whither it

[14] Secretary of War Simon Cameron's annual report in November 1861 declared, "It is as clearly a right of the Government to arm slaves, when it may become necessary, as it is to use gun-powder taken from the enemy." Cameron leaked this statement to newspapers before Lincoln had seen it. Lincoln forced Cameron to excise the passage from his report. Because of this and other embarrassments, Lincoln made Cameron minister to Russia in January 1862 and appointed Edwin Stanton to take Cameron's place as secretary of war. John G. Nicolay and John Hay, *Abraham Lincoln: A History* (10 vols.; New York, 1890), V, 125–26.

is tending seems plain. If God now wills the removal of a great wrong, and wills also that we of the North as well as you of the South, shall pay fairly for our complicity in that wrong, impartial history will find therein new cause to attest and revere the justice and goodness of God.

Yours truly
A. LINCOLN

Most Republican officials throughout the North supported Lincoln's nomination for a second term. In an effort to garner votes from Democrats who favored continued war in order to preserve the Union, the Republican party adopted a new name for the 1864 presidential election: the National Union party. Meeting in Baltimore in early June, the party quickly nominated Lincoln and, after considerable maneuvering, selected Andrew Johnson—a prowar Democrat and military governor of Tennessee—as Lincoln's running mate. The party platform called for a constitutional amendment abolishing slavery, demanded unconditional surrender of Confederate forces, applauded the wisdom of Lincoln's Emancipation Proclamation and "employment as Union soldiers of men heretofore held in slavery," and promoted such Republican projects as "the speedy construction of the Railroad to the Pacific coast," the encouragement of foreign immigration, and "economy and rigid responsibility in the public expenditures."[15] In sum, the platform endorsed the policies of Lincoln's presidency and promised to continue them.

Despite Lincoln's public optimism about Union military prospects, Grant's spring campaign had caused a bloodbath of more than 100,000 Union casualties before his troops dug in to besiege Petersburg in mid-June. As Confederate general Jubal Early's army rampaged near Washington in early July, Horace Greeley, editor of the *New York Tribune*, wrote Lincoln urging him to meet with two Confederate ambassadors who were in Canada with "full & complete power for a peace."[16] Greeley went on to "remind" Lincoln—who needed no reminding—"that our bleeding, bankrupt, almost dying country also longs for peace—shudders at the prospect of fresh conscriptions, of further wholesale devastations, and of new rivers of human blood. . . . Mr. President, I fear you do

---

[15] *CW*, VII, 381–82.
[16] William Cornell Jewett to Horace Greeley, enclosed in Greeley to Lincoln, July 7, 1864, *CW*, VII, 436.

not realize how intently the people desire any peace consistent with the national integrity and honor. . . . With United States stocks worth but forty cents in gold per dollar, and drafting about to commence on the third million of Union soldiers, can this be wondered at?"[17]

Shrewdly, Lincoln delegated Greeley to contact the Confederate representatives and sound them out. He gave Greeley a brief statement of terms for initiating serious peace negotiations, including "the restoration of peace, the integrity of the whole Union, and the abandonment of slavery, and which comes by and with an authority that can control the armies now at war against the United States."[18] Lincoln fully expected these terms to be rejected as unacceptable, and they were.

The Confederate emissaries arranged to have Lincoln's peace terms published in northern newspapers, creating unease among many war Democrats in the North. Charles D. Robinson, editor of the *Green Bay (Wisconsin) Advocate*, wrote Lincoln, explaining that as a war Democrat, he had supported Lincoln's war policies, including emancipation, but that Lincoln's recent statement of the prerequisites for peace negotiations seemed to say "that no steps can be taken towards peace . . . unless accompanied with an abandonment of slavery. This puts the whole war question on a new basis, and takes us War Democrats clear off our feet, leaving us no ground to stand upon." Robinson asked Lincoln to "suggest some interpretation . . . [that will] make it tenable ground on which we War democrats may stand."[19]

Lincoln's consultation about the Robinson letter with former Wisconsin governor Alexander W. Randall and Joseph T. Mills, a Wisconsin judge, was summarized by Mills in the following excerpt from his diary, and a version was subsequently published in the *New York Tribune* on September 10, 1864.

---

[17] Greeley to Lincoln, July 7, 1864, *CW*, VII, 435.
[18] Lincoln, "To Whom It May Concern," July 18, 1864, *CW*, VII, 451.
[19] Robinson to Lincoln, August 7, 1864, *CW*, VII, 501.

50

Interview with Alexander W. Randall and Joseph T. Mills

August 19, 1864

The President was free & animated in conversation.... [He said,] my thoughts[,] my solicitude for this great country follow me where ever I go. I don't think it is personal vanity, or ambition—but I cannot but feel that the weal [well-being] or woe of this great nation will be decided in the approaching canvas.[20] My own experience has proven to me, that there is no program intended by the democratic party but that will result in the dismemberment of the Union. But Genl McClellan is in favor of crushing out the rebellion, & he will probably be the Chicago candidate.[21] The slightest acquaintance with arithmetic will prove to any man that the rebel armies cannot be destroyed with democratic [party] strategy. It would sacrifice all the white men of the north to do it. There are now between 1 & 200 thousand black men now in the service of the Union. These men will be disbanded, returned to slavery & we will have to fight two nations instead of one. I have tried it. You cannot conciliate the South, when the mastery & control of millions of blacks makes them sure of ultimate success. You cannot conciliate the South, when you place yourself in such a position, that they see they can achieve their independence. The war democrat depends upon conciliation. He must confine himself to that policy entirely. If he fights at all in such a war as this he must economise life & use all the means which God & nature puts in his power. Abandon all the posts now possessed by black men[,] surrender all these advantages to the enemy, & we would be compelled to abandon the war in 3 weeks. We have to hold territory. Where are the war democrats to do it. The field was open to them to have enlisted & put down this rebellion by force of arms, by concilliation, long before the present policy was inaugurated. There have been men who have proposed to me to return to slavery the black warriors of Port Hudson & Olustee[22] to their masters to conciliate the South. I should be damned in time & in eternity for so doing. The world shall know

[20] The presidential election in November 1864.

[21] McClellan did become the Democratic nominee, on a platform that called for an immediate end to the war, postponing for future negotiations the question of the abolition of slavery and whether the Union would be restored or Confederate independence would be allowed. McClellan himself, as Lincoln noted, was a war Democrat who insisted that the Union must be preserved. The contrast between the Democrats' peace platform and the war candidate reflected the deep divisions among party members.

[22] Black soldiers fought in the battles for Port Hudson, Louisiana, and Olustee, Florida.

that I will keep my faith to friends & enemies, come what will. My enemies say I am now carrying on this war for the sole purpose of abolition. It is & will be carried on so long as I am President for the sole purpose of restoring the Union. But no human power can subdue this rebellion without using the Emancipation lever as I have done. Freedom has given us the control of 200 000 able bodied men, born & raised on southern soil. It will give us more yet. Just so much it has sub[t]racted from the strength of our enemies, & instead of alienating the south from us, there are evidences of a fraternal feeling growing up between our own & rebel soldiers. My enemies condemn my emancipation policy. Let them prove by the history of this war, that we can restore the Union without it. . . .

Notwithstanding Lincoln's optimistic public statements, privately he was deeply pessimistic about the prospects of his re-election. On August 23, he received a gloomy letter from the chairman of the National Union Executive Committee, Henry J. Raymond, reporting that the president's "staunchest friends in every state" unanimously agreed: "The tide is setting strongly against us." Raymond wrote that "this great reaction in public sentiment" was caused by "the want of military successes, and the impression in some minds, the fear and suspicion in others, that we are not to have peace in any event under this administration until Slavery is abandoned." Raymond urged Lincoln to counteract this sentiment and "save the country from falling into hostile hands" by making "distinct proffers of peace to [Jefferson] Davis, as the head of the rebel armies, on the sole condition of acknowledging the supremacy of the constitution, — all other questions to be settled in a convention of the people of all the States."[23] Lincoln despaired that he would not be re-elected, dooming the war for Union and freedom. He expressed his pessimism in a private note to himself.

[23] Raymond to Lincoln, August 22, 1864, *CW*, VII, 517–18.

51

Memorandum concerning Lincoln's Probable Failure of Re-election

August 23, 1864

Executive Mansion
Washington
This morning, as for some days past, it seems exceedingly probable that this Administration will not be re-elected. Then it will be my duty to so co-operate with the President elect,[24] as to save the Union between the election and the inauguration; as he will have secured his election on such ground that he can not possibly save it afterwards.

A. LINCOLN

[24] George McClellan, the Democratic candidate.

Lincoln initially accepted Raymond's advice about making an overture to Jefferson Davis, and he drafted instructions for Raymond to serve as an emissary—powerful testimony of Lincoln's political desperation. But after discussing the document the next day with Raymond and several members of his cabinet, Lincoln concluded that to send such "a commission to Richmond would be worse than losing the Presidential contest—it would be ignominiously surrendering it in advance."[25] Accordingly, the plan was scrapped.

GLORIOUS VICTORIES

Dramatic news from the battlefield transformed Lincoln's political prospects. General William Tecumseh Sherman's campaign to push south from Chattanooga toward Atlanta had been under way since mid-May (see Map 1, pages xxii–xxiii). Despite Sherman's skillful military maneuvers, progress was slowed by the terrain and by Confederate general Joseph E. Johnston's shrewd defensive tactics. Eager to stop Sherman with a bold offensive, Jefferson Davis replaced Johnston with General

[25] Nicolay and Hay, *Abraham Lincoln*, IX, 221.

John Bell Hood in mid-July. While Sherman approached Atlanta, Admiral David G. Farragut took his Union fleet into Mobile Bay on the Gulf Coast of Alabama and in three weeks of battles captured the three forts that guarded the harbor, effectively closing it to Confederate shipping. Hood delayed Sherman with costly attacks, but Sherman's relentless flanking movements forced Confederate forces to evacuate Atlanta, and Union soldiers marched into the city on September 2, 1864.

General Philip Sheridan gave Lincoln more good military news on the eve of the presidential election. In pursuit of Confederate general Jubal Early's army since early August, Sheridan led his men to a decisive victory at Cedar Creek, Virginia, on October 19. During this unrelenting campaign through the Shenandoah Valley, Sheridan, with Grant's encouragement, destroyed everything in his path—crops, barns, farm animals and implements—anything that might be used to supply hungry Confederates.

A VOTE FOR UNION, FREEDOM, AND WAR?

The 1864 presidential election amounted to a referendum on Lincoln's presidency: Should a war for freedom and Union continue with Lincoln at the helm, or should the Democratic candidate, General George McClellan, be entrusted to somehow find a way to preserve the Union and postpone emancipation pending the outcome of postwar negotiations?

At 7 P.M. on Election Day, Lincoln went to the War Department with a few other officials to await telegraphed reports of election returns. Late in the night, it became almost certain that he had been re-elected. He learned later that he had carried every state except Delaware, Kentucky, and New Jersey, for an electoral vote tally of 212 to 21, a popular vote majority of 55 percent, and the support of more than three out of four soldiers, whose votes were tabulated separately. It was a smashing victory, made possible by Lincoln's success in maintaining the support of the coalition of voters who had elected him in 1860. Lincoln reflected on the larger meaning of his victory in remarks to a jubilant crowd from the Lincoln and Johnson clubs of Washington and Georgetown. His remarks were subsequently published in the *Washington Chronicle*.

52

Response to a Crowd of Supporters
November 10, 1864

It has long been a grave question whether any government, not *too* strong for the liberties of its people, can be strong *enough* to maintain its own existence, in great emergencies.

On this point the present rebellion brought our republic to a severe test; and a presidential election occurring in regular course during the rebellion added not a little to the strain. If the loyal people, *united*, were put to the utmost of their strength by the rebellion, must they not fail when *divided*, and partially paralyzed, by a political war among themselves?

But the election was a necessity.

We can not have free government without elections; and if the rebellion could force us to forego, or postpone a national election, it might fairly claim to have already conquered and ruined us. The strife of the election is but human-nature practically applied to the facts of the case. What has occurred in this case, must ever recur in similar cases. Human-nature will not change. In any future great national trial, compared with the men of this, we shall have as weak, and as strong; as silly and as wise; as bad and good. Let us, therefore, study the incidents of this, as philosophy to learn wisdom from, and none of them as wrongs to be revenged.

But the election, along with its incidental, and undesirable strife, has done good too. It has demonstrated that a people's government can sustain a national election, in the midst of a great civil war. Until now it has not been known to the world that this was a possibility. It shows also how *sound*, and how *strong* we still are. It shows that, even among candidates of the same party, he who is most devoted to the Union, and most opposed to treason, can receive most of the people's votes. It shows also, to the extent yet known, that we have more men now, than we had when the war began. Gold is good in its place; but living, brave, patriotic men, are better than gold.

But the rebellion continues; and now that the election is over, may not all, having a common interest, re-unite in a common effort, to save our common country? For my own part I have striven, and shall strive to avoid placing any obstacle in the way. So long as I have been here I have not willingly planted a thorn in any man's bosom.

While I am deeply sensible to the high compliment of a re-election; and duly grateful, as I trust, to Almighty God for having directed my countrymen to a right conclusion, as I think, for their own good, it adds nothing to my satisfaction that any other man may be disappointed or pained by the result.

May I ask those who have not differed with me, to join with me, in this same spirit towards those who have?

And now, let me close by asking three hearty cheers for our brave soldiers and seamen and their gallant and skilful commanders.

Lincoln acknowledged the ultimate sacrifice made by so many thousands of families throughout the Union in an eloquent letter to Mrs. Lydia Bixby, a widowed mother who lived in Boston. The *Boston Transcript* soon published the letter. Significantly, Lincoln referred to Mrs. Bixby's costly sacrifice "upon the altar of Freedom," not the altar of Union. Now that he had been re-elected, Lincoln knew that still more sacrifices would be required to ensure the nation's new birth of freedom.

53

Letter to Lydia Bixby
November 21, 1864

Executive Mansion
Washington

Dear Madam,—I have been shown in the files of the War Department a statement of the Adjutant General of Massachusetts, that you are the mother of five sons who have died gloriously on the field of battle.[26]

I feel how weak and fruitless must be any words of mine which should attempt to beguile you from the grief of a loss so overwhelming. But I cannot refrain from tendering to you the consolation that may be found in the thanks of the Republic they died to save.

I pray that our Heavenly Father may assuage the anguish of your bereavement, and leave you only the cherished memory of the loved and lost, and the solemn pride that must be yours, to have laid so costly a sacrifice upon the altar of Freedom.

Yours, very sincerely and respectfully,[27]

A. LINCOLN

[26] Mrs. Bixby had five sons in the Union army, but the adjutant general had misinformed Lincoln about their deaths; only two of the five were killed.

[27] Lincoln signed this famous letter, and there is no doubt that it conveyed his sentiments, but the original letter was evidently destroyed by Mrs. Bixby. Years later, Lincoln's secretary, John Hay, claimed that he had written the letter; the evidence of this is intriguing but not conclusive. The strongest case for Hay's authorship is made by Michael Burlingame, "New Light on the Bixby Letter," *Journal of the Abraham Lincoln Association*, 16 (1995), 59–71.

8

"To Finish the Work We Are In"

Re-election boosted Lincoln's confidence that he could—as he put it in his second inaugural address—"finish the work we are in." Lincoln's re-election defeated at the ballot box the Confederates' hope that northerners would vote for peace under Democrats rather than for continuing the war under Lincoln. Having won the battle on the political front at home, Lincoln gained a decisive advantage he had lacked before re-election: time. Lincoln's re-election made time an enemy of the Confederacy. With four more years as president ahead of him, Lincoln had every reason to believe that the Confederate army could not hold out against the unrelenting attacks of Union commanders.

THE WAR CONTINUES

Lincoln expressed his renewed confidence in his annual message to Congress in early December 1864. He reviewed evidence of northern strength to show that the war could be continued "indefinitely," a statement no sensible Confederate leader could match. Reports of Union successes on the battlefield soon confirmed Lincoln's optimism.

54

Annual Message to Congress
December 6, 1864

Fellow-citizens of the Senate and House of Representatives:
. . . The war continues. Since the last annual message all the important lines and positions then occupied by our forces have been maintained, and our arms have steadily advanced; thus liberating the regions left in

rear, so that Missouri, Kentucky, Tennessee and parts of other States have again produced reasonably fair crops.

The most remarkable feature in the military operations of the year is General Sherman's attempted march of three hundred miles directly through the insurgent region.[1] It tends to show a great increase of our relative strength that our General-in-Chief[2] should feel able to confront and hold in check every active force of the enemy, and yet to detach a well-appointed large army[3] to move on such an expedition. The result not yet being known, conjecture in regard to it is not here indulged.

Important movements have also occurred during the year to the effect of moulding society for durability in the Union. Although short of complete success, it is much in the right direction, that twelve thousand citizens in each of the States of Arkansas and Louisiana have organized loyal State governments with free constitutions, and are earnestly struggling to maintain and administer them. The movements in the same direction, more extensive, though less definite in Missouri, Kentucky and Tennessee, should not be overlooked. But Maryland presents the example of complete success. Maryland is secure to Liberty and Union for all the future.[4] The genius of rebellion will no more claim Maryland. Like another foul spirit, being driven out, it may seek to tear her, but it will woo her no more.

At the last session of Congress a proposed amendment of the Constitution abolishing slavery throughout the United States, passed the Senate, but failed for lack of the requisite two-thirds vote in the House of Representatives. Although the present is the same Congress, and nearly the same members, and without questioning the wisdom or patriotism of those who stood in opposition, I venture to recommend the reconsideration and passage of the measure at the present session. Of course the abstract question is not changed; but an intervening election shows, almost certainly, that the next Congress will pass the measure if this does not. Hence there is only a question of *time* as to when the proposed amendment will go to the States for their action. And as it is to so go, at all events, may we not agree that the sooner the better? It is not claimed that the election has imposed a duty on members to change their views or their votes, any further than, as an additional element to be considered, their judgment may be affected by it. It is the voice of the people now, for the first time, heard upon the question. In a great national crisis, like ours, unanimity of action among those seeking a common end is very desirable — almost indispensable. And yet no approach to such unanimity is attainable, unless some deference shall be paid to the will of the majority, simply

---

[1] On November 15, Sherman left Atlanta, cutting his lines of communication and supply, and began his famous march through enemy territory toward Savannah.

[2] Grant.

[3] Sherman's army of more than sixty thousand battle-hardened veterans.

[4] Lincoln is referring to Maryland's new constitution, which abolished slavery.

because it is the will of the majority. In this case the common end is the maintenance of the Union; and, among the means to secure that end, such will, through the election, is most clearly declared in favor of such constitutional amendment.

The most reliable indication of public purpose in this country is derived through our popular elections. Judging by the recent canvass [election] and its result, the purpose of the people, within the loyal States, to maintain the integrity of the Union, was never more firm, nor more nearly unanimous, than now. The extraordinary calmness and good order with which the millions of voters met and mingled at the polls, give strong assurance of this. Not only all those who supported the Union ticket, so called, but a great majority of the opposing party also, may be fairly claimed to entertain, and to be actuated by, the same purpose. It is an unanswerable argument to this effect, that no candidate for any office whatever, high or low, has ventured to seek votes on the avowal that he was for giving up the Union. There have been much impugning of motives, and much heated controversy as to the proper means and best mode of advancing the Union cause; but on the distinct issue of Union or no Union, the politicians have shown their instinctive knowledge that there is no diversity among the people. In affording the people the fair opportunity of showing, one to another and to the world, this firmness and unanimity of purpose, the election has been of vast value to the national cause.

The election has exhibited another fact not less valuable to be known — the fact that we do not approach exhaustion in the most important branch of national resources — that of living men. While it is melancholy to reflect that the war has filled so many graves, and carried mourning to so many hearts, it is some relief to know that, compared with the surviving, the fallen have been so few. While corps, and divisions, and brigades, and regiments have formed, and fought, and dwindled, and gone out of existence, a great majority of the men who composed them are still living. The same is true of the naval service. . . . The important fact remains demonstrated, that we have *more* men *now* than we had when the war *began*; that we are not exhausted, nor in process of exhaustion; that we are *gaining* strength, and may, if need be, maintain the contest indefinitely. This as to men. Material resources are now more complete and abundant than ever.

The national resources, then, are unexhausted, and, as we believe, inexhaustible. The public purpose to re-establish and maintain the national authority is unchanged, and, as we believe, unchangeable. The manner of continuing the effort remains to choose. On careful consideration of all the evidence accessible it seems to me that no attempt at negotiation with the insurgent leader [5] could result in any good. He would accept nothing short of severance of the Union — precisely what we will not and cannot give. His declarations to this effect are explicit and oft-repeated. He does not attempt to deceive us. He affords us no excuse to deceive ourselves.

[5] Jefferson Davis.

He cannot voluntarily reaccept the Union; we cannot voluntarily yield it. Between him and us the issue is distinct, simple, and inflexible. It is an issue which can only be tried by war, and decided by victory. If we yield, we are beaten; if the Southern people fail him, he is beaten. Either way, it would be the victory and defeat following war. What is true, however, of him who heads the insurgent cause, is not necessarily true of those who follow. Although he cannot reaccept the Union, they can. Some of them, we know, already desire peace and reunion. The number of such may increase. They can, at any moment, have peace simply by laying down their arms and submitting to the national authority under the Constitution. After so much, the government could not, if it would, maintain war against them. The loyal people would not sustain or allow it. If questions should remain, we would adjust them by the peaceful means of legislation, conference, courts, and votes, operating only in constitutional and lawful channels. . . .

A year ago general pardon and amnesty, upon specified terms, were offered to all, except certain designated classes; and, it was, at the same time, made known that the excepted classes were still within contemplation of special clemency [Document 46]. . . . Thus, practically, the door has been, for a full year, open to all, except such as were not in condition to make free choice—that is, such as were in custody or under constraint. It is still so open to all. But the time may come—probably will come—when public duty shall demand that it be closed; and that, in lieu, more rigorous measures than heretofore shall be adopted.

In presenting the abandonment of armed resistance to the national authority on the part of the insurgents, as the only indispensable condition to ending the war on the part of the government, I retract nothing heretofore said as to slavery. I repeat the declaration made a year ago, that "while I remain in my present position I shall not attempt to retract or modify the emancipation proclamation, nor shall I return to slavery any person who is free by the terms of that proclamation, or by any of the Acts of Congress." If the people should, by whatever mode or means, make it an Executive duty to re-enslave such persons, another, and not I, must be their instrument to perform it.

In stating a single condition of peace, I mean simply to say that the war will cease on the part of the government, whenever it shall have ceased on the part of those who began it.

ABRAHAM LINCOLN

While Sherman burned a wide swath across central Georgia, Confederate general John B. Hood initiated a bold and reckless advance into Tennessee that culminated in a devastating defeat at Nashville by Union forces under General George H. Thomas.

Lincoln soon received news of an even greater military achievement. On December 22, 1864, the day after marching into Savannah, Georgia, Sherman telegraphed Lincoln, "I beg to present you as a Christmas gift the city of Savannah, with 150 heavy guns & plenty of ammunition & also about 25000 bales of cotton."[6] Sherman's army had proved that the Confederate military was incapable of protecting its homeland, profoundly demoralizing Confederate military and civilian leaders alike.

[6] Sherman to Lincoln, December 22, 1864, *CW*, VIII, 182.

55

Letter to William T. Sherman

December 26, 1864

Executive Mansion,
Washington

My dear General Sherman.

Many, many, thanks for your Christmas-gift—the capture of Savannah.

When you were about leaving Atlanta for the Atlantic coast, I was *anxious*, if not fearful; but feeling that you were the better judge, and remembering that "nothing risked, nothing gained" I did not interfere. Now, the undertaking being a success, the honor is all yours; for I believe none of us went farther than to acquiesce. And, taking the work of Gen. Thomas into the count, as it should be taken, it is indeed a great success. Not only does it afford the obvious and immediate military advantages; but, in showing to the world that your army could be divided, putting the stronger part[7] to an important new service, and yet leaving enough[8] to vanquish the old opposing force of the whole—Hood's army—it brings those who sat in darkness, to see a great light. But what next? I suppose it will be safer if I leave Gen. Grant and yourself to decide.

Please make my grateful acknowledgments to your whole army, officers and men.

Yours very truly
A. LINCOLN

---

[7] Sherman's army, which marched from Atlanta to Savannah.
[8] Thomas's army, which had been part of Sherman's command in the assault on Atlanta.

Sherman, with Grant's concurrence, proposed to follow his march across Georgia with an even more dangerous but eagerly anticipated march through the heartland of secession, South Carolina. Sherman wrote that his strategy would still be to "make a good ready and then move rapidly to my objective, avoiding a battle at points where I would be encumbered by wounded, but striking boldly and quickly when my objective is reached . . . [in order to] conduct war as though it could only terminate with the destruction of the enemy."[9]

While millions of northern soldiers braved the mortal dangers of combat, Lincoln's eldest son, Robert Todd Lincoln, remained a student at Harvard until he graduated in 1864. Criticized as a shirker, Robert wanted to enlist, but his parents feared for his safety. Although the president himself obviously could not serve in the army, he nonetheless paid $750 to a substitute—a man from Stroudsburg, Pennsylvania, named John Summerfield Staples—to serve as his personal representative in the ranks. Lincoln also interceded with Grant and asked for a safe, token position for Robert.

[9] Sherman to Henry W. Halleck, December 31, 1864, *CW*, VIII, 201.

56

Letter to Ulysses S. Grant

January 19, 1865

Executive Mansion
Washington

Lieut. General Grant:

Please read and answer this letter as though I was not President, but only a friend. My son, now in his twenty second year, having graduated at Harvard, wishes to see something of the war before it ends. I do not wish to put him in the ranks, nor yet to give him a commission, to which those who have already served long, are better entitled, and better qualified to hold. Could he, without embarrassment to you, or detriment to the service, go into your Military family with some nominal rank, I, and not the public, furnishing his necessary means? If no, say so without the least hesitation, because I am as anxious, and as deeply interested, that you shall not be encumbered as you can be yourself.[10]

Yours truly
A. LINCOLN

[10] Grant arranged for Robert Lincoln to receive a captain's commission on his staff, with the primary duty of serving as an escort for visitors to the army.

TOWARD PEACE AND FREEDOM

Union military success made the terms of peace a pressing concern for Lincoln. In early January 1865, Lincoln agreed to permit Francis P. Blair, a longtime supporter and editor of the *Congressional Globe*, to go to Richmond and sound out Jefferson Davis about possible peace negotiations. Davis told Blair that he was willing to send representatives to a "conference with a view to secure peace to the two countries."[11] Lincoln, of course, found Davis's "two countries" formula unacceptable. He sent Blair back to Richmond with an expression of willingness to meet informally with Confederate representatives "with the view of securing peace to the people of our one common country."[12] After numerous memos back and forth, Lincoln agreed to informal discussions at Hampton Roads, Virginia,[13] with three Confederate representatives: Alexander H. Stephens, the Confederate vice president and a former Whig from Georgia, whom Lincoln had known when both served in Congress almost twenty years earlier; John A. Campbell, a former Supreme Court justice, who had resigned to become assistant secretary of war for the Confederacy; and Robert M. T. Hunter, a former U.S. congressman and Speaker of the House, who served as Confederate secretary of state before being elected to represent Virginia in the Confederate Senate. Lincoln specified his conditions for the Hampton Roads discussions in a letter to Secretary of State William Seward.

[11] Jefferson Davis to F. P. Blair, January 12, 1865, *CW*, VIII, 275.
[12] Lincoln to F. P. Blair, January 18, 1865, *CW*, VIII, 220.
[13] Hampton Roads is the entrance to the harbor of Norfolk, Virginia, at the mouth of the James River.

57

Letter to William H. Seward

January 31, 1865

Executive Mansion
Washington

Hon. William H. Seward
Secretary of State
You will proceed to Fortress-Monroe, Virginia, there to meet, and informally confer with Messrs. Stephens, Hunter, and Campbell. . . .

You will make known to them that three things are indispensable, towit:

1. The restoration of the national authority throughout all the States.

2. No receding, by the Executive of the United States on the Slavery question, from the position assumed thereon, in the late Annual Message to Congress, and in preceding documents.

3. No cessation of hostilities short of an end of the war, and the disbanding of all forces hostile to the government.

You will inform them that all propositions of theirs not inconsistent with the above, will be considered and passed upon in a spirit of sincere liberality. You will hear all they may choose to say, and report it to me.

You will not assume to definitely consummate anything.

Yours &c.
Abraham Lincoln

Lincoln met with Seward and the Confederate representatives aboard the presidential steamboat, *River Queen*, at Hampton Roads on February 3. After several hours, it became clear that the Confederates were unwilling to accept Lincoln's terms. Although the meeting had been held in secret, a few days later Lincoln sent to the House of Representatives a full documentary record of the discussions, which, as he wrote, "ended without result."[14]

Lincoln made clear that Grant should press on with the more certain approach to peace, namely the destruction of Lee's army. He insisted that only he, not his military commanders, had the authority to negotiate

---

[14] Lincoln to the House of Representatives, February 10, 1865, *CW*, VIII, 285.

terms for ending the war, as he relayed to Grant via the following letter from Secretary of War Stanton.

58

Letter to Ulysses S. Grant

March 3, 1865

Lieutenant General Grant[15]
The President directs me to say to you that he wishes you to have no conference with General Lee unless it be for the capitulation of Gen. Lee's army, or on some minor, and purely, military matter. He instructs me to say that you are not to decide, discuss, or confer upon any political question. Such questions the President holds in his own hands; and will submit them to no military conferences or conventions. Meantime you are to press to the utmost, your military advantages.

EDWIN M STANTON
Secretary of War

[15] Grant had asked Stanton for instructions about how to respond to a letter from Lee asking to meet with him to discuss "the possibility of arriving at a satisfactory adjustment of the present unhappy difficulties, by means of a military convention." Grant to Stanton, March 2, 1865, *CW*, VIII, 331.

While the Union army pressed forward on the military front as Lincoln directed, Congress responded to Lincoln's request for a thirteenth amendment abolishing slavery throughout the nation. Although the president's signature was not required before submitting the congressional resolution to the states for ratification, Lincoln signed it anyway, declaring it "a great moral victory."

59

Resolution Submitting the Thirteenth Amendment to the States

February 1, 1865

A RESOLUTION

Submitting to the legislatures of the several States a proposition to amend the Constitution of the United States.

Resolved by the Senate and House of Representatives of the United States of America in Congress assembled, (two-thirds of both houses concurring), That the following article be proposed to the legislatures of the several States as an amendment to the constitution of the United States, which, when ratified by three-fourths of said Legislatures, shall be valid, to all intents and purposes, as a part of the said Constitution, namely: Article XIII. Section 1. Neither slavery nor involuntary servitude, except as a punishment for crime whereof the party shall have been duly convicted, shall exist within the United States, or any place subject to their jurisdiction. Section 2. Congress shall have power to enforce this article by appropriate legislation.

> SCHUYLER COLFAX
> Speaker of the House of Representatives
> H. HAMLIN
> Vice President of the United States,
> and President of the Senate

Approved, February 1. 1865.   ABRAHAM LINCOLN

Although Lincoln resolutely supported the end of slavery, he nonetheless favored federal compensation to masters for the loss of slave property. He had offered compensation to border-state masters back in 1862, but only in Washington, D.C., was compensated emancipation actually put into practice. There the federal government paid masters for 2,989 slaves, hiring a Baltimore slave trader to determine a reasonable value for each one. By February 1865, Lincoln was so eager to end the war that he proposed privately to his cabinet that the government compensate all slave states—including Confederate states—the amount of $400 million for their loss of slave property. Lincoln believed the proposal might drive a wedge between Confederate leaders, who refused to stop fighting, and the Confederate people, who might well respond to this incentive to abandon the war and support emancipation. Lincoln also maintained that the $400 million offer of compensation was small compared to the cost of continuing the war, which he estimated at $3 million a day. Lincoln's cabinet persuaded him that this compensation proposal would never be approved by Congress, and the proposal was quietly shelved. The proposal illustrates Lincoln's astonishing willingness to recognize masters'—even rebel masters'—property rights in slaves at the same time that he urged ratification of the Thirteenth Amendment to guarantee slaves' right to freedom.

60

Message to the Senate and House of Representatives
February 5, 1865

Fellow citizens of the Senate, and House of Representatives:
I respectfully recommend that a Joint Resolution, substantially as follows, be adopted so soon as practicable, by your honorable bodies.

Resolved by the Senate and House of Representatives, of the United States of America in congress assembled: That the President of the United States is hereby empowered, in his discretion, to pay four hundred millions of dollars to the States of Alabama, Arkansas, Delaware, Florida, Georgia, Kentucky, Louisiana, Maryland, Mississippi, Missouri, North Carolina, South Carolina, Tennessee, Texas, Virginia, and West-Virginia, in the manner, and on the conditions following, towit: The payment to be made in six per cent government bonds, and to be distributed among said States *pro rata* on their respective slave populations, as shown by the census of 1860; and no part of said sum to be paid unless all resistance to the national authority shall be abandoned and cease, on or before the first day of April next; and upon such abandonment and ceasing of resistance, one half of said sum to be paid in manner aforesaid, and the remaining half to be paid only upon the amendment of the national constitution recently proposed by congress, becoming valid law, on or before the first day of July next, by the action thereon of the requisite number of States.

The adoption of such resolution is sought with a view to embody it, with other propositions, in a proclamation looking to peace and re-union.

Whereas a Joint Resolution has been adopted by congress in the words following, towit

Now therefore I, Abraham Lincoln, President of the United States, do proclaim, declare, and make known, that on the conditions therein stated, the power conferred on the Executive in and by said Joint Resolution, will be fully exercised; that war will cease, and armies be reduced to a basis of peace; that all political offences will be pardoned; that all property, except slaves, liable to confiscation or forfeiture, will be released therefrom, except in cases of intervening interests of third parties; and that liberality will be recommended to congress upon all points not lying within executive control.

[Endorsement]

Feb. 5, 1865

Today these papers, which explain themselves, were drawn up and submitted to the Cabinet & unanamously disapproved by them.

A LINCOLN

"THAT THIS MIGHTY SCOURGE OF WAR MAY SPEEDILY PASS AWAY"

By inauguration day, the end of the war, at long last, seemed near. In his eloquent second inaugural address, Lincoln attributed "this terrible war" to God's will to end slavery, for which the entire nation must suffer. In contrast to a vengeful God, Lincoln promised a magnanimous peace, "with malice toward none; with charity for all," vanquished and victor alike. Lincoln's calm, elegiac address set a standard of presidential rhetoric that has seldom been equaled and never surpassed.

Lincoln's remarkable generosity toward rebellious southerners looked forward to a peaceful reunion of the nation. But it did not cause Lincoln to moderate his insistence on military victory; he wanted peace and reconstruction not as an alternative to war, but as its result.

61

Second Inaugural Address
March 4, 1865

[Fellow Countrymen:]

At this second appearing to take the oath of the presidential office, there is less occasion for an extended address than there was at the first. Then a statement, somewhat in detail, of a course to be pursued, seemed fitting and proper. Now, at the expiration of four years, during which public declarations have been constantly called forth on every point and phase of the great contest which still absorbs the attention, and engrosses the enerergies [*sic*] of the nation, little that is new could be presented. The progress of our arms, upon which all else chiefly depends, is as well known to the public as to myself; and it is, I trust, reasonably satisfactory and encouraging to all. With high hope for the future, no prediction in regard to it is ventured.

On the occasion corresponding to this four years ago, all thoughts were anxiously directed to an impending civil-war. All dreaded it—all sought to avert it. While the inaugeral address was being delivered from this place, devoted altogether to *saving* the Union without war, insurgent agents were in the city seeking to *destroy* it without war—seeking to dissol[v]e the Union, and divide effects, by negotiation. Both parties deprecated war; but one of them[16] would *make* war rather than let the nation survive; and the other would *accept* war rather than let it perish. And the war came.

One eighth of the whole population were colored slaves, not distributed generally over the Union, but localized in the Southern part of it. These slaves constituted a peculiar and powerful interest. All knew that this interest was, somehow, the cause of the war. To strengthen, perpetuate, and extend this interest was the object for which the insurgents would rend the Union, even by war; while the government claimed no right to do more than to restrict the territorial enlargement of it. Neither party expected for the war, the magnitude, or the duration, which it has already attained. Neither anticipated that the *cause* of the conflict[17] might cease with, or even before, the conflict itself should cease. Each looked for an easier triumph, and a result less fundamental and astounding. Both read the same Bible, and pray to the same God; and each invokes His aid against the other. It may seem strange that any men should dare to ask a just God's assistance in wringing their bread from the sweat of other

[16]The Confederacy.
[17]Slavery.

men's faces; but let us judge not that we be not judged. The prayers of both could not be answered; that of neither has been answered fully. The Almighty has His own purposes. "Woe unto the world because of offences! for it must needs be that offences come; but woe to that man by whom the offence cometh!"[18] If we shall suppose that American Slavery is one of those offences which, in the providence of God must needs come, but which, having continued through His appointed time, He now wills to remove, and that He gives to both North and South, this terrible war, as the woe due to those by whom the offence came, shall we discern therein any departure from those divine attributes which the believers in a Living God always ascribe to Him? Fondly do we hope—fervently do we pray—that this mighty scourge of war may speedily pass away. Yet, if God wills that it continue, until all the wealth piled by the bond-man's two hundred and fifty years of unrequited toil shall be sunk, and until every drop of blood drawn with the lash, shall be paid by another drawn with the sword, as was said three thousand years ago, so still it must be said "the judgments of the Lord, are true and righteous altogether."[19]

With malice toward none; with charity for all; with firmness in the right, as God gives us to see the right, let us strive on to finish the work we are in; to bind up the nation's wounds; to care for him who shall have borne the battle, and for his widow, and his orphan—to do all which may achieve and cherish a just, and a lasting peace, among ourselves, and with all nations.

[18] Matthew 18:17.
[19] Psalms 19:9.

As Confederate military prospects became gloomier, rebel leaders began to discuss seriously the possibility of arming the slaves. With the endorsement of General Lee, a bill to conscript a quota of black soldiers from each state was considered by the Confederate Congress, where the Senate passed it but the House defeated it by one vote. Lincoln commented on this act of Confederate desperation in a speech to an Indiana regiment that was subsequently published in the *New York Herald* and other newspapers.

Figure 6. *Reburial of Union Dead*
Soldiers killed in battle were often buried hastily in shallow graves that were
soon opened by rainstorms and rummaging animals. As shown in this April
1865 photograph of the Cold Harbor, Virginia, battlefield, black soldiers were
frequently assigned the heavy labor of reburying soldiers' remains in proper
graves.
National Archives W+C #258.

62

Speech to 140th Indiana Regiment
March 17, 1865

FELLOW CITIZENS: It will be but a very few words that I shall undertake
to say. I was born in Kentucky, raised in Indiana and lived in Illinois.
(Laughter.) And now I am here, where it is my business to care equally for
the good people of all the States. I am glad to see an Indiana regiment on
this day able to present the captured [Confederate] flag to the Governor

of Indiana. (Applause.) I am not disposed, in saying this, to make a distinction between the states, for all have done equally well. (Applause.) There are but few views or aspects of this great war upon which I have not said or written something whereby my own opinions might be known. But there is one—the recent attempt of our erring brethren, as they are sometimes called— (laughter)—to employ the negro to fight for them. I have neither written nor made a speech on that subject, because that was their business, not mine; and if I had a wish upon the subject I had not the power to introduce it, or make it effective. The great question with them was, whether the negro, being put into the army, would fight for them. I do not know, and therefore cannot decide. (Laughter.) They ought to know better than we. I have in my lifetime heard many arguments why the negroes ought to be slaves; but if they fight for those who would keep them in slavery it will be a better argument than any I have yet heard.[20] (Laughter and applause.) He who will fight for that ought to be a slave. (Applause.) They have concluded at last to take one out of four of the slaves, and put them in the army; and that one of the four who will fight to keep the others in slavery ought to be a slave himself unless he is killed in a fight. (Applause.) While I have often said that all men ought to be free, yet I would allow those colored persons to be slaves who want to be; and next to them those white persons who argue in favor of making other people slaves. (Applause.) I am in favor of giving an opportunity to such white men to try it on for themselves. (Applause.) I will say one thing in regard to the negro being employed to fight for them. I do know he cannot fight and stay at home and make bread too— (laughter and applause) —and as one is about as important as the other to them, I don't care which they do. (Renewed applause.) I am rather in favor of having them try them as soldiers. (Applause.) They lack one vote of doing that, and I wish I could send my vote over the river so that I might cast it in favor of allowing the negro to fight. (Applause.) But they cannot fight and work both. We must now see the bottom of the enemy's resources. They will stand out as long as they can, and if the negro will fight for them, they must allow him to fight. They have drawn upon their last branch of resources. (Applause.) And we can now see the bottom. (Applause.) I am glad to see the end so near at hand. (Applause.) I have said now more than I intended, and will therefore bid you goodby.

---

[20]The Virginia legislature passed a law on March 13, 1865, authorizing slaves to fight against the Union, and two black companies were hurriedly assembled. They never participated in combat.

As Lincoln predicted, the end was near. Grant's long siege of Petersburg finally succeeded on April 2, causing Lee to pull out of the city and retreat toward the west in an attempt to prevent Grant from capturing his entire army. Grant invited Lincoln to visit the army, and the president set out for Virginia on April 3, accompanied by his young son Tad. Lincoln went to Richmond on April 4 and walked the streets of the Confederate capital, even visiting the recently evacuated Confederate White House and sitting in Jefferson Davis's chair.

Upon receiving news that Sheridan had almost succeeded in cutting off Lee's retreat, Lincoln telegraphed his encouragement to Grant.

63

Letter to Ulysses S. Grant

April 7, 1865

Head Quarters Armies of the United States
City-Point
11 AM.

Lieut Gen. Grant.
Gen. Sheridan says "If the thing is pressed I think that Lee will surrender." Let the *thing* be pressed.

A LINCOLN

Grant needed no reminder to press on. He accepted the surrender of Lee's army in the home of Virginia farmer Wilmer McLean at Appomattox Courthouse about 1 P.M. on April 9. Lincoln learned of the surrender that night after he had returned to Washington from Virginia. The next day, he spoke briefly to a jubilant crowd gathered at the White House. His remarks were published by the *Washington Daily National Intelligencer* and other newspapers.

64

Response to a Crowd of Supporters
April 10, 1865

FELLOW CITIZENS: I am very greatly rejoiced to find that an occasion has occurred so pleasurable that the people cannot restrain themselves. [Cheers.] I suppose that arrangements are being made for some sort of a formal demonstration, this, or perhaps, to-morrow night. [Cries of "We can't wait," "We want it now," &c.] If there should be such a demonstration, I, of course, will be called upon to respond, and I shall have nothing to say if you dribble it all out of me before. [Laughter and applause.] I see you have a band of music with you. [Voices, "We have two or three."] I propose closing up this interview by the band performing a particular tune which I will name. Before this is done, however, I wish to mention one or two little circumstances connected with it. I have always thought "Dixie" one of the best tunes I have ever heard. Our adversaries over the way attempted to appropriate it, but I insisted yesterday that we fairly captured it. [Applause.] I presented the question to the Attorney General, and he gave it as his legal opinion that it is our lawful prize. [Laughter and applause.] I now request the band to favor me with its performance.[21]

[21] While the President remained in view, the band played "Dixie," followed by "Yankee Doodle"; then Lincoln called for "three good hearty cheers for General Grant and all under his command," then "three more cheers for our gallant Navy." *Washington Daily National Intelligencer*, April 11, 1865, *CW*, VIII, 393–94.

The next evening, in the midst of the joyous celebration of Lee's surrender and the impending collapse of the rebellion, Lincoln delivered what turned out to be his last public address, a serious and detailed defense of his plans for reconstruction.

65

Last Public Address
April 11, 1865

We meet this evening, not in sorrow, but in gladness of heart. The evacuation of Petersburg and Richmond, and the surrender of the principal

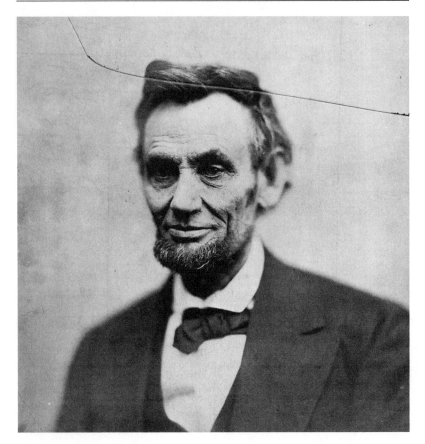

Figure 7. *Lincoln in 1865*
One of the last photographs of Lincoln, this portrait made in February
1865 documents the personal toll the war took on the president. Two and
a half months later, following Lee's surrender at Appomattox, Lincoln was
assassinated.
National Portrait Gallery, Smithsonian Institution/Art Resource, N.Y.

insurgent army, give hope of a righteous and speedy peace whose joyous
expression can not be restrained. In the midst of this, however, He, from
Whom all blessings flow, must not be forgotten. A call for a national
thanksgiving is being prepared, and will be duly promulgated. Nor must
those whose harder part gives us the cause of rejoicing, be overlooked.
Their honors must not be parcelled out with others. I myself, was near the
front, and had the high pleasure of transmitting much of the good news
to you; but no part of the honor, for plan or execution, is mine. To Gen.

Grant, his skilful officers, and brave men, all belongs. The gallant Navy stood ready, but was not in reach to take active part.

By these recent successes the re-inauguration of the national authority—reconstruction—which has had a large share of thought from the first, is pressed much more closely upon our attention. It is fraught with great difficulty. Unlike the case of a war between independent nations, there is no authorized organ for us to treat with. No one man has authority to give up the rebellion for any other man. We simply must begin with, and mould from, disorganized and discordant elements. Nor is it a small additional embarrassment that we, the loyal people, differ among ourselves as to the mode, manner, and mean, of reconstruction.

As a general rule, I abstain from reading the reports of attacks upon myself, wishing not to be provoked by that to which I can not properly offer an answer. In spite of this precaution, however, it comes to my knowledge that I am much censured for some supposed agency in setting up, and seeking to sustain, the new State Government of Louisiana. In this I have done just so much as, and no more than, the public knows. In the Annual Message of Dec. 1863 and accompanying Proclamation [Documents 45 and 46], I presented *a* plan of re-construction (as the phrase goes) which, I promised, if adopted by any State, should be acceptable to, and sustained by, the Executive government of the nation. I distinctly stated that this was not the only plan which might possibly be acceptable; and I also distinctly protested that the Executive claimed no right to say when, or whether members should be admitted to seats in Congress from such States. This plan was, in advance, submitted to the then Cabinet, and distinctly approved by every member of it. One of them[22] suggested that I should then, and in that connection, apply the Emancipation Proclamation to the theretofore excepted parts of Virginia and Louisiana; that I should drop the suggestion about apprenticeship for freed-people, and that I should omit the protest against my own power, in regard to the admission of members to Congress; but even he approved every part and parcel of the plan which has since been employed or touched by the action of Louisiana. The new constitution of Louisiana, declaring emancipation for the whole State, practically applies the Proclamation to the part previously excepted. It does not adopt apprenticeship for freed-people; and it is silent, as it could not well be otherwise, about the admission of members to Congress. So that, as it applies to Louisiana, every member of the Cabinet fully approved the plan. The Message went to Congress, and I received many commendations of the plan, written and verbal; and not a single objection to it, from any professed emancipationist, came to my knowledge, until after the news reached Washington that the people of Louisiana had begun to move in accordance with it. From about July 1862

---

[22] Salmon P. Chase, Secretary of the Treasury until July 1864, after which Lincoln appointed him Chief Justice of the Supreme Court. Chase had just written to Lincoln urging him to insist on granting suffrage to all citizens, including freedmen.

I had corresponded with different persons, supposed to be interested, seeking a reconstruction of a State government for Louisiana. When the Message of 1863, with the plan before mentioned, reached New-Orleans, Gen. Banks wrote me that he was confident the people, with his military co-operation, would reconstruct, substantially on that plan. I wrote him [Document 44], and some of them to try it; they tried it, and the result is known. Such only has been my agency in getting up the Louisiana government. As to sustaining it, my promise is out, as before stated. But, as bad promises are better broken than kept, I shall treat this as a bad promise, and break it, whenever I shall be convinced that keeping it is adverse to the public interest. But I have not yet been so convinced.

I have been shown a letter on this subject, supposed to be an able one, in which the writer[23] expresses regret that my mind has not seemed to be definitely fixed on the question whether the seceded States, so called, are in the Union or out of it. It would perhaps, add astonishment to his regret, were he to learn that since I have found professed Union men endeavoring to make that question, I have *purposely* forborne any public expression upon it. As appears to me that question has not been, nor yet is, a practically material one, and that any discussion of it, while it thus remains practically immaterial, could have no effect other than the mischievous one of dividing our friends. As yet, whatever it may hereafter become, that question is bad, as the basis of a controversy, and good for nothing at all—a merely pernicious abstraction.

We all agree that the seceded States, so called, are out of their proper practical relation with the Union; and that the sole object of the government, civil and military, in regard to those States is to again get them into that proper practical relation. I believe it is not only possible, but in fact, easier, to do this, without deciding, or even considering, whether these states have even been out of the Union, than with it. Finding themselves safely at home, it would be utterly immaterial whether they had ever been abroad. Let us all join in doing the acts necessary to restoring the proper practical relations between these states and the Union; and each forever after, innocently indulge his own opinion whether, in doing the acts, he brought the States from without, into the Union, or only gave them proper assistance, they never having been out of it.

The amount of constituency, so to to [*sic*] speak, on which the new Louisiana government rests, would be more satisfactory to all, if it contained fifty, thirty, or even twenty thousand, instead of only about twelve thousand, as it does. It is also unsatisfactory to some that the elective franchise is not given to the colored man. I would myself prefer that it were now conferred on the very intelligent, and on those who serve our cause as soldiers. Still the question is not whether the Louisiana government, as

[23] Again, Chase.

it stands, is quite all that is desirable. The question is "Will it be wiser to take it as it is, and help to improve it; or to reject, and disperse it?" "Can Louisiana be brought into proper practical relation with the Union *sooner* by *sustaining*, or by *discarding* her new State Government?"

Some twelve thousand voters in the heretofore slave-state of Louisiana have sworn allegiance to the Union, assumed to be the rightful political power of the State, held elections, organized a State government, adopted a free-state constitution, giving the benefit of public schools equally to black and white, and empowering the Legislature to confer the elective franchise upon the colored man. Their Legislature has already voted to ratify the constitutional amendment recently passed by Congress, abolishing slavery throughout the nation. These twelve thousand persons are thus fully committed to the Union, and to perpetual freedom in the state—committed to the very things, and nearly all the things the nation wants—and they ask the nations recognition, and it's assistance to make good their committal. Now, if we reject, and spurn them, we do our utmost to disorganize and disperse them. We in effect say to the white men "You are worthless, or worse—we will neither help you, nor be helped by you." To the blacks we say, "This cup of liberty which these, your old masters, hold to your lips, we will dash from you, and leave you to the chances of gathering the spilled and scattered contents in some vague and undefined when, where, and how." If this course, discouraging and paralyzing both white and black, has any tendency to bring Louisiana into proper practical relations with the Union, I have, so far, been unable to perceive it. If, on the contrary, we recognize, and sustain the new government of Louisiana the converse of all this is made true. We encourage the hearts, and nerve the arms of the twelve thousand to adhere to their work, and argue for it, and proselyte for it, and fight for it, and feed it, and grow it, and ripen it to a complete success. The colored man too, in seeing all united for him, is inspired with vigilance, and energy, and daring, to the same end. Grant that he desires the elective franchise, will he not attain it sooner by saving the already advanced steps toward it, than by running backward over them? Concede that the new government of Louisiana is only to what it should be as the egg is to the fowl, we shall sooner have the fowl by hatching the egg than by smashing it? Again, if we reject Louisiana, we also reject one vote in favor of the proposed amendment[24] to the national constitution. To meet this proposition, it has been argued that no more than three fourths of those States which have not attempted secession are necessary to validly ratify the amendment. I do not commit myself against this, further than to say that such a ratification would be questionable, and sure to be persistently questioned; while a ratification by three fourths of all the States would be unquestioned and unquestionable.

---

[24] The Thirteenth Amendment, abolishing slavery.

I repeat the question. "Can Louisiana be brought into proper practical relation with the Union *sooner* by *sustaining* or by *discarding* her new State Government?"

What has been said of Louisiana will apply generally to other States. And yet so great peculiarities pertain to each state; and such important and sudden changes occur in the same state; and, withal, so new and unprecedented is the whole case, that no exclusive, and inflexible plan can safely be prescribed as to details and colaterals. Such exclusive, and inflexible plan, would surely become a new entanglement. Important principles may, and must, be inflexible.

In the present *"situation"* as the phrase goes, it may be my duty to make some new announcement to the people of the South.[25] I am considering, and shall not fail to act, when satisfied that action will be proper.

---

[25] Lincoln left no record that documents the gist of the announcement he had in mind. The eminent Lincoln scholar David Herbert Donald points out that Lincoln probably was considering a plan to allow state legislatures to assemble and formally vote to withdraw from the Confederacy as a practical and expedient way to speed reconstruction and restore civil order in the defeated South. David Herbert Donald, *Lincoln* (New York, 1995), 583–85.

Three days later, a relaxed and cheerful President and Mrs. Lincoln went to Ford's Theater to enjoy a performance of the comedy *Our American Cousin*. During the third act, a little after 10 P.M., actor John Wilkes Booth, a fanatical Confederate sympathizer, made his way into the presidential box, sneaked up behind Lincoln, and shot him in the back of the head. In the pandemonium, Booth escaped.[26] The comatose Lincoln was carried to a private home across the street from the theater; he died there a little before 7:30 A.M. on April 15. At the deathbed, a tearful Secretary of War Stanton solemnly pronounced the benediction, "Now he belongs to the ages."[27]

[26] He was subsequently tracked down near Bowling Green, Virginia, and killed on April 26 as he tried to get away.

[27] John G. Nicolay and John Hay, *Abraham Lincoln: A History* (10 vols.; New York, 1890), X, 302.

An Abraham Lincoln Chronology (1809–1865)

1809   *February 12*   Abraham Lincoln born in Hardin County, Kentucky, the son of Thomas Lincoln (born 1778) and Nancy Hanks Lincoln (born about 1784).

1816   Thomas Lincoln moves his family to Little Pigeon Creek, Indiana.

1818   Nancy Hanks Lincoln dies.

1819   Thomas Lincoln marries Sarah Bush Johnston.

1830   Lincoln moves with his father, stepmother, and family to Macon County, Illinois.

1831   Lincoln's father, stepmother, and family move to Coles County, Illinois. Lincoln moves to the village of New Salem in Sangamon County, where he works as a store clerk and does odd jobs.

1832   Lincoln volunteers for the Illinois militia to serve in the Black Hawk War and is elected company captain. He runs for the Illinois House of Representatives but is not elected.

1834   Lincoln elected to the Illinois House of Representatives as a Whig in one of four seats from Sangamon County. He begins to study law.

1836   Lincoln re-elected to the legislature as one of seven Sangamon County representatives. He earns a license to practice law.

1837   With another Whig, Lincoln proposes an antislavery resolution in the Illinois legislature. He moves to Springfield and begins to practice law as a partner of John T. Stuart.

1842   Lincoln decides not to run again for the state legislature. He marries Mary Todd.

1844   Lincoln sets up a law practice and takes William H. Herndon as a partner.

1846   Lincoln elected as a Whig to the U.S. House of Representatives.

1847 Lincoln goes to Washington, D.C., with his family and serves in the Thirtieth Congress.

1848 Lincoln opposes the Mexican War policy of President James Polk. He does not seek re-election to Congress. He campaigns for Whig presidential candidate Zachary Taylor and votes for the Wilmot Proviso.

1849 Lincoln returns to Springfield and resumes his law practice.

1854 Lincoln speaks out against the Kansas-Nebraska Act. He wins election to the Illinois legislature but declines to serve, so as to be eligible for election by the legislature to the U.S. Senate.

1856 Lincoln fails to be elected to the U.S. Senate. He becomes a founding member of the Republican party in Illinois and campaigns for Republican presidential candidate John C. Frémont.

1857 Lincoln speaks out against the *Dred Scott* decision.

1858 Lincoln gives his "House Divided" speech as the Republican candidate for a U.S. Senate seat. He debates incumbent Democratic senator Stephen A. Douglas.

1859 Lincoln loses the senatorial election to Douglas, campaigns for Republicans in the Midwest, and begins to be mentioned as a possible presidential candidate.

1860 *February 27* Lincoln speaks at Cooper Institute in New York City.

May 18 Lincoln wins the presidential nomination of the Republican National Convention in Chicago.

November 6 Lincoln wins the presidential election.

December 20 South Carolina secedes.

1861 *January* Mississippi, Florida, Alabama, Georgia, and Louisiana secede.

February Texas secedes. Confederate government meeting in Montgomery, Alabama, chooses Jefferson Davis as provisional president.

March 4 Lincoln inaugurated as president of the United States.

April 12 Confederates bombard Fort Sumter, South Carolina.

April 13 Major Robert Anderson surrenders the fort.

April 15 Lincoln calls for 75,000 militia.

April 17 Virginia convention adopts secession ordinance.

May Lincoln calls for more than 42,000 three-year volunteers. Arkansas, Tennessee, North Carolina, and Virginia secede. Great Britain declares neutrality.

July 21   At the first battle of Bull Run (Manassas), Union forces under General Irvin McDowell suffer defeat.

July 27   General George B. McClellan replaces McDowell as commander of the Department of the Potomac. France declares neutrality.

August 6   Congress passes the First Confiscation Act. General John C. Frémont declares martial law in Missouri and proclaims the slaves of Missouri rebels free.

September   Lincoln rescinds Frémont's emancipation order.

November   Lincoln appoints McClellan general in chief. Union forces capture Port Royal, South Carolina.

1862   *February*   General Ulysses S. Grant defeats the Confederate forces at Fort Henry and Fort Donelson, Tennessee.

March   Lincoln proposes gradual, compensated emancipation of slaves in loyal border states. McClellan starts to deploy his Army of the Potomac for the peninsula campaign.

April   McClellan begins the peninsula campaign. Grant suffers a surprise attack at Shiloh, Tennessee, but forces a Confederate retreat. Lincoln signs a law abolishing slavery in the District of Columbia. Union forces capture New Orleans.

May   McClellan advances toward Richmond.

June   Lincoln signs a law prohibiting slavery in federal territories. McClellan begins an attack that becomes the Seven Days' Battles. He retreats under a counterattack by General Robert E. Lee.

July   Lincoln calls for 300,000 men to enlist for three years. He visits McClellan and the Army of the Potomac, dug in at Harrison's Landing, Virginia. He appoints General Henry Halleck general in chief. He signs the Second Confiscation Act, which provides freedom for slaves of rebel masters.

July 22   Lincoln reads a draft of the Preliminary Emancipation Proclamation to his cabinet.

August   Lincoln calls for 300,000 militia to serve for nine months. McClellan begins to withdraw the Army of the Potomac from the peninsula. Union forces defeated at the second battle of Bull Run.

September   Lee begins an invasion of the North by crossing the Potomac River into Maryland.

September 17   McClellan repulses Lee's northern advance at the battle of Antietam.

September 22   Lincoln issues the Preliminary Emancipation Proclamation.

November   Grant begins a campaign to capture Vicksburg, Mississippi. Democratic candidates make gains in the congressional elections. General Ambrose E. Burnside replaces McClellan as commander of the Army of the Potomac.

December 1   Lincoln urges Congress to pass a constitutional amendment allowing gradual, compensated emancipation.

December 13   Burnside attacks Confederate defenses at Fredericksburg, Virginia, and is badly beaten.

1863   *January 1*   Lincoln issues the Emancipation Proclamation. Later that month, General Joseph Hooker replaces Burnside as commander of the Army of the Potomac.

March   Lincoln signs a law introducing conscription.

April   Grant crosses the Mississippi River south of Vicksburg.

May 1–4   Lee defeats Hooker at Chancellorsville, Virginia.

May 22   Grant begins a siege of Vicksburg.

June   Lee begins a second campaign to invade the North. Lincoln calls for 100,000 militia. General George G. Meade replaces Hooker as commander of the Army of the Potomac. West Virginia admitted to the Union.

July 1–3   Meade defeats Lee at Gettysburg and turns back his invasion of the North.

July 4   Grant captures Vicksburg.

July 9   General Nathaniel P. Banks captures Port Hudson, Louisiana, establishing Union control of the Mississippi River.

July 13–16   Draft riots occur in New York City.

September 19–20   At Chickamauga, Georgia, the Confederates defeat the Union forces, which retreat to nearby Chattanooga, Tennessee.

October   Lincoln elevates Grant to command all Union forces in the West. Lincoln calls for 300,000 volunteers.

November 19   Lincoln delivers the Gettysburg Address.

December 8   Lincoln issues the Proclamation of Amnesty and Reconstruction.

1864   *March*   Lincoln promotes Grant to general in chief of the army and appoints General William T. Sherman commander of the armies in the West.

May 5–21   Grant attacks Lee at the battles of the Wilderness and Spotsylvania. Sherman launches a campaign against Atlanta.

June Lincoln nominated for a second term by the National Union party convention. General Jubal Early initiates a Confederate offensive in the Shenandoah Valley.

June 18 Grant begins a siege of Petersburg, Virginia.

July Lincoln refuses to sign the Wade-Davis bill. He calls for 500,000 volunteers. Early reaches the outskirts of Washington, D.C., but is forced to retreat.

August General Philip H. Sheridan takes command of Union forces in the Shenandoah Valley. Democrats nominate General George McClellan for president.

September 2 Sherman captures Atlanta.

October 19 At Cedar Creek, Virginia, Sheridan expels the Confederate forces from the Shenandoah Valley.

November 8 Lincoln re-elected president.

November 15 Sherman begins the March to the Sea.

December Lincoln calls for 300,000 volunteers.

December 21 Sherman captures Savannah.

1865 *February 1* Congress submits the Thirteenth Amendment, abolishing slavery, to the states for ratification.

February 3 Lincoln meets with Confederate representatives at Hampton Roads, Virginia.

March 4 Lincoln inaugurated for a second term.

April 2 Grant captures Petersburg, and Lee retreats toward the west, while the Confederate government evacuates Richmond.

April 3 Union forces capture Richmond.

April 4 Lincoln visits Richmond.

April 9 Lee surrenders to Grant at Appomattox Courthouse, Virginia.

April 14 Lincoln is shot by John Wilkes Booth and dies the next day.

April 26 Booth killed by federal pursuers.

May 4 Lincoln buried in Springfield, Illinois.

December 18 Thirteenth Amendment ratified.

Questions for Consideration

1. In what ways did Lincoln's early life influence his later ideas and behavior? How did his personal traits shape his performance as president?
2. Why did Lincoln revere the federal Constitution? How did his views of the Constitution affect his political and military decisions?
3. Why did Lincoln oppose the extension of slavery into federal territories? According to Lincoln, how did slavery differ from free labor, both in day-to-day practice and in long-term social and political repercussions?
4. Did Lincoln believe in human equality? Why? Did he consider blacks equal to whites? How did his views compare to those of his contemporaries?
5. Why did Lincoln place such a high value on the Union? What were the consequences of his devotion to the Union during his presidency?
6. How did Lincoln view the South? Did his views change? How did his views of the South influence his policies as president?
7. Why did Lincoln become a Republican? How did his leadership of the Republican party shape his actions as president?
8. How did Lincoln's political ideas influence his military strategy? How did military developments shape his presidential policies? What was his understanding of his responsibility as commander in chief?
9. Why was Lincoln often disappointed by the actions of leading generals? What qualities did he value in military commanders?
10. How did Lincoln's ideas about slavery change? Why? Did his ideas about African Americans change? Why? How did Lincoln think freedom would change the lives of slaves?
11. Why did Lincoln issue the Emancipation Proclamation (Document 34)? Did it serve the purposes he intended? What were its short-term and long-term consequences? Does Lincoln deserve to be called "the Great Emancipator"?
12. How did Lincoln's ideas about the Union and the Constitution mesh with his concepts of freedom, democracy, and equality?

216

13. To what degree was the Gettysburg Address (Document 42) a departure from Lincoln's previous thinking about the meaning of the Civil War? What messages was Lincoln trying to communicate in the address?

14. Did Lincoln's ideas about religion influence his thinking about slavery and the Civil War? If so, how?

15. What plans did Lincoln have for reconstruction? What were his goals for reconstruction? To what extent would former slaves be equal to whites?

16. In what ways did Lincoln's second inaugural address (Document 61) outline his views of the problems and possibilities of peace and reunion? What were the strengths and weaknesses of his approach to peace and reunion?

17. Do you think Lincoln achieved what was realistically possible during his years as president? Or did he fail to accomplish certain goals that were within reach? If so, what were those goals, and how might he have achieved them?

18. In Lincoln's eyes, what was the significance of the Civil War in the larger realm of world history? What was at stake in the outcome? Were other issues at stake that he neglected to mention or perceive?

19. How do the qualities of Lincoln's writings and speeches compare to those of more recent presidents? What accounts for the differences?

20. What was Lincoln's legacy to succeeding generations? How do his thoughts and deeds continue to influence the ways Americans think and act?

Selected Bibliography

Jean Harvey Baker, *Mary Todd Lincoln: A Biography* (1987).

Herman Belz, *Abraham Lincoln, Constitutionalism, and Equal Rights in the Civil War Era* (1998).

Ira Berlin et al., eds., *Freedom: A Documentary History of Emancipation* (4 vols.; 1982–1993).

David Blight, *Race and Reunion: The Civil War in American Memory* (2001).

Michael Burlingame, *Abraham Lincoln: A Life* (2 vols.; 2008).

Oliver Vernon Burton, *The Age of Lincoln* (2007).

Dudley Taylor Cornish, *The Sable Arm: Negro Troops in the Union Army, 1861–1865* (1956).

David Herbert Donald, *Lincoln* (1995).

Don E. Fehrenbacher and Virginia Fehrenbacher, eds., *Recollected Words of Abraham Lincoln* (1996).

Eric Foner, *The Fiery Trial: Abraham Lincoln and American Slavery* (2010).

William E. Gienapp, *The Origins of the Republican Party, 1852–1856* (1987).

Doris Kearns Goodwin, *Team of Rivals: The Political Genius of Abraham Lincoln* (2006).

Alan C. Guelzo, *Abraham Lincoln: Redeemer President* (2003).

———, *Lincoln's Emancipation Proclamation: The End of Slavery in America* (2006).

Steven Hahn et al., eds., *Freedom: A Documentary History of Emancipation, 1861–1867*, Volume I, *Land and Labor, 1865* (2008).

Harold Holzer, ed., *The Lincoln Mailbag: America Writes to the President, 1861–1865* (1998).

Fred Kaplan, *Lincoln: The Biography of a Writer* (2008).

Philip B. Kunhardt III et al., *Looking for Lincoln: The Making of an American Icon* (2008).

James M. McPherson, *Battle Cry of Freedom: The Civil War Era* (1988).

———, *Tried by War: Abraham Lincoln as Commander in Chief* (2008).

Mark E. Neely Jr., *The Fate of Liberty: Abraham Lincoln and Civil Liberties* (1991).

———, *The Last Best Hope of Earth: Abraham Lincoln and the Promise of America* (1993).

Phillip S. Paludan, *The Presidency of Abraham Lincoln* (1994).

Merrill D. Peterson, *Lincoln in American Memory* (1994).

John Stauffer, *Giants: The Parallel Lives of Frederick Douglass and Abraham Lincoln* (2008).

Ronald C. White Jr., *A. Lincoln: A Biography* (2009).

Gary Wills, *Lincoln at Gettysburg: The Words That Remade America* (1992).

Douglas L. Wilson, *Honor's Voice: The Transformation of Abraham Lincoln* (1998).

Douglas L. Wilson and Rodney O. Davis, eds., *Herndon's Informants: Letters, Interviews, and Statements about Abraham Lincoln* (1998).

———, eds., *The Lincoln-Douglas Debates* (2008).

Kenneth J. Winkle, *The Young Eagle: The Rise of Abraham Lincoln* (2001).

Index

abolitionists, 17, 38. *See also* antislavery
   movement
Address on Colonization to a Delegation of
   Black Americans (Lincoln), 125–29
Address at Cooper Union (Lincoln), 49–56
Africa, 125
African Americans, 162. *See also* slaves
   citizenship of, 42
   colonization of, 17, 28–29, 88–89, 123,
      125–29, 134, 137
   Constitution and, 17, 24–29, 42
   Declaration of Independence and, 27–28,
      38, 39, 40, 41, 43, 44
   Democratic party and, 29
   displacement of white laborers by, 138
   Dred Scott decision and, 24–29
   education of, 167, 174
   emancipation of, 131–42, 140, 144–48
   equality of, 17, 27–29, 38, 40, 41–42,
      43–44, 113
   federal employment of, 124
   following emancipation, 148
   intermarriage with whites, 27, 42, 43
   public views on, 26–27
   reconstruction and, 174
   Republican party and, 28–29
   resistance to admitting into society, 125,
      126, 137–39, 145, 156, 158
   resistance to fighting for, 109, 159
   rights of, 23
   social equality of, 17, 40, 42, 43
   status of former slaves, 166
   violence toward, 155
   voting rights, 26, 175n10, 207n22, 208–9
   work contracts, 167, 167n5
African American soldiers
   in Confederate army, 201, 203n20
   Confederate executions of, 145–46, 146n7
   fugitive slaves, 88n13, 115, 124
   Kentucky's dissatisfaction with, 177–80
   numbers of, 169, 182
   performance of, 145
   reburial of fallen soldiers by, 202f
   in Union army, 88n13, 115, 124, 140,
      144–48
   value of, 159, 169, 179, 182–83, 203
Alabama, 58, 73, 141, 174, 198

"American System," 11
amnesty, 172n8, 190
   defined, 172n8
   proclamation of, 172–74
Anaconda strategy, 72
"An act to make an additional Article of
   War," 132–33
"An Act to suppress Insurrection, to punish
   Treason and Rebellion," 133
anarchy, secession as, 67
Anderson, Robert, 74, 117, 117n3, 212
Anglo-African Institute for the Encourage-
   ment of Industry and Art, 125n12
Annual Message to Congress (Lincoln)
   1861, 85–93
   1862, 134–40
   1863, 168–72
   1864, 188–91
Antietam, battle of, 105, 109
antislavery movement, 94. *See also*
   abolitionists
Appeal to Border-State Representatives to
   Favor Compensated Emancipation
   (Lincoln), 122–23
Appomatox Courthouse, 204, 215
Arkansas, 70, 76, 141, 169, 173–74, 189, 198
"armed neutrality" policy, 77
Army and Flotilla at Cairo, Illinois, 96
Army at & about Fortress Monroe, Virginia,
   96
Army near Munfordsville, Kentucky, 96
Army of Northern Virginia, 151
Army of the Cumberland, 111n32
Army of the Potomac, 85, 96, 97–99, 103,
   143, 149–50, 154, 213, 214
Army of Virginia, 103
Army of Western Virginia, 96
Articles of Association, 65
Articles of Confederation, 80
Atlanta, Sherman's campaign, 184–85

Baker, Edward D., 112, 112n33
Ball's Bluff, battle of, 97
banks, 11
Banks, Nathaniel P., 100, 151, 153, 167n2,
   175n9, 208, 214
   Lincoln's letter to, 167–68

221